Reflections on Renewal

Reflections on Renewal

Lay Ecclesial Ministry and the Church

Edited by
Donna M. Eschenauer
and
Harold Daly Horell

A Michael Glazier Book

LITURGICAL PRESS
Collegeville, Minnesota

www.litpress.org

A Michael Glazier Book published by Liturgical Press

Cover design by David Manahan, OSB.

1 2 3 4 5 6 7 8 9

Library of Congress Cataloging-in-Publication Data

Reflections on renewal : lay ecclesial ministry and the church / Donna Eschenauer and Harold Daly Horell, editors.
p. cm. — (A Michael Glazier book)
Includes bibliographical references.
ISBN 978-0-8146-8016-2 — ISBN 978-0-8146-8018-6 (ebook)
1. Co-workers in the vineyard of the Lord. 2. Lay ministry—United States. 3. Lay ministry—Catholic Church. 4. Catholic Church—United States. 5. Catholic Church. United States Conference of Catholic Bishops. Committee on the Laity. I. Eschenauer, Donna. II. Horell, Harold Daly.

BX1920.R37 2011
253—dc23 2011023256

Contents

Foreword

I had the privilege to serve on the committee that guided the development of Co-Workers in the Vineyard of the Lord. Some committees are fun to work on and some are not so much fun, but I can honestly say that this particular committee was one of the most energizing and exciting committees that I have ever worked on for the United States Conference of Catholic Bishops (USCCB). There was a tremendous amount of dialogue and collaboration. The document and its formulation helped me initiate an institute in lay ecclesial ministry.

To begin, I want to reflect on the past of lay ecclesial ministry. I suggest that lay ecclesial ministry is not new; it was part of the church from its very beginning. Jesus, as we know, gave certain responsibilities to the twelve apostles who participated in his mission. However, we also see very clearly in Luke's Gospel, chapter ten, that Jesus sent out the seventy-two in pairs ahead of him to every place he intended to visit. There was a real sense of collaboration and sharing in that mission. He sent them out with authority. With the mission to care for the people in general, especially the sick, Jesus sent them to announce that the Reign of God is at hand.

When we look at Paul's own ministry as an apostle in Romans, chapter sixteen (I love this quote), Paul says, "Greet Prisca and Aquila, my co-workers in Christ Jesus, who risked their necks for my life, to whom not only am I grateful but also all the churches of the Gentiles" (vv. 3-4). Additionally, in Paul's letter to the Corinthians he talks about the various ministries; specifically he mentions the ministries of teaching, administration, and healing. I suggest that in many ways lay ecclesial ministry, this sharing in the mission and the ministry of Christ, is not new.

To put this into a Christian theological context, we believe that all of us, through our baptism, are called to live in the triune God; we are called to share in the life of the risen Christ, and to be a witness of that life to the world. Through our baptism, God calls us to build and to form community with one another. We are called to live out that baptismal commitment to transform the world so that the Christ living in us may be given to others. This transformation is the responsibility and the mission of *all* the baptized.

From among the baptized, we believe that some are called and sent to lead and to serve God's people in a more committed way, to make the ministry and the mission of Jesus Christ present today by their lives. I would say that historically there have been times in the church when lay ecclesial ministry has been strong: lay ecclesial ministers have worked very collaboratively with the ordained. There are other times in the church when ordained ministry was seen as the *only* ministry.

We live in a time when we must ask, "How do we bring lay and ordained ministries together?" The goal of lay ecclesial ministry is to foster the mission and the ministry of Jesus Christ. Through lay ecclesial ministry, we are encouraging the ordained and the laity to work together and truly be co-workers in the vineyard of the Lord. The church will become richer and more alive as lay ecclesial ministry continues to develop.

I want to turn now to look at the present reality. What *is* lay ecclesial ministry? First, it means that we have laypeople in the church who are given the authority and responsibility of service and leadership. Second, what they do is ecclesial; it has a place within the community of the church. Their ministry *is* in communion with the church. The ministry serves the church and makes present the mission and the ministry of Jesus Christ. It is ecclesial because it is grounded in the church, and because it is discerned, authorized, and supported by the church at large. It is ecclesial ministry because it shares in and fosters the three-fold ministry of Jesus Christ: his ministry of priesthood (prayer, and offering oneself in prayer); the prophetic role of teaching and preaching the word of God; and the role of leader or shepherding. The present reality is that our church is very, very blessed by a large number of lay ecclesial ministers in the world.

Who are these people? They are pastoral associates, catechetical leaders, youth ministry leaders, school principals, directors of liturgy, pastoral musicians, and others. These ministers serve at the parish level, but we cannot neglect that there are many lay ecclesial ministers in hospitals, nursing homes, prisons, and clinics. In recent times, the number of lay ecclesial ministers has grown significantly. When Co-Workers was written, there were over thirty thousand lay ecclesial ministers, working at least twenty hours a week, in paid positions throughout the United States and another twenty-six hundred parish volunteers who worked at least twenty hours. There are also over two thousand lay ecclesial ministers in hospitals, health care, college campuses, prisons, seaports, and airports in our country. The National Catholic Educational Association reminds us that there are just over seven thousand principals of Catholic elementary schools and high schools. The church would not fulfill its mission if it were not for lay ecclesial ministers. Lay ecclesial ministers, working in the church and with others in ministry, make the church and the mission of Christ more alive, more visible, and more active.

Moving on to the present reality, I suggest that while we find great effectiveness in lay ecclesial ministry, we also need to look at where lay ecclesial ministry is not effective, perhaps even ineffective. We have to be honest in looking at that reality. What makes the difference? First, lay ecclesial ministry is effective where we have people who are rooted personally in prayer and who are educated and formed. Their gifts and their faith are recognized. They are invited by the church and sent by the church to take on ministerial responsibilities, and they become extremely close collaborators with others who are in ordained ministry. A person who is an effective lay ecclesial minister is committed to continuing education and is accepted and respected by other people in ministry. In addition, their gifts are used, their charism is obvious, and they see themselves as sharing in the ministry of Christ himself. I believe those characteristics are present where we have effective lay ecclesial ministry.

Nevertheless, I suggest that we have to look at the opposite side of that. Where is there ineffective lay ecclesial ministry? It seems to me that some ministers, paid or not paid, are not adequately prepared. They do not have the spiritual formation, the theological formation, the human formation, and the pastoral formation to do the task that we have entrusted to them. In some cases, their education in theology is either weak or non-existent. Very often, they have received no spiritual formation. They have generous hearts but have not been formed, spiritually or theologically. In order to teach reading, math, and science, a teacher has to be certified by the state. Imagine my surprise when I discovered that in one of our schools the religion teachers had not been certified. In one case, the teacher had never taken a theology course. Those who are directing or serving on staffs and leadership in social ministry, religious education, worship, campus ministry, youth ministry, prison chaplaincy, and healthcare need more than good will; they need to be prepared—truly formed in faith. Those who are not effective in lay ecclesial ministry very often do not see or understand the mission of the church, but they often see their role to be one of control, or perhaps they have a need for this. It seems to me that when people are ineffective, they do not have the ability (or have not been taught how) to collaborate with others. They tend to be more interested in their own turf than the mission and ministry of Christ.

I suggest that there are some definite challenges before us, as we move forward and as we try to live out what has been put before us in Co-Workers. Specifically, I am suggesting that there are ten challenges that we face. For some of these, I have partial answers; for others, I have no answers, but by prayer, the guidance of the Spirit, and by living the challenges out, I believe that we will be shown the way.

The first challenge I suggest is that the church must continue to encourage lay ecclesial ministry. As we continue to move forward, we must refine the definition of lay ecclesial ministry. I think the definition we have in Co-Workers is a wonderful beginning, but as we move forward, we do need to ask the questions, "Can we develop that definition better? Can we describe lay ecclesial ministry better?"

Second, we believe, and it is clearly stated in the document, that people are called to lay ecclesial ministry; that it is a vocation, a calling, a vocation within a vocation. Our first vocation is obviously the call to be baptized, and then of course the other vocations are the states in life. However, we believe that when a person is called by the church and sent, they have a vocation. This recognition, however, needs further studying, research and dialogue. How does vocation fit into this reality? What does that mean for our church? We would say that first, people either sense the call of God within themselves, or someone first invites them into considering ministry, and then they come to a realization of the call. That call must be discerned in prayer. If a person believes that the call may be truly God's call to ministry, they would then enter into a period of preparation in order to exercise ministry. At some point the church has to say, "not only do you feel called to lay ecclesial ministry, but we as church, the people of God, along with other leaders of the church, see in you the gifts necessary to do ministry, and we need your gifts in order to fulfill the mission of Christ among us." I think that this point needs further dialogue, study, and research because some people become uncomfortable when we talk about lay ecclesial ministry as a vocation.

Third, we must have, and I do not think I can emphasize this enough, not just formation programs but quality formation programs. I did not say education—but formation. Lay ecclesial ministers, those who are called by God and sent by the church, need to be formed. There are four pillars of formation: the human, the spiritual, the theological, and the pastoral. We need to ask the question (and this will vary from diocese to diocese, perhaps region to region): what are the prerequisites for candidates before formation programs accept them? What about a degree? Is that essential or not? How do we help a person have a balanced understanding of theology and of the church?

I would like to dwell just a little bit on these four pillars: the human, the spiritual, the theological, and the pastoral. All of us are probably most familiar with the theological. We have many schools, universities, and programs in dioceses that are providing theological education. However, as we know, to be a lay ecclesial minister, theological education is not enough. The knowledge of theology has to be integrated into our spirituality, into our relationship with God. A person in lay ecclesial ministry formation should have a spiritual director and should have courses in spirituality. Pastoral formation concerns how we communicate, how we lead God's people. I would suspect that the part of the formation that may be a surprise and may sound different is the dimension of human formation, so I would like to note the basic ingredients of human formation: "a basic understanding of self and others, psychological health, a mature sexuality, physical health, knowledge of one's personal gifts and special charisms and their relationship to the ministry, recognition of the traits and the abilities one lacks, understanding of family systems and dynamics, ability to learn from both praise and criticism, appreciation and valuing of racial, ethnic, and cultural diversity, a genuine respect and concern for others, virtues of Christian discipleship."[1] (When I read that, I am tempted to think to myself, "I should not be a minister!")

Fourth, I think we need to continue to talk about the important relationship between the ordained and the lay ecclesial minister. It would seem to me that the bishop, the priest, the deacon, and the lay ecclesial minister, though they have different functions and ministries, need one another. The lay ecclesial minister shares in the ministry of the bishop and collaborates with others. The lay minister is entrusted with specific responsibilities and leadership that make the church more alive. The purpose of focusing on lay ecclesial ministry is not to raise up an elite group or a different class, but is to recognize lay people who are giving themselves in leadership and service. Such ministry is truly ecclesial; it is connected to the very heart of the church, and it is the ministry of Christ. We need more discussion on the relationship between the bishop, priest, deacon, and the lay ecclesial minister.

Fifth, it seems to me that bishops, priests, and deacons, should be encouraged to see the need for lay ecclesial ministry, and to understand how it enhances who we are as a church. It is important to use opportunities to show seminarians the importance of lay ecclesial ministry, and this emphasis should be a part of their formation program. Likewise, the emphasis should be a part of the formation program for permanent deacons, and it would be a good topic to use for a convocation of priests. Commissioning for lay ministry makes the most theological sense if done by the bishop. After people go through formation and upon the completion of formation and education, the bishop should accept them, and their credentials, and their gifts. He should recognize their charisms, and then authorize them within the diocese, the local church, to do ministry. This commissioning needs further discussion and research.

Sixth, where there is fear of lay ecclesial ministry and resistance, it is important that these realities are faced and discussed. Not to address these fears will cause tension in ministry, greater division, and "turfism."

Seventh, as mentioned earlier, all ministry is a sharing in the ministry of the bishop. It would seem appropriate for the bishop or his delegate to do the commissioning. Another question that requires discussion is, "How long is one commissioned and is it advisable to see permanency in such ministry?"

Eighth, as we continue to recognize the important reality of lay ecclesial ministry, we must practice what we preach, specifically in the area of just salaries and in benefits. That needs discussion. I do not have the answers to some of these questions, but I think they are important questions to be asked for the good of the church.

Ninth, how do we evaluate the ministry of lay ecclesial ministers? This is a complicated and important question. How do we help people grow in ministry?

Tenth, what process should be followed when a person requests a transfer from one parish or one ministry to another. What about the issue of termination when a person is not effective in ministry? These are complicated questions that need further deliberation!

Lay ecclesial ministry in the Catholic Church, in the United States, has an extremely bright future. There was a study done that was just published recently on young adult Catholics and their future in ministry.[2] The Emerging Models of Pastoral Leadership sponsored the study and focused on the next generation of pastoral leaders. Without getting into too much detail, the study was based on interviews of college and university students from nineteen colleges, three of them Catholic; over a thousand people were interviewed. Then they conducted separate interviews of people who were involved in young adult groups in the dioceses and they interviewed over twelve hundred people. Interestingly, one-third of the college students who were interviewed and who were active in campus ministry said that they seriously were considering lay ecclesial ministry as a future vocation. One-half of those involved in young adult groups in dioceses said that they were interested in considering lay ecclesial ministry as a way of life, as a vocation. Eighty percent of those who were interviewed said that they believe lay ecclesial ministry is a vocation and a call from God. That 80 percent said, "I believe God is calling me and has given me gifts in order to do ministry," is, I think, a significant sign of how the Spirit is working in the church today. You may ask, "Well, what areas of ministry were they mostly interested in?" As one might expect, they answered that they were primarily interested in youth ministry or young adult ministry—that is where they are. Second on their list was religious education. The third most popular area of ministry was being a teacher or administrator of a Catholic school. And fourth, they were interested in becoming pastoral counselors or spiritual directors. Those were the four major ones. The question was also asked in this survey, "What would discourage you from becoming a lay ecclesial minister?" There were two major issues: first: "the wages might just be too low and I might not be able to support a family, or live properly myself," and the second was, "will my gifts really be used?" "Will my gifts really be recognized and used?"

Interestingly, they were not discouraged when the interviewer said, "Well, you know you're going to have to go into a formation program." That was not a point of discouragement. Even the issue of job security and moving from place to place was not an issue. Their main motivation was the desire to live their faith actively, to share their faith, and to pass it on to others.

In conclusion, it seems to me that we are at a crossroads. When we look at the past, we see some periods in the history of our church when lay ecclesial ministry has been strong, and we need to revisit those times and learn from them. What about the present? I believe that Co-Workers in the Vineyard of the Lord points us in a very positive direction; it gives us a vision. Someday we will rewrite Co-Workers as a document, but we will rewrite it by the way in which we live, and by the way in which we work together in ministry. We know that the Spirit of God leads us individually and is certainly leading the church. We must ask the enlightenment of the Holy Spirit so that we can know where the Spirit is calling us and how the Spirit is calling us. We need to be able to name our fears, claim our questions, and dialogue instead of becoming alienated. The Spirit is alive and will work in us and through us.

Archbishop Gregory Aymond

Notes

1. USCCB, Co-Workers in the Vineyard of the Lord: A Resource for Guiding the Development of Lay Ecclesial Ministry (USCCB, Washington, DC: 2005), 36-37.

2. Dean R. Hoge and Marti Jewell, *The Next Generation of Pastoral Leaders: What the Church Needs to Know* (Chicago: Loyola Press, 2010).

INTRODUCTION

The Fordham University Convocation

Donna Eschenauer

Reflections on Renewal: Lay Ecclesial Ministry and the Church is a venture committed to deepening the ongoing reflection about lay ecclesial ministry, and at the same time, it is committed to contributing to the work of renewal. Our book firmly supports the 2005 document, Co-Workers in the Vineyard of the Lord: A Resource for Guiding the Development of Lay Ecclesial Ministry from the United States Conference of Catholic Bishops (USCCB), as a vital resource for the development of lay ecclesial ministry. The authors, however, address critical issues about ministry to stimulate greater awareness and scholarly research in the twenty-first century. Overall, *Reflections on Renewal: Lay Ecclesial Ministry and the Church* serves the work of the church. The essays offer insights for fostering a broader perspective of ministry and greater collaboration among all ministers.

This collection of essays was inspired by Co-Workers in the Vineyard of the Lord, the annual convocation sponsored by Fordham University's Graduate School of Religion and Religious Education (GSRRE). Our book is grounded in Fordham University's commitment to the church and its mission in the world. On April 4, 2008, the first Co-Workers in the Vineyard of the Lord convocation commemorated the fortieth anniversary of the GSRRE, honoring the vision of the founding dean, Fr. Vincent Novak, SJ. Faculty, students, lay ministers, bishops, priests, and representatives from several colleges, universities, and dioceses gathered to reflect on the USCCB document: Co-Workers in the Vineyard of the Lord. Since that time, the GSRRE continues to hold its annual convocation on this most important issue in the church. Of particular significance, because of the Co-Workers conferences, a pastoral consortium of Jesuits from various colleges and universities was formed.

Additionally, one cannot forget Fordham University's treasure in the astute wisdom and influence of Cardinal Avery Dulles. Without his intervention, the document Co-Workers may not have emerged in the way it did. In *Forward in Hope: Saying Amen to Lay Ecclesial Ministry,*

Bishop Matthew Clark captures a pivotal moment in the document's development. He writes:

> In the midst of my brother bishops' deep discussion over what exactly 'ministry' is and whether or not the term can or should be associated with people who are not ordained, Cardinal Dulles rose to the floor. He spoke very strongly that such use of the word *ministry* was not a new development for the Church but rather has been part of our tradition for centuries. He spoke eloquently, as always, that we shouldn't fear using this kind of language about the laity, that this seemingly brand-new thing was not new at all.[1]

Today, the GSRRE's vision, reflecting the Second Vatican Council, continues to energize religious education in all its forms (that is, in the classroom, the parish, family life, and in other arenas), and through its academic programs and events the GSRRE seeks to energize lay ecclesial ministry.

Personal experience prompts my own passion for lay ecclesial ministry. For over twenty years, I have worked full-time in a large suburban parish. As a laywoman, it is with deep joy that I serve the people of God on a daily basis. When I enter my office building, a poster announcing the newly ordained of our diocese hangs on the wall with the caption: "these men have answered a call to serve." This statement is true, and I honor the call of the ordained. However, as I read the sign I think to myself, "I too have answered a call to serve."

Thousands of laypeople have answered a call to serve the church. This call is rooted in a serious recognition of one's baptismal vocation to carry on the mission of Jesus Christ. In Co-Workers, the bishops affirm the universal call to holiness and the particular call of non-ordained persons to service in the church.

We are privileged to have Archbishop Gregory Aymond's encouraging closing remarks from the 2008 convocation in the Foreword of this book. Archbishop Aymond served on the committee that guided the development of *Co-Workers;* he describes his experience as energizing and exciting. While addressing the present and future of lay ecclesial ministry, Aymond also looks to its past and insists lay ministry is not new, rather it has been part of the church from the beginning.

The book is divided into two parts. The essays in part one (chapters one through four) affirm the work of Co-Workers. The first few chapters explore how the document provides a foundation for discussions of lay ecclesial ministry and the status of laypeople in the church. The essays in part two (chapters five through thirteen) address critical concerns, raise questions for deeper conversation, and offer possible pathways for the ongoing development of ministry in general, and especially what is currently called lay ecclesial ministry.

Part One begins with "The Development of Lay Ecclesial Ministry in the United States" (chapter one) by Richard McCord. McCord provides the story of lay ecclesial ministry in the United States. He concisely examines the meaning of lay ecclesial ministry, highlights its growth, presents some characteristics of its development, and offers questions for its future growth.

In chapter two, "How Co-Workers Came to be Written," Amy Hoey, RSM, outlines the collaboration in the development of the document. She summarizes the deliberations that took place when Co-Workers was written, and provides a historical context with a brief look at the years between 1980 and 2005, citing other significant documents that emerged during that period. Hoey makes a most important point: lay ecclesial ministry is not a response to the declining number of priests; rather it is the work of the Holy Spirit among us today.

Chapter three, "From Communion to Mission: The Theology of Co-Workers in the Vineyard of the Lord," by Edward Hahnenberg, is a striking reflection on the dynamic of God's work in the emergence of lay ministry. Hahnenberg views the theology of Co-Workers through the prisms of communion and mission. He discusses the rich significance of communion, or interrelationship, among the diverse ministries in the church. In addition, the theology expressed in Co-Workers, writes Hahnenberg, is Trinitarian. According to Co-Workers, ministry is essentially about healthy *interpersonal* and *ecclesial* relationships of service. In the same vein, Hahnenberg emphasizes that mission is the context of communion, and the goal of all ministry. In the end, he affirms that baptism commissions the communion of ministers for mission.

In chapter four, "Engaging in a Collective Gasp: A Historical Perspective on Co-Workers in the Vineyard of the Lord," Anthony Ciorra examines the history of ministry from the Council of Trent to the Second Vatican Council. He offers an ecclesiology for lay ecclesial ministry that is rooted in the work of Cardinal Avery Dulles. Ciorra also proposes that the lives and mission of two giants in our church, St. Francis of Assisi and St. Ignatius of Loyola, can serve as patron saints for lay ecclesial ministry.

Part two of the book deepens and guides the flow of the conversation toward genuine renewal. Kieran Scott's chapter, "Swimming Against the Tide: Language and Political Design in Lay Ecclesial Ministry" (chapter five), is pivotal to this book. He skillfully and prophetically explores the relationships between language, practice, and the institutional order of the church. Using philosophical analysis, Scott constructively attends to the importance of language modification and its direct effect on institutional renewal. Such attention to language is often neglected in the pastoral and educational ministries of the church. The chapter also explores the dilemma associated with the phrase "lay ecclesial ministry." Like others, Scott recognizes the ambiguity of this phrase and argues that our language reflects our ecclesiology and the ministerial nature of the church. With sound conviction, Scott proposes a reshaping of ministerial language for the health, survival, and mission of the church.

Bishop Howard Hubbard's essay, "Lay Ministry and the Challenges Facing the Church" (chapter six) pays tribute to a century-long process of renewal resulting in the explosion of lay ministries since Vatican II's proclamation of the church as "the people of God." This shift renews our understanding of baptism and the universal call to active participation. The notion of lay ministry then evolved more deeply through postconciliar documents and the work of the USCCB. Like Hoey, Bishop Hubbard stresses that lay ministry is not the result of the decline in vocations to the ordained or vowed life, but results from appreciating laypeople's gifts and charisms for building the Kingdom of God. Embracing this vision and moving forward are not without challenges. From his personal experience as a diocesan bishop, Hubbard explores the challenges and tensions associated with the responsibility of fulfilling the mission and ministry of the church.

In chapter seven, "Being a Minister and Doing Ministry: A Psychological Approach," Lisa Cataldo draws on psychoanalytic theory to examine how the inseparable models of being and doing underlie both lay and ordained ministry. Exploring the necessary elements of being and doing that are integral to the call to ministry, Cataldo engages the work of theologian Edward Hahnenberg and two psychoanalysts Donald Winnicott and Heinz Kohut. Moreover, she cautions that splitting these two elements is dangerous. Overall, Cataldo examines how the categories of *being and doing* and *lay and ordained* can be vehicles for realizing more fully our shared vocation as baptized persons.

"A Latino/a Perspective on Co-Workers in the Vineyard of the Lord" (chapter eight) addresses a timely and important issue for the church in the United States. Claudio Burgaleta explores how Co-Workers adequately addresses the situation of Latino/a lay ministry in the United States, while at the same time he presents a constructive critique for further responding to the growing Hispanic presence in the church. Burgaleta offers important statistics that help us to understand the different aspects of the Latino/a Catholic community in the United States. He applauds the document's awareness of an already multicultural church that invites local adaptation. However, Burgaleta contends that the rich Latino/a charismatic experience merits greater attention in future revisions of this document. In addition, like Kieran Scott and others, Burgaleta proposes reconsideration of the term "lay ecclesial minister."

"The Sacraments of Initiation: A Guiding Theme for the Future Development of Lay Ecclesial Ministry" (chapter nine) by Donna Eschenauer further develops the emerging understanding of lay ecclesial ministry. The chapter takes a liturgical perspective that fosters a spirit of participation, imagination, and celebration. Inspired by the Rite of Christian Initiation of Adults, mandated for use in the United States in 1988, Eschenauer explores the three sacraments of initiation—baptism, confirmation, and Eucharist—and shows how they ground lay ecclesial ministry.

Chapter ten, "Co-Workers in the Vineyard of the Lord and an Evolving Ministry," by Zeni Fox, explores whether Co-Workers can assist the ongoing evolution of ministry in the years ahead. Offering a succinct assessment of the document, Fox probes lay ecclesial ministry by looking at the origins of Co-Workers and developments in lay ministry. She applauds the theological vision of the document while acknowledging the need for greater clarity regarding the lay ecclesial minister. She concludes with some issues that require further reflection.

"Formation of Lay Ecclesial Ministries: Rooted in a Genuinely Lay and Ecclesial Spirituality" (chapter eleven) by Janet Ruffing, RSM, examines the emerging vocation of lay ecclesial ministers and proposes a better way to understand lay spirituality. She emphasizes vocational discernment, saying that for many laywomen and laymen, their vocation is to church ministry. Ruffing suggests that discipleship and conversion are a way of life. In addition, she reflects on the value of striving to nurture a paschal spirituality nurtured through the Gospel throughout the liturgical cycle of feasts and seasons.

Michael P. Horan's "Ministry in Service to an Adult Church: How Lay Ministry Fosters Mature Faith in the Catholic Parish" (chapter twelve) looks at lay ecclesial ministry through the lens of religious educational and pastoral theology. Horan pays particular attention to lay ministers as public professional leaders. He also considers the lay minister as a "living parable," stirring people to conscious faith. Like others, he challenges the ambiguity of the term "lay ecclesial minister." Significantly,

Horan picks up on the blurring of the distinction between volunteer lay ministers and professional lay ministers. He notes that professional lay ministers tend to be more concerned than volunteers with developing ministerial skills, establishing specific educational and professional goals, and seeking ecclesial leadership roles and authorization for their ministry. Horan also argues that clearer distinctions between volunteer, professional lay, and ordained ministry are needed if we are to encourage collaborative ministry in the church today.

Harold D. Horell concludes the book with "A Cause for Rejoicing: Hopes and Horizons for Lay Ecclesial Ministry" (chapter 13). The chapter reflects on critical issues concerning the development of ministry, especially lay ecclesial ministry. With honest sensitivity to justice, Horell affirms the signs of hope in the Spirit's presence and action within the church. Undoubtedly, this is a cause for rejoicing! The essay specifically explores how the sacraments of initiation provide a common foundation for all ministries, presents an understanding of ministerial functions and roles that can enable us to develop a better understanding of lay ecclesial ministry, and examines how the involvement of laymen and laywomen in the secular world affects the ongoing development of lay ecclesial ministry. Each of these issues is explored in the light of the challenges and signs of renewal found within the church today. The chapter concludes by considering the importance of being open to the continuing guidance of the Spirit in further developing lay ecclesial ministry.

In order to promote deeper reflection on the various aspects of Co-Workers in the Vineyard of the Lord, each chapter concludes with reflection questions that serve as a springboard for conversation about future development and renewal.

The pages that follow are grace-filled endeavors that capture the significance of Co-Workers for the mission of the church. Each essay brings the reality of lay ecclesial ministry to the forefront and at the same time urges us to stop and ask critical questions that can lead us toward holistic growth and development. The essays presented in this volume prompt vital reflection regarding the responsibility of all the baptized. Perhaps the most compelling gift of Vatican II is an on-going appreciation that the baptismal vocation is central to renewal and, most important, that lay and ordained ministers should genuinely collaborate. In this regard, I am reminded of a homily preached at the Easter Vigil many years ago. The pastor humbly pronounced this statement: "Peter's baptism tonight is more important than my ordination." His intent was not to lessen the importance of ordination. Rather, he was acknowledging that he was ordained because of his baptism. In the same vein, lay ecclesial ministry, in all its forms, acknowledges that all of the baptized are called to serve.

Since April 2008, Fordham University continues its commitment to Co-Workers in the Vineyard of the Lord. This book reflects the sustained efforts of faculty, alumni, and students of the Graduate School of Religion and Religious Education and their persistent dedication to educating leaders for sound mission in the church and society.

Notes

1. Bishop Matthew H. Clark, *Forward in Hope: Saying Amen to Lay Ecclesial Ministry* (Notre Dame, IN: Ave Maria Press, 2009), 2.

PART

I

CHAPTER ONE

The Development of Lay Ecclesial Ministry in the United States

H. Richard McCord

The story of the birth and growth of lay ecclesial ministry in the United States is both fascinating and far from being completed.[1] In their most extensive statement on the topic, Co-Workers in the Vineyard of the Lord, the United States Catholic bishops acknowledge that the church's experience of lay ecclesial ministry and of many other forms of lay participation in church life is still maturing.[2]

With these realities in mind, I have chosen to examine this topic in broad strokes with the following progression:

- First, a brief word about the meaning of lay ecclesial ministry itself
- Second, some highlights of its growth and development over the past few decades
- Third, some observations about the characteristics of this development
- Fourth, a few questions about future growth

Lay Ecclesial Ministry: Its Meaning

To understand the nature and boundaries of lay ecclesial ministry I will take as my starting point what the bishops say in Co-Workers. Lay ecclesial ministry is a generic, categorical term for a population of laypeople who carry out such roles as pastoral associate, parish catechetical leader, director of youth ministry, school principal, director of music and liturgy, RCIA director, and so on.[3]

These roles and others like them can be included under the umbrella term, "lay ecclesial ministry," because they share four characteristics:

- *leadership* in a particular area of ministry

- *authorization* of the hierarchy to serve publicly in the local church as leaders
- *close collaboration* with the pastoral ministry of bishops, priests, and deacons
- *preparation and formation* appropriate to the level of responsibility assigned to them

These characteristics are meant to delineate a relatively small number of laywomen and laymen who serve—mostly as employees and full-time—at parish, diocesan, and other levels of institutional church life.

Their number is small when compared to the many, many thousands of laypersons who serve in church ministries on a volunteer and occasional basis, for example, reading or serving at Mass, helping to distribute Holy Communion, teaching in catechetical programs, visiting the sick and elderly, working with youth groups, assisting in charitable programs, and so on.

In Co-Workers, the bishops recognize and express gratitude for all of these ways in which laypeople participate in building up the church community and carrying out its mission. The bishops also acknowledge the individual and collective service laypeople bring to the transformation of family, work, and society in the world.

Lay ecclesial ministry is part of the total fabric of lay involvement in the Christian life of discipleship, but lay ecclesial ministry also stands in a special relationship to discipleship. It was for this reason, among others, that the bishops decided to address lay ecclesial ministry, to reflect on its growth and significance, and to help guide its development.

Lay Ecclesial Ministry: Its Growth and Significance

The reality of lay ecclesial ministry (even before this term was invented) had begun to emerge in the American Catholic Church by the early 1970s, principally in the roles of parish directors of religious education and youth ministers. In 1980, the bishops' conference, in a statement entitled Called and Gifted: The American Catholic Laity, drew specific attention to the growing number of laypeople who "have prepared for professional ministry in the Church." They called these men and women "ecclesial ministers" and welcomed them as a gift to the church.[4]

In 1990, the bishops began to study the development of these professional pastoral ministries in parish life. They commissioned the first study of what so far have been three national studies carried out in seven-year intervals. It is from this research data that we can assemble our best picture of the trends and patterns in lay ecclesial ministry.[5] What are some highlights?

First, there is continuing growth in the ranks. The number of people employed at least twenty hours a week in parish pastoral leadership positions increased 42 percent from 1990 to 2005. The total now stands at more than thirty-one thousand people. Today, two out of every three parishes have at least one paid lay ecclesial minister, while in1990, only 54 percent of the parishes employed one or more.[6] *Conclusion*: Lay ecclesial ministry is growing both in absolute numbers and in its presence in parish life. It is one of the standard features of pastoral ministry in the United States.

Second, there are still far more female than male lay ecclesial ministers. Laywomen (not including religious sisters) account for 64 percent of these ministers, an increase of 20 percent since 1990. Laymen make up 20 percent of the total. Seventy percent of lay ecclesial ministers are married.[7] *Conclusion*: Lay ecclesial ministry is being shaped and sustained primarily by married women. The combination of a female presence and the married vocation brings a new face to church ministry.

Third, lay ecclesial ministry is becoming more of a long-term experience. Nearly 60 percent of those lay ministers in parish positions have had previous employment experience in a parish. The average length of paid ministry experience for an ecclesial lay minister is thirteen years. Almost 75 percent of all lay parish ministers anticipate pursuing a lifetime of service in the church.[8] *Conclusion*: There is not only a clear stability in lay ecclesial ministry, but there is also a developing sense of an ecclesial vocation in those laypeople who enter ecclesial ministry and stay in it.

Fourth, lay ecclesial ministers are an aging population. From 1990 to 2005 the median age of lay ministers (not including religious) increased from forty-five to fifty-two. The median age of adult Catholics in the United States is forty-four.[9] *Conclusion*: Lay ecclesial ministers are more conscious of the significance of Vatican II than are average Catholics. The ecclesial generation gap is becoming wider and more significant.

Fifth, people of color have not filled the ranks of lay ecclesial ministry in proportion to the increase in the church's cultural diversity. The percentage of Hispanic/Latino lay parish ministers now stands at 8 percent, which is double the percentage ten years ago. As we know, Latinos/as make up 30 percent of the United States Catholic population. *Conclusion*: We have a significant gap between these two realities. Closing this gap presents multiple questions and challenges to church leaders today.

Sixth, lay ecclesial ministers are generally well educated and prepared for their work. Nearly half of them have a master's degree or better. Of those with an advanced degree, more than half hold it in a ministry-related field. These statistics include women religious but even factoring them out, the level of education still seems impressive, especially given the fact that most laypeople have had to pay for their own education. *Conclusion*: Most lay ecclesial ministers recognize the need to be well prepared for church ministry, and they are finding ways to prepare themselves, sometimes without any institutional support.

Finally, those in parish ministry have consistently expressed high levels of satisfaction with their work and with the relationships they form doing it. In fact, they feel so positive about their ministry that 87 percent say they would encourage others to enter parish ministry. *Conclusion*: Because vocational choice depends a lot on invitation and attraction, today's lay ecclesial ministers can play a significant role in attracting the next generation of lay ecclesial ministers.

The Growth of Lay Ecclesial Ministry: Some Observations

I would like to make two general observations about the story of growth in lay ecclesial ministry that I have just presented.

First, several factors in the American Catholic Church promote and support lay ecclesial ministry. Our ecclesial experience in the post–Vatican II period, especially at the parish level, has placed a high value on lay participation of all kinds. The "full, active, conscious participation" (SC 14)[10] of all the faithful was a message from the council that resonated positively with our cultural values in a participatory democracy and that was heard enthusiastically by many laypeople and clergy eager to renew a more open community in the church.

In addition, there is a spirit of pragmatism that undergirds much of what we do strategically and pastorally as a church in this country. Therefore, notwithstanding the receptivity to lay ministry that come from a renewed conciliar ecclesiology, we have been willing to entrust laypeople with ministry leadership positions because this is a pragmatic response to needs that were not necessarily present before the council. For example, we now have a much larger and more diverse Catholic population, we have far fewer priests and religious, and we have an extensive system of Catholic institutions to maintain.

Finally, in addition to the factors of participation and pragmatism, we also place high value on parish life. This remains the centerpiece of

Catholic Church life in the United States. So, it seems natural that lay ecclesial ministry is strongly embedded there and has developed many of the characteristics of parish life: for example, it relies a lot on homegrown talent; it tends to be collegial; it attracts more women than men; and it looks to certain diocesan structures and services for assistance and leadership.

In addition to these few observations about the external context for lay ecclesial ministry, I now want to make a few observations about its internal dynamic of growth. This dynamic is a "bottom-up" or "grassroots" one. No national decision or formal decree gave rise to lay ecclesial ministry. Rather, individual parish priests and bishops began to assess the needs, locate the resources, create the positions, and hire the people. From the planting of those first seeds in the ecclesiology of the late 1960s, a large tree with many branches has taken root and grown.

There are some consequences of the fact that growth has occurred in this way. First, parish life and ministry remain the principal arena of lay ecclesial ministry and, as we have seen in the three national studies, the parish is the place where we gather most of our data and pursue most of our thinking about the viability of lay ecclesial ministry.

Second, because lay ecclesial ministry grew from the bottom up, there has been a discrepancy between realities on the ground and the church's ability to think about the phenomena theologically and to regulate them. This means that we have had some confusion and tension over terminology, roles, authority, relationships, and so on. In other countries that have lay ecclesial ministers, the pattern has differed. In several cases, the national church has established a system for lay ministry, including some general titles and role descriptions. Therefore, for example, Germany has two or three broadly but clearly defined lay ministry positions into which people doing a variety of ministries are placed.[11] Here in the United States, we have pursued the opposite pattern. Many different ministries developed and were named and came to be known not so much for what they had in common but for what distinguished them from one another. It has been the task of the bishops in Co-Workers to propose some ways of understanding and ordering this diversity.

Third, there has been some regulation of lay ecclesial ministries at the national level. This regulation was initiated by national ministry associations, whose leaders and members are mainly laypeople. In the 1980s, these associations began to create national standards for certifying lay ecclesial ministers in various fields such as hospital and prison chaplaincies and catechetical, liturgical, and youth ministries. This effort has evolved and continues to become more refined. This effort is a fine example of the people in the field instituting quality controls on themselves and, in the process, establishing a necessary degree of professionalization.[12] However, the ministers in the field by themselves can only take this so far. The hierarchy needs to be engaged at various points in the process for theological as well as organizational reasons.

This brings me to my last observation. It is simply to note that the bishops, as a national body, have adopted a methodology of response in guiding the development of lay ecclesial ministry. From at least 1980 onward, their activities have been to observe (and sometimes describe) the realities; to assess them theologically and pastorally (though not always with a univocal approach); and to respond with varying amounts of practical guidance (usually non-binding), as we see in Co-Workers. This approach seems to fit well with the way lay ecclesial ministry has grown. It has also been an authentic way for the bishops to carry out their ministry of oversight—testing everything and retaining what is good—while being careful not to extinguish the Spirit. I think it can be asked, however, whether more is needed and even expected from the bishops in the future.

Lay Ecclesial Ministry: Some Questions about the Future

A mention of the future provides me with a nice transition to a few final questions. The underlying premise of each of my questions is the same, namely, that lay ecclesial ministry is an authentic development in the church's life and not merely a temporary, stopgap measure to replace fewer numbers of priests and religious.

So, first, if we think lay ecclesial ministry is here to stay, then how and by whom in the church shall it be authorized? The hierarchy and the laity have their proper roles. How are the ministries to be implemented without unwittingly creating what one bishop called "an eighth sacrament" or a fourth level of the hierarchy?

Second, if we think lay ecclesial ministry is here to stay, then do we really want high quality persons doing it, or are we content to settle for willing and well-intentioned people? Are we going to find the resources to create substantive, reputable programs of education and formation, and give people access to them while respecting a diversity of personal and pastoral situations?

Third, if we think lay ecclesial ministry is here to stay, what are the prospects for continuing to build collaborative relationships with ordained ministers? Will we, in the process, work our way out of several dead-end arguments that have stalemated the conversation about church ministry in recent years?

Finally, if we think lay ecclesial ministry is here to stay, then what do we need to do in order to ensure it has a future in the younger generation of Catholic adults, and especially with cultural groups whose population is disproportionately young? There are some promising signs of interest in all church ministries among young adults, as well as a generous spirit of service on their parts, but will this interest and spirit be welcomed and supported by institutions that do not always know how to make room for them? Just as the history of lay ecclesial ministry continues to unfold, so also must the reflection and discussion about it continue.

Reflection Questions

1. McCord points out that lay ecclesial ministry is a generic term that applies to laity serving as pastoral associates, parish catechetical leaders/directors and coordinators of religious education, directors of youth ministry, school principals, directors of music and liturgy, RCIA directors, and other ecclesial ministers. How do the lay ecclesial ministers who are part of your local church contribute to its life and vitality?
2. What educational background do lay ecclesial ministers need in order to serve the church well? How can and should the church encourage and support the education of lay ecclesial ministers?
3. McCord notes, "lay ecclesial ministers are an aging population" (5). How can the church invite more young adults to become involved in lay ecclesial ministry?

Notes

1. A good source for historical narrative and other important context is Zeni Fox, *New Ecclesial Ministry: Lay Professionals Serving the Church*, rev. and expanded ed. (Franklin, WI: Sheed and Ward, 2002).

2. USCCB, Co-Workers in the Vineyard of the Lord: A Resource for Guiding the Development of Lay Ecclesial Ministry (Washington, D.C.: USCCB, 2005), 15.

3. Ibid., 11.

4. USCC, Called and Gifted: The American Catholic Laity (Washington, D.C.: USCC, 1980), 7.

5. The most recent of the three studies from which the data in this article are taken is David DeLambo, *Lay Parish Ministers: A Study of Emerging Leadership* (New York, NY: National Pastoral Life Center, 2005).

6. Ibid., 44.

7. Ibid., 46.

8. Ibid., 71.

9. Ibid., 46.

10. *Sacrosanctum Concilium* (Constitution on the Sacred Liturgy), in *Vatican Council II: The Conciliar and Post Conciliar Documents*, ed. Austin Flannery, 1–282 (Northport, NY: Costello Publishing Company, 1987).

11. As noted in Co-Workers, 14, footnote 23, in 1977, the German bishops' conference published *Principles for the Regulation of Pastoral Services*, which identified three ministries by name: "pastoral assistant adviser" (a layperson who has completed theological studies on the university level), "community assistant adviser" (a layperson who has completed studies on the university-professional school level), and "community helper" (a layperson who has appropriate general, basic knowledge).

12. See the National Association for Lay Ministry, the National Conference for Catechetical Leadership, and the National Federation for Catholic Youth Ministry, *National Certification Standards for Lay Ecclesial Ministers Serving as Parish Catechetical Leaders, Youth Ministry Leaders, Pastoral Associates, Parish Life Coordinators* (Washington, DC: NALM, NCCL, and NFCYM, 2003). These national certification standards were approved by the United States Conference of Catholic Bishops Commission on Certification and Accreditation, April 2003.

CHAPTER TWO

How Co-Workers Came to Be Written

Amy M. Hoey, RSM

In many ways, the process of writing Co-Workers in the Vineyard of the Lord modeled its message. While the document was and exists today as one written and adopted by the United States bishops' conference, its preparation was a collaborative process, involving bishops and theologians; ordained and lay ministers; women and men; religious, single, and married people.

The subcommittee itself was a work of collaboration, constituted of bishop representatives from other United States Conference of Catholic Bishops (USCCB) committees such as those concerned with priestly life and ministry, doctrine, diaconate, vocations, laity, and pastoral practices.

From the very beginning, the style of the subcommittee was consultative and dialogic. The members of the subcommittee began with an outline of the document's contents. The outline remained fairly intact, beginning with a description of the reality of lay ecclesial ministry, exploring its theological grounding, and then addressing the four pastoral applications: pathways to lay ecclesial ministry, formation for lay ecclesial ministry, authorization for lay ecclesial ministry, and the ministerial workplace. To develop the contents, the subcommittee convened groups of bishops, theologians, seminary rectors, school of theology presidents, directors of formation programs, canonists, lay ministers themselves, attorneys, and experts in human resource management. From those conversations, the first drafts of the document were developed, drafts that were revised extensively by written consultations with all the bishops and with lay ministerial associations. The consultation with those associations was particularly significant, involving over twenty organizations, many of whom made the draft available to their executive committees, and one to its total membership. The subcommittee took those consultations seriously. When several lay associations commented that the draft contained "repetitious and defensive distinctions between lay ecclesial ministry and ordained ministry," the bishops on the subcommittee acknowledged that it did and asked for further revisions. They changed content and wording repeatedly because of the comments they received from other bishops and consultants with whom they worked. The draft on which the bishops voted in November 2005 was the seventh, and even then, in the final debate, there were changes suggested by other bishops and incorporated by the subcommittee into the final text.

At the beginning of the process, when the entire conference was deciding whether the subcommittee should go forward with the preparation of the document, one bishop raised a question about the authority of the proposed document. I remember one of the archbishops who had been a long-term advisor to the subcommittee responding to that question and saying that he thought of the document as "reflective and descriptive," rather than prescriptive or dogmatic.

In many ways, the document's preparation was also a process of theological reflection for the bishops. They were increasingly conscious of a new reality in the church: laymen and laywomen, appropriately prepared (usually at their own expense), who shared significant pastoral responsibilities in the local church's positions of leadership. Together, the bishops reflected on that reality in the light of Scripture, church teaching, and practice in order to integrate it into the American church today.

It is important to note that Co-Workers is not the first time the United States bishops addressed the issue of lay ecclesial ministry. Close to thirty years ago, in 1980, in Called and Gifted, the bishops referred to "ecclesial ministers, i.e., lay persons who have prepared for professional ministry in the Church [who] represent a new development." The bishops continued, "We welcome this as a gift to the Church."[1]

In the years between 1990 and 2005, the numbers of lay ecclesial ministers continued to grow. Three studies, two by the late Monsignor Philip Murnion of the National Pastoral Life Center (1992 and 1997) and the most recent by David DeLambo in 2005, trace the growth of parish ministers from over twenty-one thousand to over thirty-thousand, an increase of close to 40 percent in fifteen years.[2]

During those fifteen years, the thinking—and the practice—of the bishops continued to develop. The Subcommittee on Lay Ministry, which was established in 1995, sponsored a theological colloquium in 1997 to which they invited theologians and bishops who had terminal degrees in theology or canon law. The papers from the colloquium were subsequently published as Together in God's Service: Toward a Theology of Lay Ecclesial Ministry. For ten years, the subcommittee published a bi-monthly newsletter that was sent to every bishop, and held consultations with lay ecclesial ministers and those involved with their preparation for ministry. In 1999, the subcommittee presented to the USCCB a report titled Lay Ecclesial Ministry: The State of the Questions. During the discussion of that report, a significant number of bishops made it clear that they wanted further guidance from the USCCB on the topic of lay ecclesial ministry, particularly on the appropriate preparation of such individuals.

This plea was echoed by the leaders of the theological schools who were receiving increasing numbers of students preparing for leadership in church ministry but not for ordination. I remember one president told the subcommittee how his institution had struggled to adapt the Plan for Priestly Formation as they developed programs for laypeople and asked the bishops to consider the preparation of a document designed specifically for laypeople.

In his first study of parish ministers, Monsignor Murnion observed that such ministry was largely a parochial phenomenon, not related to the diocese in any specific way. Similarly, the bishops who were addressing the phenomenon were doing so individually or, in just a couple of cases, regionally. In 1997, the late Bishop Delaney of Fort Worth asked for some national guidance so that the individual bishop might be assured that his efforts to be faithful to church teaching were consistent with those of other bishops in the conference. In the introduction to Co-Workers, the bishops address that concern with these words: "We intend *Co-Workers in the Vineyard of the Lord* to be a common frame of reference for ensuring that the development of lay ecclesial ministry continues in ways that are faithful to the Church's theological and doctrinal tradition and that respond to contemporary pastoral needs and situations."[3]

A consistent theme in Called and Gifted and Co-Workers is one of welcome and gratitude toward lay ecclesial ministers. Co-Workers is unambiguous in affirming lay ecclesial ministers: "We . . . offer this document to lay ecclesial ministers themselves to encourage and assist them, to express gratitude to them and to their families and communities, and to convey an understanding of how their service is unique and necessary for the life and growth of the Church."[4]

The numbers of lay ecclesial ministers grew, and they had developed an increasing sense of their own professionalism. Several lay ministerial associations (the National Association for Lay Ministry, the National Conference for Catechetical Leadership, the National Federation for Catholic Youth Ministry, in addition to associations of health care chaplains, prison and seaport chaplains) had developed competency standards for certification. They submitted the competency standards to the USCCB Commission on Certification and Accreditation and received Commission approval. In addition, several formation programs sought and received accreditation from the commission. All of this activity meant that an arm of the bishops' conference was already considering issues related to lay ecclesial ministry although there were no statements about the theological underpinnings for such ministry, which is why it was so necessary for the bishops to come to some agreement about the theology of lay ecclesial ministry. I remember one cardinal-advisor to the subcommittee who would say repeatedly, "Get the theology right, and everything else will flow from that." It was, not surprisingly, the theology section of Co-Workers that drew the most comments and suggestions from the bishops throughout the entire process of its preparation.

Another reason that the subcommittee believed it was necessary to prepare the document was that the Program of Priestly Formation was nearing another revision,[5] and the National Directory for the Formation, Ministry, and Life of Permanent Deacons in the United States[6] had been recently approved. Most parish staffs consist of priests, deacons, and lay ecclesial ministers who work together to accomplish the mission of the parish. All three groups, the subcommittee believed, should have documents that describe their role and, as much as possible, a common language and categories for formation. That is why the subcommittee deliberately chose to describe the formation of lay ecclesial ministers using the four pillars of human, spiritual, intellectual, and pastoral formation that had been used in the other two documents. The bishops were, at the same time, very clear that it was laypeople, not prospective priests or religious, who were being formed. This unique focus is especially evident where the bishops write these words: "Formators (those responsible for the human, spiritual, intellectual and pastoral formation) will want to recognize and tap the life experiences of lay ecclesial ministers; for example, their broad and varied family relationships, the ordinary responsibilities of daily chores, or the financial challenges of educating children or providing for retirement."[7] The difference is specifically evident in their comments at the end of the section introducing spiritual formation where they write: "The multiple demands of family and community responsibilities may occasionally challenge some lay ecclesial ministers in their effort to set aside regular time and space for spiritual practices. However, when daily life is lived intentionally and reflectively in light of the Gospel of Jesus Christ, it is a school of holiness."[8]

One important distinction among the three documents needs to be noted here. The documents for priests and deacons have the force of particular law and are based on Roman documents from the Congregation of the Clergy. Co-Workers is not a local specification of any universal church document, although it is clearly based on magisterial teaching. Neither does it have the force of particular law. Again, I remember Bishop Delaney during a subcommittee discussion of this issue saying that the document would not be binding on any individual bishop but would have the weight of its own internal authority.

Co-Workers is descriptive and reflective in nature; its tone might best be described as invitational. The document offers goals, not mandates; it describes rather than prescribes. These distinctions are particularly evident in the section on formation, during the writing of which the bishops tried to be true to the wide diversity of this country. In that section, they write:

> Level of preparation and extent of formation are important questions that have no single answer. Lay ecclesial ministers, their supervisors, and diocesan bishops above all are best able to discern local needs and to set standards and expectations accordingly, seeking always to provide what would best serve a given pastoral setting or community. What follows in this document may, at present, be feasible in some situations and less so in others. Inadequate and faulty preparation harms rather than helps the mission of the Church. Usually, a master's degree, or at least a bachelor's degree, in an appropriate field of study is preferable.[9]

Because the document does not have the force of law, it gives to the individual diocesan bishop or his delegate the responsibility, "in accord with the norms of canon law, to identify the roles that most clearly exemplify lay ecclesial ministry." The document acknowledges immediately that the "application of the term may vary from diocese to diocese."[10]

My limited experience and observation is that bishops have been slow to identify these roles. Less than one year after the document was approved, one bishop, speaking at a conference at Loyola University in Chicago, noted that varying applications in such a mobile society would not be helpful. The term "lay ecclesial ministry" does not come trippingly off the tongue, and I have yet to meet any bishop who would not prefer another term if one could be found which adequately conveys the intended meaning. Nonetheless, the term *lay ecclesial ministry* is being used more and more widely and often to identify, at least informally, a ministry that encompasses significant leadership within a faith community. The formal recognition of lay ecclesial ministers, however, seems to be progressing very slowly.

Throughout all their work, the bishops who worked most closely on the document were quite clear that lay ecclesial ministry is not a response to the declining number of priests. Too often, Co-Workers is discussed in that context, not in the context of the work of the Spirit among us today. At one of the regional consultations held by the subcommittee, a theologian urged the bishops to move very slowly with such a document. The theologian suggested that the Holy Spirit seemed to be doing something quite remarkable in the church today, so to fit these laypeople into a structure, which seems to be radically changing, might not be ultimately helpful for anyone. My recollection is that the bishops on the subcommittee listened carefully, agreed with his assumption, but continued with the development of the document because of their desire to validate and recognize the developments of the previous thirty years.

Let me call your attention to the subtitle of the document, A Resource to Guide the Development of Lay Ecclesial Ministry. It is intended as a resource, a stimulus for reflection and action. The subcommittee hoped that our understanding of lay ecclesial ministry would continue to develop as people reflected upon the document, and gathered to discuss lay ministry and the formation of laypeople for ministry. The subcommittee never had any illusions that they were writing the last word on lay ecclesial ministry. Actually, the conclusion commits the bishops to "revisit" and "refine" Co-Workers "within the next five years."[11] By my calculations, we are more than halfway there!

That same conclusion also points to the need for "a more thorough study of our theology of vocation," but that is another, although closely related, issue.

I think we have explored sufficiently the document's task as guide, not commander. The word *development* in the subtitle is particularly meaningful. In his *America* article on theology since Vatican II, Roger Haight omitted any reference to the significant developments in the theology of ministry since Vatican II, but he did write something that I found helpful. He made this statement: "Theological progress differs from development in technology, where one way of doing things supplants another—the computer making the typewriter obsolete. Instead, in theology one stage takes the former into itself, slowly widening its horizon and deepening perceptions, allowing a complexification of issues that leads to greater understanding."[12]

That complexification and greater understanding were borne home to me early in my work for the subcommittee. I met a bishop in whose diocese I had ministered at one time, and he asked me how the work for the subcommittee was going. I responded, "OK, but when I get discouraged that it's taking so long, I console myself by thinking that if it took the church two centuries to figure out ordained priesthood, I shouldn't be surprised that it's taking thirty years to work out lay ecclesial ministry." He looked at me a little wistfully and said, "What makes you think we've worked out priesthood!"

As we continue our conversations about Co-Workers in the Vineyard of the Lord, let us be grateful for all who contribute to the development of lay ecclesial ministry by their episcopal leadership, their theological reflection, and especially by their lives of service in the faith community.

Reflection Questions

1. How might Co-Workers shape or continue to influence the ways you think about lay ecclesial ministry? How might Co-Workers help to shape the ongoing development of lay ecclesial ministry in your parish or diocese?
2. What can it mean for laywomen and laymen serving as ministers (pastoral associates, directors or coordinators of religious education, youth ministers, school principals and in other ecclesial ministries) to think of themselves as lay ecclesial ministers who are part of a process of change that is significantly reshaping how ministry is understood?
3. From its opening words, Co-Workers is built around the theme of God calling and our responding. In the conclusion, the document notes that there is "a need for a more thorough study of our theology of vocation."[13] How would you like to see a theology of vocation continue to develop within the church?

Notes

1. USCC, Called and Gifted: The American Catholic Laity (Washington, DC: USCCB, 1980), 4.

2. Philip Murnion, *New Parish Ministers: Laity and Religious on Parish Staffs* (New York: National Pastoral Life Center, 1992); Philip Murnion and David DeLambo, *Parishes and Parish Ministry: A Study of Parish Lay Ministry* (New York: National Pastoral Life Center, 1999); and David DeLambo, *Lay Parish Ministers: A Study of Emerging Leadership* (New York: National Pastoral Life Center, 2005).

3. USCCB, Co-Workers in the Vineyard of the Lord: A Resource for Guiding the Development of Lay Ecclesial Ministry (Washington, D.C.: USCCB, 2005), 6.

4. Ibid., 14.

5. The latest such program is the USCCB, Program of Priestly Formation, 5th ed. (Washington, DC: USCCB, 2006).

6. USCCB, National Directory for the Formation, Ministry, and Life of Permanent Deacons in the United States (Washington, DC: USCCB, 2005).

7. Co-Workers, 35.

8. Ibid., 38.

9. Ibid., 34.

10. Ibid., 11.

11. Ibid., 67.

12. Rodger Haight, "Lessons From an Extraordinary Era: Catholic Theology Since Vatican II," *America* (March 17, 2008): 12.

13. Co-Workers, 67.

CHAPTER THREE

From Communion to Mission

The Theology of Co-Workers in the Vineyard of the Lord

Edward P. Hahnenberg

The best theology is a theology rooted in reality. It is a theology that starts with the world—one that begins with experience. Christians believe that God is not absent from history but mysteriously present within it. God is not locked up in some far-off heaven. God is surprisingly—even scandalously—loose in the world. Thus the task of the theologian is to be on the lookout for the hidden God, to watch for where God might be at work, and to find the words to describe what God is doing.

What is God doing? In the realm of ministry, what has God been up to? Over the past forty years, it seems that God has been busy raising up new ministries and new ministers to meet new needs and to offer new ways of living out the Gospel call. One important dynamic in this evolving reality is the rise of "Lay ecclesial ministers," professionally prepared laypeople who exercise ministerial leadership in parishes, dioceses, and other institutions. In 2005, the United States Catholic Conference of Bishops addressed these ministers in their document Co-Workers in the Vineyard of the Lord. This document did not create lay ecclesial ministries. Instead, these ministries emerged from the ground up. In the words of Zeni Fox, lay ecclesial ministry was a lot like Topsy, it "just growed."[1] After the Second Vatican Council, liturgical changes needed explanation and implementation. Religious education shifted away from an emphasis on rote memorization of catechism answers. As fewer children attended Catholic schools, parish religious education programs grew and became more holistic and inclusive—often focusing on personal and social as well as intellectual development. Pastors hired their best volunteers to coordinate these programs, creating new positions and a new model for the parish staff. Colleges and universities offered degrees in theology for laymen and laywomen. Countless women religious sought out new ways to serve the community. This is the history that gave rise to lay ecclesial ministry. In Co-Workers, the bishops look out over this history and conclude: "Lay ecclesial ministry has emerged and taken shape in our country through the working of the Holy Spirit."[2] They seem to have seen what God is doing, and now they are talking about it.

How do the bishops talk about lay ecclesial ministry? How do they invite us to talk about it? More importantly, how might this ongoing conversation serve to foster, further, and make more fruitful this ministry for the life and mission of the church? This essay explores the theology articulated in Co-Workers. Rather than simply summarize what the document says, we will study Co-Workers through two lenses: *communion* and *mission*. These lenses, lifted up together, help us to see both what is significant in this text and what lies beyond it. Through them, we glimpse both where our theology of lay ecclesial ministry has arrived and where it might lead in the future.[3]

Communion and Mission in Co-Workers

The pairing of "communion and mission" will be familiar to those who had the stamina to keep up with the extraordinary output of official teaching documents under Pope John Paul II. The terms "communion" and "mission" appear throughout the late pope's writings. They even serve as the basic structuring principles for his apostolic exhortations on the laity, on the formation of priests, and on consecrated life.[4] These complementary concepts gave John Paul II a clear and constructive way of organizing any number of issues. He found great fruit in this twofold dynamic of the Christian life: communion and mission, gathering and sending forth, calling and commissioning, contemplation and apostolic activity.

Though they are not the primary structuring principles, communion and mission are mentioned repeatedly in Co-Workers. Early on in drafting the document, the bishops' subcommittee on lay ministry held a consultation with a diverse group of bishops and theologians. In exploring how to shape the theological section of the text, this group quickly came to a consensus. The reality of lay ecclesial ministry first had to be described and affirmed. Then this reality had to be placed in a broader theological context. The group realized that lay ecclesial ministry could only be properly understood within the context of a more inclusive theology of ministry. However, such an inclusive theology of ministry required attention to a theology of church and mission. Additionally, attention to church mission demanded some reflection on the activity of God for us through the dual mission of Christ and the Spirit. In sum, reflection on the reality of lay ecclesial ministry led the bishops to recognize wider theological implications, expanding outward from ministry to mission to the very nature of God.

As the bishops crafted the document, the basic concern to situate lay ecclesial ministry within a broader theological context served as a guide. The final text begins by describing the reality today. It then offers a series of theological reflections that move from God to church to ministry. In each section, communion and mission appear. The Trinity is described as a loving communion of persons that reaches out in mission in order to draw humanity into the divine life. The church is called, following the language of John Paul II, "a mystery of Trinitarian communion in missionary tension."[5] Ministry is presented as serving the church communion and its mission. Finally, lay ecclesial ministry finds its place as one ministry among many within this dynamic movement. What holds the theological section of Co-Workers together are these themes of communion and mission, themes that evoke a fundamentally relational approach to ministry, rooted in the communion and mission of the triune God.

Lay Ecclesial Ministry in Communion

The interrelationship among various ministries in the church today is a clear concern of Co-Workers. How are we going to talk about the ways in which lay ecclesial ministry relates to the other ministries that make up the church?

Several years ago, I had the opportunity to team-teach a course on ministry to graduate students at my alma mater.[6] The class contained a mix of students, including both seminarians and students preparing for lay ministry. It was a wonderful group. These were intelligent, energetic, and hope-filled Catholics committed to the church and to serving the mission of Christ. Moreover, they got along with one another! These young men and women had studied together for two years. They had shared experiences and formed friendships that freed them to be honest with one another about their hopes and their fears as future ministers in the church.

Yet, despite these almost ideal conditions for ministerial formation, there was still a kind of disconnect between the seminarians and the lay ministry students. It was not outright disagreement or open conflict. It was simply a disconnect. In our conversations, these two groups often seemed to be talking past each other. The lay students were interested in and raised questions primarily about issues of what it means *to do ministry*. They were concerned about professional effectiveness and the various roles they would play within a parish, school, or diocesan office. The seminarians were interested in and raised questions primarily about issues of what it means *to be a minister*. They were concerned about the nature of ordained ministry and the status of priests today. The lay students were concerned about function. The seminarians were concerned about identity. These differing concerns meant that the one group often missed what the other was trying to say. The breakthrough moment of the course came when we simply brought this dynamic out into the open. By naming it, each group was able to hear the other with a new awareness. Each group could acknowledge its own particular perspective, along with the blind spots that went with it.

It is no mystery why these were the questions these groups of students were asking. In many ways, given the past forty years of ministerial change, these differences are completely understandable. The course unfolded in a way that reflects what has been going on in the theological literature. Since the Second Vatican Council, theological writing on these topics could almost be divided into two separate conversations. One conversation revolves around the theology of priesthood. It is heavily christological (Christ-centered) and ontological ("being"-centered), emphasizing the priest's ability to act "in the person of Christ" and represent Christ to the community. This is the conversation taking place primarily in seminaries, bishops' committees, and Vatican offices. A different conversation revolves around the theology of lay ministry. It is heavily pneumatological (Spirit-centered) and functional ("doing"-centered), emphasizing the charisms of the Spirit flowing out of baptism and toward an individual's ministry. This is the conversation taking place primarily in universities, formation programs, and national ministry associations.

These two ongoing conversations speak to different needs, needs that were powerfully personalized for me in the concerns of my students. However, the manner in which these conversations unfolded has presented the church with a misleading choice. In looking for a comprehensive theology of ministry, it can appear that the church must pick between a "low" theology of ministry (that fails to address priestly identity), and a "high" theology of ministry (that fails to incorporate the many new ministries emerging in our church).

Even more problematic than this false dichotomy—particularly from the perspective of a theology of communion—is the way in which these two conversations, each in its own way, tend to promote individualism in ministry. This individualism is not new, but rather has deep roots in our theological tradition. For example, the recent reassertion of a heavily Christ-centered theology of priesthood relies on a theology of *in persona Christi*. It is based on the conviction that, at certain key moments in his sacramental ministry, the priest acts "in the person of Christ." This positive affirmation, however, is often clouded by a spirituality of priesthood that separates the priest from the community of faith. What began as a statement of relationship ("the priest is connected to Christ") ends in isolating individualism ("the priest is disconnected from the community"). History explains this irony. The phrase *in persona Christi* first emerged in our tradition in order to emphasize how the ordained minister helps to continue the mission of Christ. In its origins, the category was not primarily about the priest's identity, but rather about Christ's activity. In response to the Donatists, Augustine argued that the baptism performed by a sinful minister was still valid because it is not the priest who baptizes, but rather Jesus Christ who baptizes through him. The priest acts *in persona Christi*. Later, Aquinas spoke of the ordained minister as the instrument of Christ's saving grace. But from the late medieval to the modern period, this emphasis on the priest acting *for* Christ was displaced by an emphasis on the priest as "another Christ" (*alter Christus*); in other words, the ordained minister is a man "set apart" from and elevated above the community. What was originally and what ought to be a relational category has served to separate the priest from relationships with others in the church.

On the other hand, if we look at the theological conversation that describes ministry in light of the gifts of the Spirit, we see a similar individualism at work. For St. Paul, charisms and important ministries go hand-in-hand. However, later tradition was not as kind to the the charismatically inspired individual. For most of our church's history, individual charisms have been cast in opposition to church institutions. Too often, the free activity of the Spirit has been seen as a threat to the order of a hierarchically established church because the person with a distinctive spiritual charism could claim an independent inspiration, an authority that was based, not in the community, but on God alone. Thus, the legacies both of Christ-centered and Spirit-centered theologies of ministry include tendencies toward ministerial individualism: both the ordained priest and the charismatically inspired individual have been seen as empowered apart from the church community and the relationships implied by ecclesial existence.[7]

These issues introduce one of the challenges to any theology of ministry that strives to take communion seriously, as the bishops do in Co-Workers. However, the history also highlights a way forward, a way indicated by the bishops themselves when they began their theology of lay ecclesial ministry with this faith claim: "The one true God is fundamentally relational: a loving communion of persons, Father, Son, and Holy Spirit."[8] If we are to avoid an individualistic account of ministry, if we are to bring together christological and pneumatological conversations, we can do no better than to turn to the doctrine of the Trinity, a doctrine that affirms the fundamentally relational nature of God.

In Co-Workers, the bishops point toward a trinitarian theology of ministry. The bishops were aided in this effort by the widespread revival of interest in the doctrine of the Trinity that has marked Catholic theology over the past three decades. This revival had its roots in the renewal of historical studies that spread throughout mid-twentieth-century European theology. It sprouted up through the dry crust of neo-scholastic theology, a system that had reduced the Trinity to an incomprehensible syllogism. Pollinated by transcendental and personalist theologies, trinitarian theology flowered in the postconciliar period, spreading its seeds to other fields of theology. A rising realization that the doctrine of the Trinity *ought to matter* watered this growth. The German Jesuit Karl Rahner pointed out the obvious and embarrassing fact that the doctrine of the Trinity—the central belief of Christianity—had become practically irrelevant for most Christians.[9] Michael Himes later made Rahner's point in a more lighthearted way: "I have often remarked that, if this Sunday all the clergy stood up in their pulpits and told the parishioners, 'We have a letter from the pope announcing that God is not three but four,' most people would simply groan, 'Oh, will these changes never stop?' But aside from having to figure out how to fit the fourth one in when making the sign of the cross, the news would make no difference to anyone because it has become concretely irrelevant to people."[10]

For Rahner, the problem with the Trinity was not the doctrine itself. Rather, the problem was that this doctrine had become disconnected. It did not seem to make a difference. Rahner (followed by Himes and many others) argued that the doctrine of the Trinity *does* make a difference. Thus Catherine LaCugna begins her major study, *God For Us*, with a simple, powerful thesis: "The doctrine of the Trinity is ultimately a practical doctrine with radical consequences for Christian life."[11] The key for LaCugna, what makes the doctrine relevant, is the recognition that this doctrine points toward the fundamentally *relational* nature of God.

The doctrine of the Trinity is not the absurdity of an impossible math problem. It is the church's limited way of talking about the mystery of a God who breaks forth into history in the person of Jesus, a God who was and is present to people. In simplest terms, the doctrine of the Trinity states that God enters into relationship with us. God is interested in us. God wants to be our friend and so creates us and comes to us. Nevertheless, the doctrine of the Trinity says more than this. Christians believe that this loving activity of God expresses the very reality of God. *God is relationship*. God is a fundamentally relational being, a loving communion that spills over, reaching out and drawing us into the divine life.

Some theologians, including Cardinal Walter Kasper, have argued that this Christian vision of God as relationship requires reimaging all of reality in terms of relationship. If we are truly created "in the image and likeness of God," then we too are fundamentally relational beings. Kasper believes that such a vision of the world offers a life-giving alternative to the narrow individualism of so much of Western society.[12]

For our purposes here, we can be more modest. In reflecting on lay ecclesial ministry in light of a theology of communion, we can say that this revival of trinitarian theology comes at just the right time, offering words to name our reality. Trinitarian theology may not address all the ills of our individualistic culture, but it does challenge any individualistic understanding of ministry. Ministers are not primarily isolated individuals whose relationships of service are secondary or nonessential to their existence as ministers. One becomes a minister by entering into and being established in relationships of service. Like the three persons of the Trinity, the person in ministry finds her or his identity and purpose in relationship. Not only does such an insight speak to the daily experience of many lay ecclesial ministers, but also it offers a way to move beyond the current theological stalemate between ontological ("being"-focused) and functional ("doing"-focused) approaches to ministry. It opens up the possibility of bringing Christ-centered and Spirit-centered conversations together. Perhaps here is a language for talking about all ministries, ordained and lay alike, in a shared space of mutual understanding.

Nevertheless, this suggested route comes with a caution. The relational approach to ministry signaled in Co-Workers has to recognize the danger of its own appeal. I call this the problem of the "warm fuzzies." When we say that ministry is all about relationships, the natural reaction of many people—not all, but many—is a kind of warm and satisfied feeling. The language of relationship has an attractiveness that can easily overshadow its ambiguity. Yet, many of us know from our own experiences that the category of relationship is equivocal. Relationships can be affirming or abusive. They can be empowering or oppressive. Therefore, when I say ministry is based on relationships, I want to know what these relationships look like concretely in the church.

To begin to unpack a self-critical and realistic theology of ministerial relationship, we might begin by distinguishing between interpersonal and ecclesial relationships. *Interpersonal relationships* operate on the intimate level of direct, personal interaction. This is the level of basic human contact: gestures of care, offers of help, moments or months of presence to an individual in need. Interpersonal relationships are the basis of all church ministries. Here, people meet people. This is where ministry happens. It is not irreverent to acknowledge that an apology accepted can be more transformative in an individual life than a liturgy of episcopal ordination, or to see that a word of consolation can communicate the reign of God more clearly than a papal encyclical. Ministry at the level of interpersonal relationship is ministry at its most profound.

When interpersonal relationships take on a public and structural dimension, when they involve activity done on behalf of the church, and are formally integrated into the church's mission, they become *ecclesial relationships*. On moving to a new parish, a pastor does not necessarily become every parishioner's friend. That is the level of the interpersonal. Nevertheless, he does become a ministerial representative with a certain responsibility for leadership and administration on behalf of every parishioner within the community. He enters into an ecclesial relationship with the parishioners.

When trying to make ministry more effective, we tend to focus on interpersonal relationship building. This is natural and this is crucial. However, it has its downside: we do not always get along. Good relationships rely a lot on personal styles, individual histories, and natural personality differences. A healthy environment built only on good interpersonal relationships can disappear overnight with a personnel change. This reality suggests that ecclesial relationship building requires more attention. Ecclesial relationship building consists of developing structures or habits of collaboration, practices of consultation, procedures for shared decision making, explicit mission statements, common goals, workplace policies, financial support for programs, and so on. There will always be crazy people. That is a fact of life lived on the interpersonal level. However, there can be crazy structures too. Therefore, we need to attend to the ecclesial relationships at play in the ministerial work of the church.

There is much that we can do within our current canonical, disciplinary, and theological context to strengthen healthy ecclesial relationships. Co-Workers provides a solid starting point and good encouragement. Following its theological presentation in part one, part two of the document is dedicated to offering suggestions for strengthening the ecclesial relationships that impact lay ecclesial ministers. It takes up in turn (1) how individuals are drawn into ministry, (2) how they are trained, (3) how their roles are authorized, and (4) how the diocese might ensure a healthy ministerial workplace. Here the document moves beyond talking about lay ecclesial ministry to fleshing out some of the concrete implications of communion.

Lay Ecclesial Ministry on Mission

Communion among ministries is important so that the many ministers within the body of Christ might be strengthened to more effectively serve the mission of Christ. It is *mission* that provides both the context for communion and the common goal for all our ministerial efforts.

For too long our theology of ministry was hampered by the assumption that the mission of the church belonged to the experts: the clergy and the religious. When an upsurge in lay activity during the first half of the twentieth century began to challenge the prevailing expectation that laity were to play a passive role in the life of the church, the hierarchy had a difficult time seeing this change as anything more than laypeople simply helping the clergy do their job. Pope Pius XI famously defined these movements—called at the time "Catholic Action"—as "the participation of the laity in the apostolate of the Church's hierarchy."[13] The Second Vatican Council, however, offered a different vision. The council insisted that, by virtue of their baptism, the laity share directly in Christ's saving mission. Leaving behind the understanding of a proprietary apostolate bestowed on the clergy and only reluctantly parceled out to the laity, the council's *Apostolicam Actuositatem* (Decree on the Lay Apostolate) affirmed that laypeople's right and duty to serve the church's mission comes from their union with Christ: "Inserted as they are in the mystical body of Christ by baptism and strengthened by the power of the Holy Spirit in confirmation, it is by the Lord himself that they are assigned to the apostolate" (AA 3).[14]

Alongside this legacy of baptismal unity, centered on the one apostolic mission of Christ, the council also opened up a certain ambiguity about where this mission was to be exercised by the clergy and the laity respectively. In the council deliberations, the sacred ministry of the clergy was never questioned; the secular responsibilities of the laity were just beginning to be appreciated. Certain medieval spiritualities had reduced "the world" to a place of temptation, an occasion for sin, and a distraction from a life of holiness. Vatican II chose instead to speak of the world in positive terms, as the arena within which the laity live out their discipleship. In *Lumen Gentium* (Dogmatic Constitution on the Church), we find this description:

> To be secular is the special characteristic of the laity. . . . It is the special vocation of the laity to seek the kingdom of God by engaging in temporal affairs and directing them according to God's will. They live in the world, in each and every one of the world's occupations and callings and in the ordinary circumstances of social and family life which, as it were, form the context of their existence. There they are called by God to contribute to the sanctification of the world from within, like leaven, in the spirit of the Gospel, by fulfilling their own particular duties. (LG 31)[15]

In past theologies, not only had "the world" been seen in a negative light by the church, but the laity had also been defined in negative terms. That is, the laity were defined according to who they were not (the clergy) or what they could not do (teach, lead, sanctify, and so on). The council took these two negatives and made a positive by presenting the immersion of laypeople in daily life and in the affairs of the world, not as an obstacle but as an opportunity. After recognizing the laity's full membership in the people of God, and after affirming their baptismal dignity and participation in the priestly, prophetic, and kingly office of Christ, the council taught that what distinguishes the laity from clergy and religious is their "secular character." Their vocation is here, in a secular world that is the very place where God and others are served.

The ambiguity mentioned above comes not so much from the council's teaching, but from the manner in which this teaching has been received, particularly by those who harden the distinction between two separate realms of responsibility: clergy in the church and laity in the world.[16] The model of such a contrastive approach could be visualized as a dividing line, neatly demarking two separate areas filled with individuals or groups whose "proper vocation" corresponds to the realm they inhabit.

Clergy in Church	Laity in World

Dividing-Line Model

However, does Vatican II's teaching on the secular character of the laity imply that the laity should stay out of affairs within the church? Alternatively, should the clergy ignore the world?

Such a dichotomy can only come from a superficial reading of the council texts. Two points deserve mention. First, it is important to recognize that *Lumen Gentium*'s theological point about the secular character of the laity was quite modest. Despite its emphasis on this secular character, the document recognizes that some laypeople serve the church in direct ministries, just as it recognizes that many priests hold secular jobs. A simple contrastive dichotomy is simply not intended. Moreover, as Joseph Komonchak pointed out over twenty-five years ago, the theological intent of the passage from *Lumen Gentium* cited above was explicitly circumscribed.[17] When this text was presented to the council participants for a vote, the introduction read by Cardinal John Wright explained that the council was not proposing an "ontological" definition of the layperson in this passage. Instead, it was offering a "typological" description. In other words, the council did not intend to define the very essence of the lay condition. Rather, it offered a description of a type: a layperson typically is married, has a job, and lives in the world, and so on.

Second, there is a gradual evolution in the council's teaching on this point. Over the course of Vatican II's four years in session, there is a shift from describing the mission "in the world" as a responsibility of the laity to describing it as a responsibility of the whole church. In the passage from *Lumen Gentium* cited above, the laity is called a leaven in the world. However, by the time *Gaudium et Spes* (Pastoral Constitution on the Church in the Modern World) was approved at the council's final session, the metaphor of leaven had been extended to the whole church. "Thus the church, at once 'a visible organization and a spiritual community,' travels the same journey as all mankind and shares the same earthly lot with the world: it is to be a leaven and, as it were, the soul of human society in its renewal by Christ and transformation into the family of God" (GS 40).[18] Alongside *Lumen Gentium*'s teaching on the secular character of the laity is *Gaudium et Spes'* teaching on the mission of the *whole church* in the world.

We might imagine such a vision of church in the world as a set of concentric circles in which diverse ministries (both ordained and lay) serve within, on behalf of, and for a church community in order to further its mission in the world.[19]

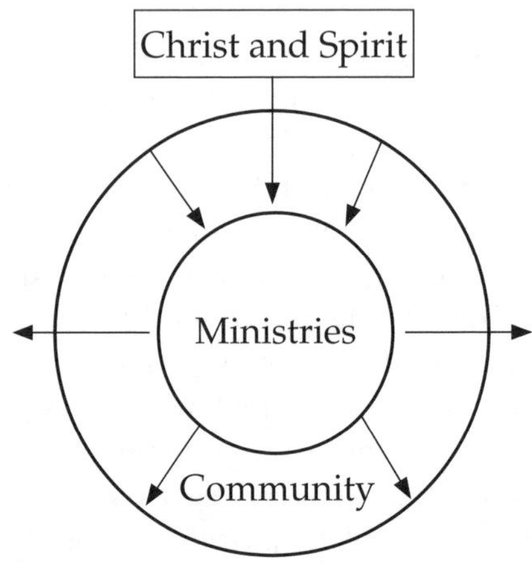

Concentric-Circles Model

The Spirit of Christ initiates and animates this ministerial community, a community that is always moving outward and forward in faithfulness to the saving mission of the triune God. Such a vision not only locates all ministries within church communion, it also helpfully subordinates all ministries to church mission. Ministry is not what is the most important. Ministry exists to serve the baptismal discipleship of all believers, so that together all of the baptized can transform the world in the light of Christ. As it has often been said, it is not so much that the church has a mission, but that the mission has a church.

By realizing our common mission in Christ, we find a more helpful starting point than one that divvies up responsibilities according to an unrealistic split between church and the world. *All believers*—clergy and laity alike—are embedded in church *and* world. All are called to impel discipleship toward transformation, and communion toward mission. We may debate the ways in which we as individuals and as groups contribute to this dynamic missionary movement, but a simple division into two spheres will not do. The best postconciliar magisterial teaching finds a way to affirm this unitary vision—holding diverse ministries and common mission in tension. In his apostolic exhortation on the laity, *Christifideles Laici* (The Lay Members of Christ's Faithful People), Pope John Paul II reaffirmed *Lumen Gentium*'s teaching on the secular character of the laity, even calling it "a theological and ecclesiological reality."[20] But the late pope placed this affirmation within the broader context of the authentic secular dimension of *the whole church*. Thus, the often-quoted concern of the late pope to avoid a "clericalization of the laity and a laicization of the clergy," must be read in light of this more nuanced understanding of clergy and laity working together to form communion and contribute to the transformational mission of Christ.

We find just such a nuanced approach in Co-Workers. In addressing the question of mission in the world, the bishops state: "All of the baptized are called to work toward the transformation of the world. Most do this by working in the secular realm; some do this by working in the Church and focusing on the building of ecclesial communion, which has among its purposes the transformation of the world."[21] Instead of defining the laity in a contrastive way as oriented toward the world (which, among other problems, leaves lay ecclesial ministry in a decidedly awkward position), and instead of ignoring the secular entirely (which, among other problems, leaves mission empty), the bishops affirm that lay ecclesial ministers serve to transform the world *precisely by their work in the church*.

Many Ministries Serving Communion and Mission

The success of the theology of Co-Workers follows from the fact that it is theology responding to reality. In an initial way, the bishops have allowed their thinking to be stretched by this new reality that has appeared in recent years: professionally prepared laypeople called to full-time ministry in the church. Co-Workers does not abandon traditional and sacramental distinctions among ministries. Indeed, the cautionary reassertion of the distinction between ordained and non-ordained that is repeated several times in Co-Workers grates against the otherwise positive tenor of the text.[22] If this essay has suggested an alternative to the parallel conversations perpetuated by a dividing-line model, my intent has not been to challenge the theological legitimacy of the distinction itself. The problem with the clergy-lay distinction is not that it is wrong. The problem is that it is too blunt of an edge to catch the real diversity in ministry today.

Despite their decision to focus Co-Workers on one particular slice of today's ministerial community, namely those thirty thousand or so ministers in the United States who can be grouped together under the heading "lay ecclesial ministers," the bishops acknowledge the many other agents who actively serve the communion and mission of the church. The theological section of Co-Workers ends with separate reflections about the relationships between lay ecclesial ministers and others in the church, such as bishops, priests, deacons, and fellow lay ministers. The document acknowledges the diversity of ministerial forms that make up today's parishes, agencies, and dioceses. And it takes up the challenge of naming this diversity—an ongoing task shared by theologians and other episcopal conferences who have also been actively reflecting on the reality of their own churches. In the 1970s, the German bishops identified lay "pastoral assistants" and "parish assistants" working alongside the ordained. In the 1990s, the Brazilian bishops distinguished between recognized, entrusted, instituted, and ordained ministries. Other examples could be added from around the world.[23] The United States bishops have opted for the language of "lay ecclesial ministry" in order to distinguish those with extensive preparation, authorization, and leadership roles from other "lay ministers" who serve in more voluntary and occasional ways. My own preference is to designate this diversity liturgically, and to speak of ordained, installed, and commissioned ministers within our local church.[24]

In the end, what is most important is not the precise set of terms but the reality to which those words point. It is a reality of diversity in ministry, noted by John Paul II, whose vision of the new millennium included an appreciation for this diversity and a confidence in the unity possible amidst it:

> The unity of the church is not uniformity, but an organic blending of legitimate diversities. It is the reality of many members joined in a single body, the one Body of Christ (cf. 1 Cor. 12:12). Therefore the church of the third millennium will need to encourage all the baptized and confirmed to be aware of their active responsibility in the church's life. Together with the ordained ministry, other ministries, whether formally instituted or simply recognized, can flourish for the good of the whole community, sustaining it in all its many needs: from catechesis to liturgy, from education of the young to the widest array of charitable works.[25]

This reality is not uniformity, but rather an organic blending of legitimate diversities, a communion of many ministries sharing one mission.

Reflection Questions

1. How are the challenges facing young priests and new lay ecclesial ministers today different? What challenges do they share? What opportunities are present for both?
2. Describe your own associations with the doctrine of the Trinity. How do you remember learning the doctrine? How have you tried to teach it? In what ways might the doctrine of the Trinity guide us in thinking about how priests and lay ecclesial ministers can and should relate to one another and to the rest of the members of a faith community?
3. What is your understanding of the mission of the church? How is the mission of the church related to the ministries of the church? How can and should ordained ministers and lay ecclesial ministers work together to further the mission of the church in the world?

Notes

1. Zeni Fox, *New Ecclesial Ministry: Lay Professionals Serving the Church* (Franklin, WI: Sheed & Ward, 2002), 4.

2. USCCB, Co-Workers in the Vineyard of the Lord: A Resource for Guiding the Development of Lay Ecclesial Ministry (Washington, DC: USCCB, 2005), 14.

3. The argument advanced in this essay is developed at length in Edward P. Hahnenberg, *Ministries: A Relational Approach* (New York: Crossroads Publishing, 2003). See also Hahnenberg, "Theology of Lay Ecclesial Ministry: Future Trajectories," in *Lay Ecclesial Ministry: Pathways Toward the Future*, ed. Zeni Fox (Lanham, MD: Rowman & Littlefield, 2010), 67–83.

4. See John Paul II, *Christifideles Laici* (The Lay Members of Christ's Faithful People) (Washington, DC: USCCB, 1988); *Pastores Dabo Vobis* (I Shall Give You Shepherds) (Washington, DC: USCCB, 1992) and *Vita Consecrata* (The Consecrated Life) (Washington, DC: USCCB, 1996).

5. Co-Workers, 19, citing John Paul II, *Pastores Dabo Vobis* (I Shall Give You Shepherds), 12.

6. See Edward P. Hahnenberg, "Ordained and Lay Ministry: Restarting the Conversation," *Origins* 35 (June 23, 2005): 94–99.

7. On the integration of christological and pneumatological approaches to ministry, see Richard Gaillardetz, "Shifting Meanings in the Lay-Clergy Distinction," *Irish Theological Quarterly* 64 (1999): 115–39.

8. Co-Workers, 17.

9. Karl Rahner, *The Trinity*, trans. Joseph Donceel (New York: Herder and Herder, 1970), 10–11.

10. Michael J. Himes, *Doing the Truth in Love: Conversations about God, Relationships and Service* (New York: Paulist Press, 1995), 16.

11. Catherine Mowry LaCugna, *God For Us: The Trinity and Christian Life* (New York: HarperSanFrancisco, 1991), 1.

12. Walter Kasper, *The God of Jesus Christ*, trans. Matthew J. O'Connell (New York: Crossroads Publishing, 1984), 290.

13. Pius XI, *L'Osservatore Romano* (Discourse to Italian Catholic Young Women), (March 21, 1927), 14.

14. *Apostolicam Actuositatem* (Decree on the Lay Apostolate), in *Vatican Council II: The Conciliar and Post Conciliar Documents*, ed. Austin Flannery, 766–98 (Northport, NY: Costello Publishing, 1987).

15. *Lumen Gentium* (Dogmatic Constitution on the Church), in *Vatican Council II: The Conciliar and Post Conciliar Documents*, ed. Austin Flannery, 350–440.

16. Though falling short of a rigid dichotomy, the tendency toward such a hardening of the distinction between clergy and laity can be found in the 1997 Congregation for the Clergy, et al., "On Certain Questions Regarding the Collaboration of the Non-ordained Faithful in the Sacred Ministry of Priests," *Origins* 27 (November 27, 1997): 397–409. See Gaillardetz, "Shifting Meanings in the Lay-Clergy Distinction," 117–19.

17. Joseph A. Komonchak, "Clergy, Laity and the Church's Mission in the World," *The Jurist* 41 (1981): 422–47.

18. *Gaudium et Spes* (Pastoral Constitution of the Church in the Modern World), in *Vatican Council II: The Conciliar and Post Conciliar Documents*, ed. Austin Flannery, 903–1001.

19. This graphic depiction of concentric circles is taken from Yves Congar, "My Path-Findings in the Theology of Laity and Ministries," *The Jurist* 32 (1972): 169–188, at 178.

20. John Paul II, *Christifideles Laici*, (The Lay Members of Christ's Faithful People) 15.

21. Co-Workers, 8.

22. These references are also reflective of the reality of lay ecclesial ministry, which operates at present within a canonical system and institutional structure that too often is clearer about who these ministers are not, than who these ministers are.

23. Edward P. Hahnenberg, "Think Globally, Act Locally: Responding to Lay Ecclesial Ministry," *New Theology Review* 17 (2004): 52–65.

24. Hahnenberg, *Ministries: A Relational Approach*, 176-210. See parallel proposal by Richard R. Gaillardetz in "The Ecclesiological Foundations of Ministry within an Ordered Communion," in *Ordering the Baptismal Priesthood: Theologies of Lay and Ordained Ministry*, ed. Susan K. Wood (Collegeville, MN: Liturgical Press, 2003), 26–51.

25. John Paul II, *Novo Millennio Ineunte* (At the Beginning of the New Millennium), 46, in *Origins* 30 (January 18, 2001): 491–508, at 503.

CHAPTER FOUR

Engaging in a Collective Gasp

A Historical Perspective on Co-Workers in the Vineyard of the Lord

Anthony Ciorra

The more I study and reflect on the United States bishops' document Co-Workers in the Vineyard of the Lord, the more these two distinct but related images come to mind: a wheelbarrow and a trapeze.

There is a story about the great magician, Rodolfo, who at the turn of the last century planned to cross Niagara Falls on a tightrope. The crowds gathered as he was about to perform his extraordinary feat. He asked the people, "Do you really think I will be able to do this?" A single voice cried out, "You are the great Rodolfo; you can do anything." He then placed a wheelbarrow on the tightrope to balance it. Heavy winds emerged and the tightrope and wheelbarrow began to shake. He then asked the crowd, "Do you still think that I can do this?" The same voice yelled back, "Of course, we do. You are the great Rodolfo; you can do anything." Then Rodolfo answered, "You are exactly the person that I have been looking for. Please, get into the wheelbarrow." As the man climbed into the wheelbarrow, there was a collective gasp that reflected the fear for his safety.

The second image is the trapeze. I was recently watching a group of trapeze artists practicing their art in a tent on the Westside highway in Manhattan. I was especially interested since I can remember going to the circus as a young boy and wanting to join as a trapeze artist. I always had a touch of resentment that my parents would not let me go away at the age of ten to follow my dream. As I watched each group of artists go to the platform to begin their journey to the other side, I anxiously watched as they let go of the first rope. There was a fraction of a second before they clutched the rope on the other side, and in that brief moment, one could hear a collective gasp that reflected the fear that the artist would not make it across.

In continuing the conversation of what has come to be called lay ecclesial ministry, Co-Workers gives greater official recognition to lay ministry in the church. This kind of recognition is a new development in the history of ministry in the Roman Catholic Church. There are various degrees of understanding and acceptance of this recognition in both clerical and lay circles. Those who carry the new title "lay ecclesial minister" are *in the wheelbarrow* and *on the trapeze*. As many of us cheer them on, we can hear *the collective gasp* as something new is struggling to emerge from the ecclesial womb.

The bishops state in their document, "Lay ecclesial ministry has emerged and takes shape in our country through the working of the Holy Spirit."[1] I suggest that the ecclesial gasp we hear is the "groaning of the Spirit" as God's new creation in ministry is emerging from the womb. It is the same Spirit who hovered over the chaos in Genesis to bring about the creation of the world. Lay ecclesial ministry comes from God, and it is God's gift for the church in the United States to meet the new needs of the twenty-first century.

The purpose of this essay is to explore, historically, the emergence of the collective gasp within the church in response to the new reality of lay ministry. We will take the sixteenth century as the starting point on our path to the wheelbarrow and the trapeze rope. We will then explore how the push or quantum leap for lay ministry began in the checkered theology of the Second Vatican Council and culminated in the majority-endorsed document of the American Catholic bishops, Co-Workers in the Vineyard of the Lord. The essay will root the new reality of lay ecclesial ministry in Cardinal Avery Dulles' sixth model of the church, "Community of Disciples." I will suggest that a spirituality for this new ecclesial reality can be found in the vision of St. Francis of Assisi and in the *Spiritual Exercises* of St. Ignatius Loyola. At the end of the essay, I will draw a parallel between the struggle to accept lay ecclesial ministry and two other struggles in the church: the historical struggle in the church to accept new models of ministry in religious communities, and the struggle to discern a new category for lay spirituality in secular institutes.

From the Council of Trent to the Second Vatican Council

The Council of Trent (1545–1563) taught that ministry was the domain of the hierarchy. One had to be a cleric (bishop or priest) to have a publicly recognized ministry in the church. (The diaconate was not a functioning ministry in the church at the time of the Council of Trent.) The pope and the bishops held the power of the keys and shared this power only with male, celibate, ordained priests. There were numerous religious communities founded in the subsequent four hundred years. Religious brothers and sisters, however, were canonically laypeople. Within clerical communities, the primary role of religious brothers as laity was to support the ministry of the ordained members, most often by doing manual labor. The priest members were then freed to do the more important work of the ministry—especially reciting the Divine Office and celebrating the sacraments. Most of the active communities of sisters that were founded over the next few centuries taught in schools, administered hospitals, or participated in other socially oriented works. What the sisters did was not called ministry but rather "apostolic works." Moreover, this understanding of the role of religious brothers and sisters was to become the model for later lay involvement in the church: laity shared in the apostolate to the degree that they were invited to or allowed to by the bishops. Additionally, lay involvement in the church was counterbalanced by the belief that the primary work of the laity was in the world, whereas the work or ministry of the ordained priest was in the church. The priest brought the laity sacraments and had jurisdiction over them. The axiom that later emerged is that the role of the laity was to "pray, pay, and obey."

The skewed stance taken by the Council of Trent was, in large part, a reaction to the Protestant reformers, who in their zeal to affirm the priesthood of all believers, often minimized the distinctiveness of holy orders. In effect, the reformers taught that the ordained priesthood was not a class of men who had been set apart to take a primary leadership role in the church, but that, instead, there was a priesthood of all believers, whereby all shared in the one priesthood of Christ.

In reaction to the Protestant reformers, the council fathers who gathered at Trent felt the need to protect ordained priesthood within the Roman Catholic Church. The fathers were rooted in a scholastic theology that taught that the ordained person experienced an ontological change and had an indelible mark inscribed on his soul through the sacrament of holy orders. The triad of pope, bishop, and priest, all male celibates, celebrated the sacraments. The fullness of orders resided with the bishop who shared or delegated his power to the priest. The council taught that dioceses, headed by bishops, should be divided into parishes, where priests were appointed by the bishops to administer the sacraments and be responsible for the spiritual well-being of the laity. This is how all ministries were structured for the next four hundred years. In effect, the Reformers emphasized the role of baptism as being primary for ministry, whereas the council subordinated baptism to holy orders.

This particular theology continued to gain momentum at the First Vatican Council (1869–70). The context for the continuation of a defensive and protective theology of holy orders was the age of "isms" that characterized the nineteenth century: deism, atheism, rationalism, Gallicanism, nationalism and indifferentism. These serious trends could have damaging consequences for religion and society. In responding to these trends, the council fathers adopted a defensive posture and decided to rely on the power of the institutional church, in other words, the power of the keys that was held by the hierarchy. Pope Pius IX institutionalized this defensive attitude in his doctrine of infallibility. With the pope's declaration of the doctrine of infallibility, power from the top down as articulated at the Council of Trent was reaffirmed and practiced for the next one hundred years. Consequently, ministry was linked to jurisdiction. It was only a few decades later that Pope Pius XI affirmed this trend in his decree *Non Abbiamo Bisogno* (On Catholic Action in Italy) in which he clearly taught that laity share in the "apostolate" (not ministry), not by baptism or gifts of the Spirit, but rather by mandate from the office of the bishop.

Despite the direction taken from the Council of Trent up to Vatican I, currents in biblical, liturgical, and patristic studies coupled with the emphasis on democratic principles in the United States gradually surfaced a role of greater lay involvement in the church. Pope Pius XII recognized these undercurrents and planned to convene a council in the 1940s. However, the urgencies caused by the Second World War overrode these internal ecclesial issues. In addition, the pope's deteriorating health after the war placed these issues on hold.

Pope John XXIII lived through the early decades of the twentieth century and understood the pastoral needs of the church well. He called Vatican II in 1962. The then-dominant theology of ministry was transformed by key council themes: the restoration of the place of baptism, the universal call to holiness, and the emphasis on the biblical theme of the church as the "people of God." The doors to ministry began to open up with the restoration of the diaconate in 1969 and the inauguration of extraordinary ministers of the Eucharist in 1974.

Yves Congar wrote that there are two doors to ministry. The first is the door of the hierarchal priesthood, whereby ministry to the church belongs to the clergy and ministry in the world belongs to the laity. The second door is the door of community, whereby the whole church shares the mission of Christ. I propose that, at Vatican II, the first door remained open and the second door was opened halfway. Thus, beginning at Vatican II, there was a new wave of ministry in the church that received various degrees of acceptance depending on how a person or a group approached the two doors of ministry. Those who favor the hierarchical priesthood have sometimes tried to push the door of community closed. In contrast, those who have sought to encourage lay ministry have frequently tried to open the door of community more widely.

The dilemma we face is that there are conflicting statements in the documents of Vatican II about the relationship between discipleship and ministry. Sometimes ecclesial ministry is presented as being open to all, while in other instances it is presented as being the domain of the hierarchy. Additionally, in chapter two of *Lumen Gentium* (Dogmatic Constitution on the Church), "The People of God," the council placed all ministry in the context of baptism and discipleship. The document refers to the "people of God," "the Christian faithful," and the "priesthood of all believers." Hence, there was no agreement about the name for Christian discipleship. The simultaneous use of these three terms, especially in discussions of ministry, continues to be ambiguous. In some instances "people of God" refers to hierarchy and in other instances, it includes the laity.[2]

The documents of Vatican II sometimes give the impression that there is a clear though not exclusive division between the ministry of the laity and the ministry of the ordained. For instance, *Lumen Gentium* states:

> Their secular character is proper and peculiar to the laity. . . . But by reason of their special vocation it belongs to the laity to seek the kingdom of God by engaging in temporal affairs and directing them according to God's will. They live in the world, that is, they are engaged in each and every work and business of the earth and in the ordinary circumstances of social and family life which, as it were, constitute their very existence. (LG 31)

The document also states:

> Although those in holy orders may sometimes be engaged in secular activities, or even practice a secular profession, yet by reason of their particular vocation, they are principally and expressly ordained to the sacred ministry. (LG 31)

Note that the above passages identify the primary ministry of the laity as being in the world while the primary, though not exclusive, ministry of the clergy is in sacred, ecclesial ministry.

At other times, the documents of Vatican II downplay the significance of the distinction between clergy and laity, and offer an expansive and inclusive sense of Christian discipleship. This more holistic sense of discipleship was incorporated into the revised Code of Canon Law. It defines *Christifidelis*, the Christian faithful, in this way:

> The Christian faithful (*Christifidelis*) are those who, inasmuch as they have been incorporated in Christ through baptism, have been constituted as the people of God; for this reason, since they have become sharers in Christ's priestly, prophetic and royal office in their own manner, they are called to exercise the ministry which God has entrusted to the Church to fulfill in the world, in accord with the condition proper to each one.[3]

Note that in this passage the Code includes all the baptized, lay and ordained, in the Christian faithful, and states that all the faithful are called to ministry in the church for the sake of the world. The Code picked up this theme from *Lumen Gentium* when it articulated the "priesthood of all believers," stating that all Christians shared in the one priesthood of Christ. It was in this spirit that the document clearly stated: "There is, therefore, one chosen People of God. . . . There is a common dignity of members deriving from their rebirth in Christ, . . . a common vocation . . . there remains, nevertheless, a true equality between all with regard to the dignity and to activity which is common to all the faithful in building up the Body of Christ" (LG 32).

There continues to be no clearly articulated teaching or consensus in the church about how, exactly, all people share in the one priesthood of Christ. Are those in the hierarchy more fully disciples, more holy, or more baptized? Moreover, some still define laity as being involved in "catholic action" or the "apostolate" in the world, but not ministry. Mixed-messages continue to appear in postconciliar documents so that in some instances the work of the laity is placed only in the world, while in other instances, laypeople are called to share ministry in the church with the hierarchy. It is unfortunate that Vatican II did not clear up these issues.

Evolving Affirmation: From "Called and Gifted" to "Co-Workers in the Vineyard of the Lord"

In the years following Vatican II, new understandings of spirituality and ministry began to gain more traction in the Catholic community. There was tension in that some still held on to the medieval dualism according to which "spiritual things belong to the priest, and temporal things to the layman."[4] Yves Congar was a pioneer in his efforts to strike the balance between the laity's mission in the world and their participation in God's work in the church. Congar's theology influenced *Apostolicam Actuositatem* (Decree on the Lay Apostolate) that acknowledged laypeople's mission both in the church and in the world.

The renewed role of the laity was evident, especially in the United States and other countries with democratic roots. When John Paul II called the Synod on the Laity in 1987, over two hundred thousand laypeople in the United States participated in local sessions in preparation for the synod. Although the tension of both sides of the argument was represented at the synod, John Paul II in *Christifidelis Laici* (The Lay Members of Christ's Faithful People) leaned toward the position of placing the laity back into the world and out of the sanctuary.

It was finally in 1988 that Bishop Timothy Harrington of Worcester, Massachusetts, noted at the National Conference of Catholic Bishops that laypeople were beginning to take a more active role in the ministry of the church. He proposed a study that was delegated to Msgr. Philip Murnion of the National Pastoral Life Center. Murnion's research noted that there were twenty-one thousand lay and religious ministers working at least twenty hours per week in various pastoral positions in over half the parishes in the United States. This trend snowballed: currently there are over thirty thousand lay parish ministers working at least twenty hours per week in paid positions. Current studies note that most lay ministers view their work as a vocation, a call from God and one that is permanent.

It is noteworthy that, prior to Vatican Council II, there was little if any official recognition of laity being involved in ministry, especially ecclesial ministry. Following the council, lay ministries began to emerge rapidly, beginning with directors of religious education (DREs) and then lay ministries such as these: youth ministry, social justice ministry, liturgical coordinators, RCIA directors, music ministers, and lay pastoral associates. The most significant development in the theology of ministry in the second millennium is this opening of the door to the community model of ministry.

These themes and trends are captured in one way or another in the four documents coming from the United States Bishops on lay ministry: Called and Gifted (1980); Called and Gifted for the Third Millennium (1995); Lay Ecclesial Ministry: The State of the Questions (1999); and Co-Workers in the Vineyard of the Lord: A Resource for Guiding the Development of Lay Ecclesial Ministry (2005). Despite the ambiguities that remain about ministry in the church and ministry to the world, these documents concede that laypeople have a role in the church. Co-Workers states:

> The basic call is the same for all followers of Christ, namely 'that all Christians in whatever state or walk of life are called to the fullness of Christian life and to the perfection of charity and this holiness is conducive to a more humane way of living even in society here on earth.' This fundamental belief, announced with urgency by the Second Vatican Council, continues to be expressed not only through Church teaching but also, in diverse ways, through the lives of the Christian faithful. . . The possibility that lay persons undertake Church ministries can be grounded in Scripture and the teachings of the Church, from St. Paul to the Second Vatican Council and in more recent documents.[5]

The term chosen to express this new reality is lay ecclesial ministers. Although there is dissatisfaction with the term itself, the more important thing is that this represents a clear affirmation of lay ministry in the church. Just as there continues to be a tension over theologies of ordained ministry, the same tension exists in definitions of lay ministry. However, the American bishops made a clear choice when they wrote:

> The ministry is *lay* because it is a service done by laypersons. The sacramental basis is the Sacraments of Initiation, not the Sacrament of Ordination. The ministry is *ecclesial* because it has a place within the community of the Church, whose communion and mission it serves, and because it is submitted to the discernment, authorization, and supervision of the hierarchy. Finally, it is *ministry* because it is a participation in the threefold ministry of Christ, who is priest, prophet, and king. 'In this original sense the term *ministry (servitium)* expresses only the work by which the Church's members continue the mission and ministry of Christ within her walls and in the whole world.' We apply the term 'ministry' to certain works undertaken by the lay faithful by making constant reference to one source, the ministry of Christ.[6]

Despite its shortcomings and lack of universal acceptance, Co-Workers affirms that the work of lay ministry is a call from God, a work of the Holy Spirit, and has a place not only in the world, but also in the church. The tension continues but the progress is stunning. In observing the reception of Co-Workers one can see the collective gasp as the church continues to ask, "What is the Spirit saying to the world today through the church in the United States, particularly through the lives of lay men and women?"[7]

An Ecclesiology for Lay Ministry

The opening sentence of Co-Workers says it all: "God calls. We respond."[8] From a Roman Catholic perspective, God calls and we live our response in our personal lives, in the church, and in the world. One's ecclesiology will determine one's perspective on the ecclesial relationships among the various ministries. From the Council of Trent until the twentieth century, some four hundred years, there was a single model of the church. The church was defined as a perfect society, complete in itself, and subordinate to no other. Robert Bellarmine helped craft this highly structured ecclesiology as a response to the attacks of Protestant reformers. This defensive ecclesiology emphasized a church of hierarchy that simply did not allow the sharing of power or service with the laity. Works that might have been the domain of laity were transferred in most instances to the new religious orders that were founded at that time. Although there were lay members in some of these religious orders (lay brothers or sisters) the church allowed them to share in its ministry because they were viewed as being a "little more than laity," in light of their vowed commitment.

The *aggiornamento* of Vatican II opened new windows into ecclesiology. Cardinal Avery Dulles in his now classic book, *Models of the Church*, initially identified five models that could be found in the various council documents. He later added another model, calling the church a "community of disciples," in a second edition of his work: in this additional model lay ecclesial ministry finds a home. I suspect that it was Dulles' inclusion of this model in his theological framework that freed him to speak publicly at the bishops' conference in favor of lay ecclesial ministry. There are many who were present at that meeting who think it was Dulles' intervention that encouraged the majority of the bishops to vote in favor of Co-Workers.

Cardinal Dulles' attraction to the term "community of disciples" is rooted in the Vatican II *Presbyterorum Ordinis* (Decree on the Ministry and Life of Priests), that tells priests "they share the status of disciples together with all Christ's faithful. The fact that the vast majority of Christians are lay persons does not mean that they escape the burden of discipleship."[9] Pope John Paul II also references this text in his first encyclical, *Redemptor Hominis* (The Redeemer of Man).[10]

In *Models of the Church*, Cardinal Dulles reflects on the multiple gifts and vocations that are present within the community of disciples. Although he writes about this in several of his other models, in his discussion of the community of disciples model there is an egalitarian dimension and a greater focus on the importance of gathering the community around the Master. Dulles points out that the Master invites disciples into a relationship with himself, and then sends them forth to "make disciples of all nations, baptizing them in the name of the Father, and of the Son, and of the holy Spirit" (Matt 28:19). All, then, are called to evangelization. Dulles writes, "In recent centuries, when the Church has been highly institutionalized the task of evangelization has been considered the responsibility of priests and religious, assisted by a few coerced volunteers. Moving away from this model, Vatican II several times asserts 'that every disciple of Christ has the obligation to take part in the spreading of the faith'."[11]

The community of disciples is one where all have a place at the table and all gather around the Master, who is the source of all life and ministry. Indeed, this is a perfect ecclesial model for lay ecclesial ministry.

Patron Saints for Lay Ecclesial Ministers

St. Francis of Assisi and St. Ignatius Loyola are perfect models for all collaborative ministries, but they are special guides for lay ecclesial ministers. Although they lived three centuries apart, these two men were kindred spirits, soul brothers in every sense of the word. St. Francis of Assisi had a vision for ministry that was several centuries ahead of his times. What he began in the thirteenth century, St. Ignatius finished in the sixteenth century.

These two great men shared a common ground: passion for the Lord that was translated into compassion for others. The vision of both of these saints led them into the marketplace. St. Francis embraced Christ in the lepers; St. Ignatius found God in all things. For Francis it was "My God and My All;" for Ignatius it was "For the greater honor and glory of God."

The church of Innocent III in the thirteenth century was a church of hierarchy and power. St. Francis lived on the margins of that church. Yet, he was faithful and is called the "vir catholicus" in the church's liturgy. His was not the church of the mighty and powerful, but rather the tiny, poor church of the Portiuncula, not even the size of a garage. He lived in the tension, the gasp of which we speak, in his rejection of a clerical caste system and his embrace of a gospel brotherhood that included women and men, clerical and lay. His was a cosmic brotherhood that embraced all of humankind, a brotherhood in which all were called to serve together in fulfilling Christ's mandate.

St. Francis received this mandate directly from Christ when he was praying before the crucifix of *San Damiano* and he heard a voice speak to him, "Francis, repair my Church." Francis took this literally and went around Assisi repairing old, fallen churches. Eventually he came to realize that the rebuilding he was called to do was a spiritual renewal of the church: his call was about rebuilding the hearts of people, and overturning the social structures of his times by breaking down the walls that would categorize and divide people. St. Francis loved and deeply respected priests. His inclusion of laymen and laywomen in his community and its gospel mission did not detract from the dignity and importance of the ordained priesthood. His was not a spirituality of subtraction, but one of inclusion, where no one group dominated the other.

St. Francis saw himself and his followers as "lesser brothers." I dare to suggest that this is a wonderful way to build a theology of ministry where lay and cleric, male and female are "lesser brothers/sisters" or minors. St. Francis' vision of minority was at the heart of his understanding of relationships. As Leonardo Boff notes in a discussion of liberation that is inspired by St. Francis:

> Relationships must not be hierarchal, from the unequal distribution of power, but absolutely fraternal, everyone being brothers and sisters, even where there are different functions, as it says in the *Regula non-bullata*: "brothers who preach, pray, and work, clerics and lay; that there is no prior, but rather ministers and servants. This fraternity, which gives shape to the Church, must be open to all without distinction, even to 'thief or robber, to the friend or adversary.[12]

St. Francis' vision was inclusive and outward looking. His vision of gospel fraternity led the community he founded into ministry, into service of others, especially to those who were lepers and outcasts of society. In this sense, he was not only the *vir catholicus* but also the *vir apostolicus*. Unfortunately, during his lifetime the institutional church took over his community, imposing a hierarchy, a focus on priesthood, and a monastic structure that fractured his vision of relatedness.

Four hundred years later, it was St. Ignatius of Loyola who continued where St. Francis left off. Like Francis, he wanted his companions to live in the world, unencumbered by structures that would hinder their ministry. I think it is fair to say that St. Ignatius was influenced by his military background more than was St. Francis. This influenced his zeal for the apostolate.

The *Spiritual Exercises*, especially the "Rules for Discernment," are at the heart of Ignatian spirituality. The *Spiritual Exercises* are available to all; there are no classes or ecclesial distinctions. St. Ignatius understood our common call to discipleship through baptism, and that each of us is sent forth to do the work of the kingdom. Like Francis, Ignatius made no distinctions; he did not introduce a class system into ministry.

Fr. Adolfo Nicolás, the current Superior General of the Jesuits, elaborated on these themes taught in the thirty-fourth and thirty-fifth congregations of the Society of Jesus. He quotes his revered predecessor, Fr. Pedro Arrupe, "Such companionship in mission depends critically on relationships based on mutual trust, nurtured by frequent exchanges, structured in flexible ways and forming a community of service."[13]

In a recent address that he gave at Loyola Marymount University in Los Angeles, Fr. General Nicolás points out that he prefers the terms "co-workers" and "companions" rather than "partners in ministry." He thinks that the term "partners" could appear paternalistic and possibly imply "junior." He notes that the phrase "co-workers in the vineyard" makes it clear that lay ministry is God's work and not ours. He also notes that at the thirty-fourth Congregation the Society spoke of cooperation with the laity in ministry. He predicts that in the coming years this will become even more pronounced, and he calls upon us to assist in that development.[14]

Expanding St. Ignatius' vision, Nicolás suggests that laity and clergy have to be co-responsible for the tasks of ministry. He says, "We have to admit that the full assimilation and meaning and true spirit of mutually respected collaboration has come slowly to us . . . . and that we must be friends and partners in ministry." I think that Nicolás builds on St. Ignatius and carries his vision into the twenty-first century when he prophetically said, "The new question is how Jesuits can serve women and men in their ministries."[15]

Nicolás notes that the thirty-fifth Congregation proclaimed, "Collaboration is at the heart of mission." He challenges Jesuits to collaborate with laypeople and to allow them to lead. He further claims that we must "remain rooted in the graces of the *Spiritual Exercises* and to find ways to make this apostolic resource available to those with whom we cooperate in mission." He beautifully says that we should share the gift of the *Spiritual Exercises*, their potential to guide formation in discernment and mission.[16]

Thus, these two great men, one living in the thirteenth century, and the other in the sixteenth century can be an excellent resource for a spirituality of lay ecclesial ministry and collaboration of laity and ordained in ministry. I am confident that, if we select St. Francis of Assisi and St. Ignatius of Loyola as our guides on the journey of ministry, the doors of community will open even wider in the years ahead.

Conclusion: Change and Resistance

The Catholic Church has survived and thrived for two thousand years precisely because of its ability to adapt and change. Nicholas of Cusa, in the sixteenth century, coined the phrase "coincidence of opposites." He described how Christ, on the cross, embraced both the "vertical" and "horizontal." The message of the cross is one of inclusively; it is the place where differences melt in the arms of a loving and inclusive God. The emergence of lay ecclesial ministry "out of nowhere," and the tension that exists as this new form expresses itself, is another example of a coincidence of opposites being brought together by the power of the Spirit.

I draw a parallel with new forms of religious life and secular consecration. Historically, we looked to religious life as the venue for seeking the more perfect way, the way to holiness and union with God. The first instinct of the Council fathers at Vatican II was to include the call to holiness in the document on religious life. But after serious reflection and dialogue, the Council fathers wisely chose to place the call to holiness in *Lumen Gentium*. In effect, they recovered the centrality of mission as rooted in the sacraments of initiation. I would like to place lay ecclesial ministry in the context of this shift in the council's plan. Although it is not a new form of religious life, lay ecclesial ministry is a new form of ministry; it opens ministerial roles to laypersons who historically had been assigned only to clerics and vowed religious.

It is important to note that evolving structures of religious life, including new ways of doing ministry, were not always enthusiastically received. For example, the monastic orders of the fifth century and the mendicant orders of the thirteenth century caused a radical shift in the way ministry was done in the church. Benedictine monks went around the world as missionaries. Their vision for ministry was informed by the new rule of St. Benedict. No sooner had the dust settled on the monastic vision for ministry, than the Franciscan movement and Order of Preachers emerged in the thirteenth century. Their mode of ministry differed from monks, canons, and diocesan clergy. In fact, the Franciscans and Dominicans were seriously attacked for their lack of structure and the free way they roamed the streets outside of monastic enclosures. Like lay ecclesial ministry, these new forms of ministry were not planned; they just happened. A gasp was heard as these new forms climbed into the wheelbarrow of change.

Various ecclesial movements are emerging phenomena in the church today. Some of these movements are known as secular institutes in which laity and clergy alike live the vowed life in the context of the world. This new way of living the vowed life and doing ministry is sometimes met with resistance. Historically, the church has had a tendency to try to stop new movements or to institutionalize them. Many communities of religious women began in what we would now call secular institutes. The church imposed structures in order to contain and control these movements.

We can apply these other examples to lay ecclesial ministry. The natural impulse is to resist what is new; if it does not go away, the next instinct is to try to control or contain it. The challenge for us is to stay with the gasp and embrace the "Gamiliean" principle—let lay ecclesial ministry happen. If it is of God, it will thrive; if not, it will die a natural death (Acts 5:34-39).

I conclude by quoting the great Jesuit Pierre Teilhard de Chardin. There were those who resisted the change he suggested out of fear; they went so far as to silence him. I invoke his wise words as we live with a new form of ministry, lay ecclesial ministry. He writes:

> Above all trust in the slow work of God. We are quite naturally impatient in everything to reach the end without delay. We should like to skip the intermediate stages. We are impatient of being on the way to something unknown, something new. And yet it is the law of progress that it is made by passing through some stages of instability—and that it may take a very long time.
>
> And so I think it is with you. Your ideas mature gradually—let them grow, let them shape themselves, without undue haste. Don't try to force them on, as though you could be today what time . . . will make of you tomorrow.
>
> Only God could say what this new spirit gradually forming in you will be. Give Our Lord the benefit of believing that his hand is leading you, and accept the anxiety of feeling yourself in suspense and incomplete.[17]

Reflection Questions

1. To what extent does the image of crossing Niagara Falls on a tight rope in a wheelbarrow help us to understand recent historical developments in lay ecclesial ministry?

2. Can you think of another image that illustrates the *newness* of lay ecclesial ministry? This image would stand in contrast to the notion of ministry as a prerogative of the ordained that was prevalent from the Council of Trent to the Second Vatican Council.
3. To what extent do you think Franciscan and Ignatian models of ministry present helpful guiding images for thinking about the development of lay ecclesial ministry? What other persons or movements (especially laypeople and movements such as, for example, Dorothy Day and the Catholic Worker movement) could provide models for the further development of lay ecclesial ministry?

Notes

1. USCCB, Co-Workers in the Vineyard of the Lord: A Resource for Guiding the Development of Lay Ecclesial Ministry (Washington, DC: USCCB, 2005), 14.

2. *Lumen Gentium* (Dogmatic Constitution on the Church), in *Vatican Council II: The Conciliar and Post Conciliar Documents*, ed. Austin Flannery, 350-440 (Northport, New York: Costello Publishing Company, 1987).

3. *Code of Canon Law* (Washington, DC: Canon Law Society, 1983), Can. 204

4. Yves Congar, *Lay People in the Church: A Study for a Theology of Laity*, trans. Donald Attwater (Westminster, MD: Newman Press, 1959), 15.

5. USCCB, Co-Workers, 7–9.

6. Ibid., 11-12.

7. USCCB, Called and Gifted for the Third Millennium (Washington, DC: USCCB, 1995), 1.

8. Ibid., 7.

9. Dulles, Avery Cardinal, *Models of the Church* (New York: Doubleday, 2001), 205.

10. John Paul II, *Redemptor Hominis* (The Redeemer of Man*)* (Boston: Pauline Books and Media, 1979), 21.

11. Dulles, 212.

12. Leonardo Boff, *Saint Francis: A Model for Human Liberation* (New York: Crossroads, 1982), 122.

13. "Companions in Mission: Pluralism in Action," Address given by Very Reverend Adolpho Nicolas, SJ. Loyola Marymount University, February 2, 2009.

14. Ibid.

15. Ibid.

16. Ibid.

17. Pierre Teilhard de Chardin, "Patient Trust," in *Hearts on Fire: Praying With Jesuits*, ed. Michael G. Harter (Chicago: Loyola Press, 2005): 102–3.

PART

II

CHAPTER FIVE

Swimming Against the Tide
Language and Political Design in Lay Ecclesial Ministry

Kieran Scott

"When I use a word," Humpty Dumpty said, in rather a scornful tone, "it means just what I choose it to mean – neither more nor less."
"The question is," said Alice, "whether you can make words mean so many different things."
"The question is," said Humpty Dumpty, "which is to be master—that's all."

—*Lewis Carroll*

This essay explores the mutually reinforcing relation between language, the ministerial practices of participants, and the institutional order that houses and embodies both. It is a study of how language both embodies and reinforces patterns of power in an institution. The essay investigates the link between the current language, ministerial classifications, and institutional form and design in the Roman Catholic Church. The essay is based on four interlocking premises:

1. A change of language is inextricably tied to institutional change. When applied to the church this means that the ongoing renewal and reform of the church, and the effectiveness of its mission and ministry in the world, is linked, in turn, to the reform and renewal of its established language pattern and form.
2. The nomenclature "lay ecclesial ministry" is an obstacle to ministerial renewal and Roman Catholic Church reform and needs problematizing. The term masks and perpetuates a medieval form of Roman Catholic institutional life.
3. Constructively, what is required is a reshaped ministerial language that correlates with a re-patterned ministerial design. This reshaping is vital to alleviate the dissonance experienced in the practice of church ministry today and the requisite reordering and interplay between diverse ministerial forms.

4. Finally, flowing logically from the first three, and intertwined with them, is the urgent and indispensable need to redesign the current pyramidic hierarchical ordering and polity in the Roman Catholic Church. This redesign is needed to bring the church more in accord with "our modern social imaginary."[1]

These four premises, I believe, are valid and defensible. Each is part of a whole—a larger context of change needed in the Roman Catholic Church. My fundamental assumption is: what is required in our time is a calm, patient, and courageous confrontation with the inadequacy of our linguistic form for relating ministry and polity in the church. We need a form of organization and language that cuts across the divisions of clergy/laity, married/single, men/women, religious/secular, and professional/nonprofessional. The nomenclature "lay ecclesial ministry" plays into these divisions and, indeed, solidifies them.

This essay proceeds to explore and probe, in turn, each of the four premises and their relationship to each other.

1. Language and Organizational Change

A change of language is at the center of any institutional change. Language is never neutral. It functions to give form to our experience of the world. It acts as choreography for the body. Our thinking and our knowing in all human endeavors is shaped by the language we dwell in and the metaphors we employ. Language, as Martin Heidegger noted, is "our house of being."[2] We live, move and have our being within linguistic systems. The language we create and choose can catalyze or polarize our capacity to perceive and receive what is there—no matter how plain or abundant the evidence.

Heidegger reminds us: language serves to cover as well as to uncover phenomena. We must always ask what a language habit hides as well as what it exposes. Words can prompt memories, images and insights. They can also mystify or cloud one's perspective and impressions. Our thinking (and practice) is curtailed within the perimeters of our language. Language reveals and conceals. It enslaves and liberates. The limits of our world are linguistic limits.

Ludwig Wittgenstein began his career by describing language as the logical representation or "picturing" of the world.[3] He understood words to be kinds of windows or transparencies through which to view reality. Later, Wittgenstein came to think of language more as a set of related practices than as a picture. He examined language as a movement, as a "game." To understand a language (or a word) we first need to understand the "game" in which it is situated, with its rules, boundaries, and back and forth flow. We understand the meaning of a word only when we understand its use in a particular context. Included in that context are attendant practices related to the communicative act. Both constitute the arena of the language-game. Words, then, are wells of meaning where thought is born. Language is a practice (game) of life.[4]

However, institutions within society, the church included, prevent certain kinds of change by not allowing for the language that would be necessary to raise questions regarding that kind of change. If there are no words available to formulate the right questions, then, no new answers are possible. Organizations that are pyramidic, bureaucratic, and biased about class remain almost impermeable to criticism and intractable to change when they remain trapped within their own language system. Rhetorical systems get built up and are used to hide and legitimate our need to control others. Then, as Gabriel Moran wrote, "Whoever owns the words owns the world."[5] Whoever controls the language system controls the worldview of the organization.

The first step in institutional reform, then, is linguistic resistance to the prevailing operating terms and categories. This is easier said than done! Nothing is harder than getting human beings to alter the way they speak when these factors exist:

1. The present is somewhat still tolerable.
2. The cost of change seems exceedingly high.
3. The worst has not happened yet—it is still in the future.

But as Peter Steinfels notes, we (Roman Catholics) are a people adrift.[6] Structural change is the great unfinished business of the Second Vatican Council. This structural change is stalled due to the current linguistic canopy covering our ecclesial life. The Roman Catholic Church needs to find a reshaped rhetorical form to engage the postmodern mind. A point of entry in this search, this essay argues, is to challenge the terminology "lay ecclesial ministry" as adequately descriptive of the remarkable ministerial developments in the American Roman Catholic Church in recent decades. Ministerial development and reform are inherently tied to institutional development and reform. And both, as Wittgenstein noted above, function within a context, a language-game, and its set of related practices.

2. Problematizing "Lay Ecclesial Ministry"

In the United States Catholic bishop's document, Co-Workers in the Vineyard of the Lord: A Resource for Guiding the Development of Lay Ecclesial Ministry (2005), "lay ecclesial ministry" is a generic term encompassing and describing several professional roles: pastoral associate, parish catechetical leader, youth ministry leader, school principal, director of music and liturgy, and participants who exercise pastoral care, and so on. The term itself is not a specific title. The bishops note, "We do not use the term in order to establish a new rank or order among the laity. Rather we use the terminology as an adjective to identify a developing and growing reality, to describe it more fully."[7]

The document proceeds to define concisely each word in the term—pointing out that each reflects key realities. The work is "lay" because it is done by "laypeople." It is "ecclesial" because it is done in, for and on behalf of the church. Finally, it is "ministry," because it participates in the threefold ministry (priest, prophet, king) of Jesus Christ.

Initially, the words and the term seems clear and precise, delineating and giving order to our ministerial lives together. But such is not the case. To date, there is considerable ambiguity about who is a "lay ecclesial minister." Amy Hoey notes there is awkwardness to the term. She writes, "The term lay ecclesial ministry does not come trippingly off the tongue, and I have not met any bishop who would not prefer another term if one could be found which adequately conveys the intended meaning."[8] The reservations some of the bishops have for the term, however, come from a different ideological vantage point than some pastoral ministers. In light of her extensive lived pastoral experience, Sylvia McGeary writes, "there was an intuitive sense that something was not right with the meaning of lay ecclesial ministry."[9] McGeary proceeds to unmask the politics of naming undergirding the creating of the term.

The search for a proper term or a more adequate language may be dismissed by some as mere semantics. Richard Gaillardetz, however, is not convinced. Gaillardetz reflects on the flourishing new ministerial reality in the Catholic Church over the last thirty-five years. It raises, he notes, a host of questions. Among them are questions about the definition of lay ministry; its scope, its limits, and its relationship to all other ministerial forms. "These questions," Gaillardetz writes, "are reflected in the struggle to find a nomenclature adequate to this new situation: Should we speak of 'lay ministry,' 'the lay apostolate,' 'lay ecclesial ministry,' 'non-ordained ministry,' or perhaps 'the ministry of the baptized?' This particular question might seem fairly insignificant, a matter of titles,"

Gaillardetz observes, "but in fact our nomenclature generally reflects an operative view of the Church."[10] In a word, our language reflects our ecclesiology, our perception of church—its ministerial nature, its political design and its mission in the world.

We ought not accept whatever ecclesiastical language seems fashionable today. We need to think through some phrases and claims that surround the ideas of "lay ecclesial ministry." There is a need to expose the controlling assumptions in the use of the term. Jurgen Habermas has pointed out that we should seek out the human interest behind any kind of knowledge. This means, in our patterned speech, we should seek to unearth and lay bare the relationship of one person to another in any social form or structure.[11] There is a need, then, to uncover and clear the thick institutional brush and undergrowth that now covers the church's institutional form. Its current linguistic self-definition, McGeary asserts, is a "stumbling block to any fruitful discussion regarding the ways in which ministry can be most effectively carried out in the church in the twenty-first century."[12] So, ironically, the term "lay ecclesial ministry," on the one hand, epitomizes the vital ministerial dynamic at the center of the United States Roman Catholic Church, and, on the other hand, it exposes the dilemma of the form of its current institutional polity.

Five years on, many wonderful things are being done under the rubric lay ecclesial ministry.[13] The people who work under its canopy are among the most idealistic and dedicated serving in the life of the church. I do not question the motives, the professional competencies or the religious convictions of the thirty-thousand plus who identify themselves as such. In the long-term, especially in the cause of church reform, it is, at best, a transitional term. However, caution is needed. With the fervor, passion and commitment driving the emergence of this phenomenon, I am reminded of the words of an old song that suggests that smoke can get into your eyes when you are in love. Karl Marx named this "mystification." When the term lay ecclesial ministry is simply superimposed on the current clergy-laity division, church ministries do not work very well. Not surprisingly, this superimposition is just what happens unless there is strong resistance to the entrenched language of clergy-laity in the Roman Catholic Church. The clergy-laity tensions are and should be undergoing drastic changes. However, the category of the laity is itself a major impediment and the guiding imagery underneath the words. The category prevents the emergence of new ministerial ways of doing things. There is a world behind the words and their relation to each other.

In the Roman Catholic Church, clergy-lay implies a rigid caste system, especially based on sexual exclusion. A member of the Roman Catholic Church is either a member of the clergy or a layperson. The categories have remained unchanged for centuries, and the language shows no tendency to change. It reinforces the very splits that need eliminating. A third category, "the religious" was in time absorbed into the other two.[14] Co-Workers, in fact, linguistically incorporates all the non-ordained (e.g. canonical religious sisters and brothers) into the laity. This linguistic absorption reinforces, and, at the same time, hides an impenetrable dualistic system.

Historically, this division of clergy-laity was not part of the Christian Church's original constitution. This language had emerged in the early church, but it was only in the twelfth century that a two-class system was finally set in place. Paul Lakeland writes,

> It is helpful to think of distinct stages in the development of a 'lay/clergy' structure in the church. The first stage corresponds to the first two centuries of the church, when there was no clergy and there was no laity. The terms were not much used and, when they were, did not correspond to the way they are used today. The ideas of clergy and laity in any terminology were foreign to the early Christian. A second stage in which ideas of laity and clergy slowly formed can be discerned in the third century and reached its full realization only in the twelfth. From that time onward, the laity are considered in a primarily negative fashion, as those who lived in the world in a lower state of holiness than the clergy.[15]

This twofold division of all Christians was generally accepted only from 1100 to Vatican II. Initially, a clergy-laity structure was a stopgap measure. It was the result of the early church's unimaginable missionary success. A minority of well-educated members became readers or clerics. The rest of the people (laity/*laos*) received basic instruction from the readers. A church divided into readers and non-readers may have been a necessity of another age. It is clearly inadequate in today's world.

A two-class system usually means that one group has something the other group lacks. The term "laity" originally meant "people," but it came to be defined as a deficiency. To this day, both in church circles and in the world of secular professions, a layperson is someone who lacks competencies, knowledge, or skills.[16] A perusal of the *Oxford* and *Webster* dictionaries define "lay" by asserting what it is not, rather than what it is: lay means "not in clerical orders," "not ecclesiastical," "not of or from a profession," "unprofessional," "not having special training or knowledge," "uncultivated." The functional, operating force of this negative meaning has flowed over into all the professions, including the profession of church ministry. The opposite of professional is lay. There is no positive meaning of lay. Wittgenstein made this observation: "If you want to know the meaning of a word look to its use."[17] The split cannot be overcome by "upgrading the laity" or "the liberation of the laity." There is nothing to build up. By definition, a layperson is someone who is deficient in something. The word provides no basis for creating a new relationship.

Vatican II's *Lumen Gentium* made an effort to heal the split. It understood the term "laity" to mean "all the faithful except those in Holy Orders and those who belong to a religious state approved by the Church" (LG 31).[18] The laity, it said, participates in the people of God by baptism. Nevertheless, the council could not overcome a language of negation in defining "laity." There was no available language for overcoming the division. In the 1987 Synod of Bishops, attempts were made to resolve this problem by giving a positive meaning to the word "laity." It defined laypeople by means of their "secularity" or involvement "in the world."[19] This raised a host of other anomalies. Were laypersons in the world but clerics were not? Do the secular and the sacred function in different arenas? Bishop Geoffrey Robinson asserts that this perspective fosters a debilitating dualism between clergy/laity. He writes, "This must be called a misguided attempt to give a positive meaning to an essentially negative term." He asserts, "It is not possible to give a positive definition to an essentially negative term.[20] The nomenclature "lay ecclesial ministry," then, simply perpetuates this negativity and class division.

In some circles, however, there is an emerging perspective that the term needs to be reconsidered. Richard Gaillardetz writes, "The term 'lay' is only with difficulty shorn of its past historical associations with a kind of ecclesial passivity. To define ministry as 'lay' is almost reflexively to define it by what it is not, a ministry proper to the ordained. . . . Since the time of the council, laudable attempts have been made to develop a positive theology of 'lay ministries,' and/or 'lay ecclesial ministries.'" "I suggest," he concludes, "that qualifying ministry as 'lay' tends to vitiate the construction of such a theology."[21] Paul Lakeland adds his voice. The very division between the two groups, clergy and laity, he notes, is at the root of the many problems and challenges facing the church. "It will be necessary perhaps," he writes, "to abandon the very terms themselves."[22] Finally, and briefly, when a word is one of a pair, addressing the first has implications for the second. The clergy-lay duality borders on a dualism. This division is reflected in the imagery beneath the words. Too often we make the mistake of accepting this imagery instead of challenging the categories. Clergy-lay gives rise to the following imagery: one is "elevated" or "admitted" into the clerical state and "reduced" or "demoted" to the lay. The image moves upward and higher, and, the reverse, downward and lower. The net effect is a pyramidal hierarchical church—split between priest and people. The language transmits implicit values and behavior models to all who use it. It evokes dysfunctional relations on both sides of the divide. Edward Hahnenberg asks, "How can we help clergy and laity work together?" The question, he notes, is "so deceptively simple." On the other hand, he writes, "[the question] masks a mess of complicated issues that touch on institutional structures, psychology, patterns of socialization and socializing, the exercise of authority, theological vision and so on."[23] These are not simple issues! Nor is the answer a simple one. However, I would venture a forthright answer: eliminate the category clergy-lay and create new terms for the emerging forms of ministries in our midst. A new pattern of church life emerges when some key terms change to name and correlate with our new ministerial practices. This is what we explore in the next section of the chapter.

3. Linguistic Renaming and Ministerial Ordering

No adequate theology of ministry or comprehensive ordering of ministry is present in the Co-Workers document. Roman Catholic efforts in recent decades have crystallized around the term "ministry." The authors of Co-Workers, after some hesitation by the United States bishops, move in the same direction. Initially, the United States Catholic Church imported the word ministry from Protestant churches. The move was fine but not sufficient. In Protestant circles, the word ministry is hampered by its narrow base. It has never been sufficient to overcome the split of clergy and lay.

It is important to keep in mind that the word ministry has almost no currency in American English usage outside of church circles. The case is different for English spoken in Britain. Ministry in the United Kingdom has political and educational significance. For example, the British have a Prime Minister and a Minister of Education. The language of ministry, however, has acquired ascendancy in Roman Catholic circles. In Walter Brueggemann's terms, it now functions as the prevailing language "behind the wall."[24] Recent theological efforts have re-rooted the term in scripture and have established it as a categorical common base for all the baptized.[25] In light of these developments, to place the qualifier "ecclesial" within the term "lay ecclesial ministry" seems redundant. All church ministries are precisely as referenced; namely, all are ecclesial.

The effort to develop a theology of ministry, re-rooted in baptism, sends nervous chills down the spine of Vatican officials and episcopal conferences. Their fear is a collapse of distinction between ordained ministry and the ministry of all the baptized. The alarm bell sounded with the 1997 publication of a Vatican decree titled, "Some Questions Regarding the Collaboration of Non-Ordained Faithful in Priests' Sacred Ministry."[26] A certain blurring had occurred, they feared, between the clergy and the laity in some Western and Central European pastoral initiatives. The decree sought to reestablish the sharp distinction in terms of roles, titles, and functions. The goal was to guard the special place of ordained ministry, its unique possession of sacred power, and to reassert that the fullness of ministry resides in the ordained. The result was a very negative document that portrayed the non-ordained to be rivals of the ordained or usurpers of their prerogatives. The document's focus was to carve out anew the activities and ministries reserved for the clergy and beyond the purview of the laity. The net effect was to heighten the distinction between the two.

While Co-Workers is much more positive in tone and affirming of diverse ministries and charisms in the church, it too acts as guardian of a firm distinction—if not a separation. The document states: "within this broad understanding of ministry, distinctions are necessary . . . The primary distinction lies between the ministry of the lay faithful and the ministry of the ordained, which is a special apostolic calling. Both are rooted in sacramental initiation, but the pastoral ministry of the ordained is empowered in a unique and essential way by the Sacrament of Holy Orders."[27] Those who are ordained to the priesthood, the document notes, "receive in the Sacrament of Orders a participation in the priesthood of Christ that is different—not simply in degree but in essence—from the participation given to all the faithful through Baptism and Confirmation."[28] The terms utilized in the document warrant noting, namely, "essentially different," "uniquely constitutive," "in the forefront of the Church," as applied to the ministry of the ordained.

Pope Benedict XVI endorsed this perspective in an address to bishops from northeastern Brazil on September 17, 2009, in Castel Gandolfo. Benedict insisted on a strict demarcation between clergy and laity. He warned the bishops not to allow the severe shortage of priests to blur the difference between the roles of the laity and ordained clergy. The distinction, he said, was "one of the most delicate issues in the existence and life of the Church" today. "It is necessary," he noted, "to avoid the secularization of priests and the clericalisation of the laity." The role of the laity, he continued, was to take the "anthropological vision and social doctrine of the church" into society and politics. The "specific identity and indispensable role" of the ordained minister was "the proclamation of the gospel and for the celebration of the sacraments, especially the Eucharist."[29] This assertion and accentuation of a separate and distinctive ordained ministerial identity "stems in part," according to Katherine Schuth, "from the increasing number of lay ecclesial ministers who are required to take on more and more ministries that were once the domain of priests."[30] This has led people, in some quarters, to regard the non-ordained as participating in ministry competitively, relative to the ordained. One important issue at stake in this debate is the meaning and function of ordination. A critically needed result of these discussions is a new theology of ordination. In this regard, Bradford Hinze writes, "the theology of ordination and of offices and their exercise must be reformulated within a larger field of vision. This will require that the theology and exercise of office holders in the church be repositioned and more fully articulated in terms of a set of relations with all of the baptized faithful."[31] This essay proceeds to take a step in that direction by viewing ministry through the lens of the term "uniqueness."

Ministerial Uniqueness

The word "unique" is filled with ambiguity, but carries a richness and a thickness that lends itself to critical distinctions. Unique is one of the chief ways people wrestle with the paradoxical relation of sameness and difference.[32] From the beginning, unique denotes difference. Nevertheless, *how* things (people, movements, ministries) differ is vital. The *how* of uniqueness runs in two opposite directions. These opposing directions give rise to two strongly contrasting meanings of uniqueness. In one case, what is unique differs from all others by a process of exclusion; in the other, the word differs by a process of inclusion. Both interpretations represent very different ways of engaging the world. Both also represent two very different ways of relating ordained and non-ordained ministry.

a) Exclusively Unique

When we speak of something being unique, we are dealing with cases of limits. That is, there are always degrees of difference. Nothing is ever absolutely unique. In this first meaning of uniqueness, one moves toward uniqueness by a process of exclusion. A thing is unique if it is separate, isolated, sharing no common traits with other things. Here, one protects one's (individual) uniqueness by (intentionally) preventing others from intruding into one's space. For example, in the sequence 3, 3, 3, 9, 3, the number 9 is unique. If we change the sequence to 3, 3, 3, M, 3, then M is even more unique—it is different in kind.[33] In Vatican, episcopal documents, and papal pronouncements, noted above, it is the claim to difference *in kind* that distinguishes ordained ministry from the ministry of all the baptized. Ordained ministry, the writers assert, is different—different in essence, substantively, ontologically different. In terms of uniqueness, it is exclusively unique. Vatican II, however, reoriented our thinking on Christian vocation by renewing an ancient theology of baptism as the foundation of all callings in the church. However, in the post–Vatican II restorationist move, noted above, difference rather than the common calling of baptism demarcated ministerial vocation. The emphasis is on the need to keep distinctions sharp and the differences among "states of life" visible. This claim to exclusive uniqueness pushes away the similarities ordained ministry has with the ministry of all the baptized. Ordained ministry is defined over against all other diverse ministerial forms. In doing so, the exclusive uniqueness erects an unbridgeable demarcation barrier between clergy and laity. In a word, exclusive uniquenes conflates small differences in degree into large differences in kind, and, in doing so, legitimates the existing system of clerical privilege and class structure. To state it another way, to superimpose the term pastoral or church ministries onto the clergy-laity division simply does not work well, because it offers no linguistic or collaborative way forward.

b) Inclusively Unique

As noted above, in the two uses and meanings of the term unique, there is a simple assertion of difference. But *how* things (people, events, ministries) are different is the key. *How* they are different reflects two ways of encountering the world. How they are different sends us in two opposite directions—one toward exclusion and the other toward inclusion. The inclusive meaning of unique takes the latter path. Here, the paradox of sameness and difference is maintained by affirming that the real is relational. Here, a thing is unique because of its non-isolation. A thing becomes its unique self as it interacts with everything in its environment. To be is to be in communion. The greater the openness and receptivity to others, the more distinct, the more unique, is the self. Of course, there are varying degrees of openness. However, a person, a movement, or a ministry becomes more unique by letting more of the world flow in.

A letter sequence can capture this inclusive way of being in the world. Moran writes, "In the sequences a, ab, abc, abcd, the fourth member of the set is inclusively unique. It is different from all the others because it includes all the others. In fact, each member is unique. However, each successive member in the sequence becomes more (inclusively) unique."[34] This, I propose, is the direction the development of a theology of ministry ought to take. Therefore, instead of ordained ministry pushing away the similarities it shares with the other diverse forms of ministry, its distinctiveness ought to depend on opening and responding to the plurality of forms all around it. Ministry is diverse in its forms, but, of its historical and geographic nature, needs to be inclusively relational. To re-appropriate this original Christian impulse, a new linguistic starting point is needed to re-shape a comprehensive ministerial language for our time.

Reshaping a Ministerial Language

Comprehensive church reforms have always been progressive and traditional simultaneously. The reforms have been liberal (open to development) and, at the same time, deeply conservative. The strategy has been neither to reject tradition nor to foreclose it, but to be radically traditional. Radical here means a return to classical sources (ressourcement) and origins. Re-appropriating the insights in some of our original Christian sources and writings, then, may hold the exit key out of our current linguistic cul-de-sac.

Thomas O'Meara has developed a comprehensive theology of ministry. He begins by grounding his work in New Testament sources, particularly Paul's Corinthians (12:4-30) and Acts (2:32, 42-47). "Ministry," writes O'Meara "is a horizon within the life of the Christian Community."[35] It is an ecclesial reality, the work of the church community. This work is constituted by a core set of practices: teaching, preaching, worship, social outreach, pastoral care, and administration. These set of practices have been continuous throughout the tradition and, at the same time, adaptive to the historical and cultural conditions of time and place.

While each of the ministerial practices is distinct, taken together as a whole, the practices build up the Body of Christ and incarnate it in the world today.[36] Seminal to O'Meara's conceptual shift (away from reducing ministry to the ordained priest) is his emphasis on baptism as ministry's foundational sacrament. Baptism grounds all ministerial forms, ordained and non-ordained. From this common base and calling, distinctions in roles and identities can be made. "Ministries differ in importance," O'Meara notes, "and distinctions among ministries (and ministers) remain, but they are, according to the New Testament, grounded upon a common faith and baptismal commissioning."[37] Ministry, then, is pluriform and multiform (rather than dual in form) and is rooted in our common baptism.

However, there is a tendency (and temptation) today to inflate the meaning of the term ministry. A misguided use of the term is to spread it over everything a person/parishioner does as a Christian. Ministry, on the other hand, needs form, institutional form. Form in ministry is crucial in relationship to the church's overall institutional form and in reshaping it. (This is explored in section four below). If the term ministry is to have substantive meaning, it has to involve designation and commitment by the local church, and accountability by individuals involved. A vital move in this direction calls for conceptual clarity with appropriate design and ordering of baptismal ministry. We find key elements of that design especially in Jewish and Christian histories.

Historically, in Jewish and Christian culture, there are two overarching components of any genuine ministry, namely, the *priestly* and *prophetic*. The *priestly* and *prophetic* are always in tension, which alerts us to the *political* dynamics in ministry. These (priestly, prophetic, and political components) are variations of the threefold ministry of Jesus and benchmarks for all ministries in the church. Tension between the priestly and prophetic is needed and good. Politically, when these two important forces (and practices) are held in creative tension, positive conditions are created. This is the mark of religious intelligence and a mature religious community.

The two overarching components of church ministry—the priestly and prophetic—should not be associated with any class or the prerogative of any persons. Both are roles and functions to perform. They describe a set of practices and the quality of a community's life. Traditionally, the priestly role is concerned with the past (as it flows into the present). This work is the work of "traditioning," in other words, conserving, guarding and passing on the tradition. This responsibility is currently expressed by specific activities or practices *within* priestly ministry. These are the chief practices: a) catechetical instruction (*didache*); b) acting in ritually remembered ways (*leiturgia*); and c) gathering up the community (*koinonia*).[38] Some people may be gifted, trained, or credentialed to exercise these roles. Others may be appointed, ordained, or elected to the priestly role. However, the focus on "priestliness" should be on the character of the community, and its distinctive practices, not the position of the individual ordained priest. The community, if it is inclusively unique, will generate a wide sharing of priestly possibilities.

Priestly ministry, however, needs a corrective balance with prophetic practices. When this corrective is absent, priestly ministry can collapse into self-absorption, bypass the chastening work of critical examination, and become idolatrous. Kenan Osborne writes, "In the conserving, guardianship role, priesthoods are prone to try and maintain traditions with which they are comfortable even when cultural change makes the outward forms of the tradition seem antiquated and uninspiring."[39]

Traditionally, the prophetic role is concerned with the present and its orientation toward the future. The work is the work of transforming, challenging, and calling into account. It is "disruption for justice."[40] This responsibility is expressed by specific activities *within* prophetic ministry. These are the chief practices: a) pushing back the current boundaries of the tradition (*diaconia*); b) speaking the word no one wants to hear (*kerygma*); and c) challenging society by disquieting actions (*diaconia*). Prophetic practices provoke engagement with issues. It is a ministry of "troublemaking."[41] Prophetic practices occur when the community emphasizes that it has a responsibility beyond itself, criticizes its current order, and confronts and condemns personal and structural evil. Biblical prophets called people back to renew their covenantal promises. Their words and deeds were never currently fashionable. We should expect no different today. It is the work of the fearless, risking for a new future. It is directed toward mending a broken world. It is an array of practices for a just and compassionate church and society. However, once again, we need to resist the temptation of exclusively identifying "propheticness" with any category or classification of persons (for example, a band of rebels). Some people may have the charisma to work in this area; others may have credentials to do so; still others may be commissioned or ordained to do so. However, if the community is inclusively unique, it will generate a wide sharing of prophetic possibilities.

A final word here: No one ministerial work is exclusively priestly or exclusively prophetic. Instead, they tend to overlap. In addition, an individual could step in and out of both roles. One might be prophetic in one part of life and priestly in another part. A parish or congregation may likewise emphasize different aspects at different times. The key to a mature religious life, however, requires a constant movement and interplay between these two ministerial polarities. They are not contradictions, but complementary opposites in need of integration in our personal and communal lives.

4. Institutional Re-Ordering and Re-Design

Ministry, as O'Meara demonstrates, has historically undergone a metamorphosis.[42] Its development has been pluriform and multiform. Ministries now exist and function within a network of relationships. However, not every ministerial relationship is the same. Richard Gaillardetz writes, "There are certain ministries in the church which, because of their public nature bring about a certain 'ecclesial re-positioning' or reconfiguration. In other words, the people who take on such a ministry find themselves in a new relationship within the church. . . . These ministers are public persons who in some sense are both called by the community and accountable to the community. . . Some will be repositioned by virtue of ordination into apostolic leadership, others into alternative ministries with or without ordination."[43] However, how are we to envision this new repositioning or reconfiguration?

The authors of Co-Workers suggest a pattern of a circle of ministry in an "ordered, relational, ministerial community."[44] A number of scholars have developed this image into the "concentric circles" model.[45] This model, rooted in a trinitarian theology, seeks to capture the unity (oneness) and the diversity ("manyness") of ministry positions today. This "relational ontological" approach, Gaillardetz writes, is to be preferred over a "powers" approach. He asserts, "A theology of ministry based on power . . . inevitably puts various ministries in a competitive relationship with one another. Each is defined by what one group can do that another cannot. . . . A powers-oriented theology of ministry encourages a view of hierarchy conceived as a top–down command structure . . . a spiritual trickle-down theory."[46] It is at this point, I believe, that systemic structural reform and significant ministerial repositioning fails to have deep traction in the *ecclesia*. The two boulders in the road, in Gaillardetz's statement, are these: 1. his negative conception of human power, and, 2. his reductionist image of hierarchy.

Power, for many in the church, is a dirty word. Liberals are particularly suspicious of the word. Church officials like to substitute the word service in its place, and play delusional games as if power (and politics) does not operate at every level of the church's life. Power here connotes force and command, coercion and domination. It is a negative to eliminate. This understanding, however, only leads to impotence. Power is ubiquitous. It is an inescapable dimension of human relations. It is fluid, flowing through the entire network of human (ministerial) relations. It is what Daniel Finn calls "the software of daily life."[47] Its reality must be attended to if it is to play a part in the reshaping of ministerial relations and the institutional re-patterning of the Roman Catholic Church. Moreover, "power" has the capacity to do so. This is the chief reason: the real paradox of human power is that power can be almost the exact opposite of force and control. Human power can be an invitation to cooperation, interdependence and receptivity.[48] People in our churches and society yearn for expressions of power that are mutual and communal. They may find it in a refashioned meaning of hierarchy and in its embodied communal forms.

Hierarchy is a form of order and design. It describes an authority pattern in an institution. The Roman Catholic Church is exhibit A in a *type* of hierarchy, namely, hierarchy as pyramid. The image is clear and unambiguous. All power flows from the top-down. Worldwide, at every level of its life today, the Roman Catholic Church has a problem with this form of hierarchy. To attempt to place concentric circles of ministers into this pyramidic structural form simply will not work. This institutional pattern reproduces class structure and authoritarian concepts of leadership. It obstructs any deep-rooted reform. However, the church needs order and patterns of power and authority for carrying out its work. Its challenge is to re-imagine a different form and structure of hierarchy that honors the past and, at the same time, resonates with our postmodern sensibilities.

"Hierarchy," Gabriel Moran writes, "need not imply an exercise of power from the top to the bottom."[49] Hierarchy can be based on participation in power. The term "hierarchy" literally means "sacred order." Moran traces how the term hierarchy, first coined by Pseudo-Dionysius, a Syrian monk of the fifth century, referred to the divine plan of creation: God at the center, surrounded by a choir of angels. Further out on the circumference come the humans and then the other earthy creatures.[50] Moran writes, "The image of the divine or sacred order was circles inside circles." "This image," he claims, "makes a lot of sense today for ecology as well as theology, for organizational theory as well as metaphysics."[51] It is also the image captured in Ezekiel's mystical vision of divine order: "a wheel within a wheel" (Ezek 1:15-16; NRSV).

For over half of its history, hierarchy in the Catholic Church referred to a system or pattern of order. It was a *what* rather than a who—a *design* rather than a designated group. The current practice, originating in the twelfth century, of referring to bishops as "the hierarchy," Moran writes, makes no sense historically, logically, or practically. Linguistically, it presents an insuperable obstacle to ministerial and church reform.[52] However, recovering a richer meaning of hierarchy as circles within circles, with men and women imagined at the center of life and at the center of ministry, allows us to envision hierarchy as a sharing of power with mutuality and reciprocity.

The Roman Catholic Church is hierarchical, a holy order. The key to its survival, health and mission is to replace its medieval, institutional (hierarchy) pattern with another institutional (hierarchy) pattern. A Christian Church that wishes to engage in education today has to examine its whole organizational pattern. Redesigning its structure as concentric circles of interdependent communities, with each part of the body having its role to play (1 Cor. 12: 4-30), and each church minister commissioned to uniquely and inclusively practice their vocation, is the vital ministerial reconfiguration needed today. Within this institutional reshaping of its holy order, the term "lay ecclesial ministry" can be laid to rest in the Roman Catholic communion.

Reflection Questions

1. Are you aware of other linguistic shifts in our culture (socially, sexually, or politically) in the latter half of the twentieth century? What impact, if any, have they made?
2. The metaphor "people of God" shifted to the center of the Roman Catholic imagination after Vatican II. What practical effects did it have?
3. What language might you consider as a replacement for "lay ecclesial ministry"?
4. What changes must come about for genuine renewal and collaboration of all ministers?
5. What pattern of power and authority do you envision for the cultivation of ministerial best practices?
6. What suggestions might you offer for ongoing conversation and future documentation on the topic of lay ecclesial ministry?

Notes

1. Charles Taylor, *A Secular Age* (Cambridge: Harvard University Press, 2008), 159–212.

2. Martin Heidegger, *Being and Time* (New York: Harper and Row, 1962), 203.

3. See chapter three of Ludwig Wittgenstein, *Tractatus Logico-Philosophicus*, repr. of original 1921 ed. (London: Routledge & Kegan Paul, 1981).

4. Ludwig Wittgenstein, *Philosophical Investigations* (New York: MacMillan, 1953), 10-11, 22-23.

5. Gabriel Moran, *Religious Body: Design for a New Reformation* (New York: Seabury Press, 1974), 31.

6. For a complete discussion, see Peter Steinfels, *A People Adrift: The Crisis of the Roman Catholic Church in America* (New York: Simon and Schuster, 2003).

7. USCCB, Co-Workers in the Vineyard of the Lord: A Resource for Guiding the Development of Lay Ecclesial Ministry (Washington, D.C.: USCCB, 2005), 11.

8. Amy Hoey, "How Co-Workers Came To Be Written," in chapter 2 of this collection, 15.

9. Sylvia McGeary, "A Critical Reflection: Naming Lay Ecclesial Ministry – the Political and Personal Narratives," *The Journal of Adult Education*, 4 no 2: 167.

10. Richard Gaillardetz, "The Ecclesiological Foundations of Ministry within an Ordered Communion," in *Ordering the Baptismal Priesthood*, ed. Susan K. Wood, (Collegeville, MN: Liturgical Press, 2003), 26.

11. For a complete discussion, see Jurgen Habermas, *Knowledge and Human Interests* (Boston: Beacon Press, 1971).

12. McGeary, "A Critical Reflection,"166.

13. Dennis Coday, "Document Delivers on its Promise," *National Catholic Reporter* (September 2010): 1-2.

14. Kenan B. Osborne, *Orders and Ministry* (Maryknoll, NY: Orbis Books, 2006), 62.

15. Paul Lakeland, *The Liberation of the Laity: In Search of an Accountable Church* (New York: Continuum, 2003), 10.

16. Maria Harris, "Questioning Lay Ministry," in *Women and Religion: A Reader for the Clergy*, ed. Regina Coll (New York: Paulist Press, 1982), 99.

17. Ludwig Wittgenstein, *Philosophical Investigations*, par. 212.

18. *Lumen Gentium* (Dogmatic Constitution on the Church) in *Vatican Council II: The Conciliar and Post Conciliar Documents*, ed. Austin Flannery, 350–440 (Northport, NY: Costello Publishing, 1996).

19. See John Paul II, *Christifideles Laici* (The Lay Members of Christ's Faithful People) (Washington, DC: USCCB, 1988), 34–36.

20. Geoffery Robinson, *Confronting Power and Sex in the Church* (Collegeville, MN: Liturgical Press, 2008), 295.

21. Gaillardez, "The Ecclesiological Foundations of Ministry within an Ordered Communion," 43-44.

22. Paul Lakeland, "Maturity and the Lay Vocation: From Ecclesiology to Ecclesiality," in *Catholic Identity and the Laity,* ed. Tim Muldoon (Maryknoll, NY: Orbis Press, 2009), 242.

23. Edward Hahnenberg, "The Vocation to Lay Ecclesial Ministry," *Origins* 37, no.12 (2007): 177-182.

24. Walter Brueggemann, "The Legitimacy of a Sectarian Hermeneutic: 2 Kings 18-19," in *Education for Citizenship and Discipleship,* ed. Mary C. Boys (New York: Pilgrim Press, 1989), 4.

25. See Thomas O'Meara 1999 and Kenan Osborne 2006.

26. See *Origins* 27 (November 27, 1997): 397-410.

27. USCCB, Co-Workers, 20.

28. Ibid., 24.

29. Robert Mickens, "The Pope Insists On Strict Demarcation Between Clergy and Laity," *The Tablet: The International Catholic Weekly* (September 26, 2009): 31.

30. Katherine Schuth, "A View of the State of the Priesthood in the United States," *Louvain Studies* 30 (2005): 8-24.

31. Bradford Hinze, *Practices of Dialogue in the Roman Catholic Church* (New York: Continuum, 2006), 265.

32. See Gabriel Moran *Uniqueness: Problem or Paradox in Jewish and Christian Traditions* (Maryknoll, NY: Orbis Press, 1992), 5.

33. Moran, *Uniqueness,* 19.

34. Ibid., 20.

35. Thomas O'Meara, *Theology of Ministry* (New York: Paulist Press, 1999), 5.

36. Ibid., 21.

37. Ibid., 29.

38. Harris, *Fashion Me a People: Curriculum in the Church* (Louisville, KY: Westminister/John Knox Press, 1989), 43-45.

39. Osborne, *Orders and Ministry,* 27.

40. Walter Brueggmann, *The Creative Word: Canon as a Model for Biblical Education* (Philadelphia, PA: Fortress Press: 1982), 40-66.

41. Harris, *Fashion Me A People,* 145.

42. O'Meara, *Theology of Ministry,* 80-138.

43. Gaillardetz, "Shifting Meanings in the Lay-Clergy Distinction," *Irish Theological Quarterly* 64 (1999):115-139.

44. Co-Workers, 21.

45. See Thomas O'Meara, 157; Edward Hahnenberg (2003), Chap. 3; Thomas Groome, "The Future of Catholic Ministry: Our Best Hope," in *Priests for the 21st Century,* ed. Donald Dietrich (New York: Crossroads Publishing Co, 2006), 169, 184.

46. Gaillardetz, "The Theology Underlying Lay Ecclesial Ministry," *Origins* 36, 9 (July 2006):138-143.

47. Daniel Finn, "The Catholic Theological Society and the Bishops," *Origins* 37, 6 (June 2007): 88-95.

48. Kieran Scott, "Illness and the Paradox of Power: A Spirituality of Mortality," in *Spiritual and Psychological Aspects of Illness*, eds. Beverly A. Musgrave and Neil J. McGettigan (Mahwah, NJ: Paulist Press, 2010) 103-06.

49. Moran, *Believing in a Revealing God* (Collegeville, MN: Liturgical Press, 2009), 70.

50. Ibid., 70.

51. Gabriel Moran, *Fashioning A People Today: The Educational Insights of Maria Harris* (New London, CT: Twenty-Third Publications, 2007), 23.

52. Moran, *Believing in a Revealing God*, 69.

CHAPTER SIX

Lay Ministry and the Challenges Facing the Church

Bishop Howard J. Hubbard

The Flowering of Lay Ministries

It is indisputable that there has been an explosion of lay ministries since the conclusion of the Second Vatican Council. This phenomenon was brought home to me very powerfully this past year at a liturgy in our diocese commemorating the one-hundred-fiftieth anniversary of one our parishes. In the entrance procession there were banners representing the various ministries exercised within the parish. I counted thirty-one banners that proclaimed the array of liturgical, catechetical, and service ministries in the parish. If that same motif had been employed at the parish's hundredth anniversary, there probably would have been five banners for five groups: the Altar Rosary Society, the Holy Name Society, the St. Vincent de Paul Society, the Parent Teachers Association, and the Ushers Guild.

Yes, the past four decades have witnessed the flowering of lay ministries. In the liturgical life of the church laypeople proclaim the Scripture and act as extraordinary ministers of the Eucharist, which in many places includes taking communion to the sick. All of the liturgical rites have been revised to provide for a more active participation by the worshiping community, while implementation of the *Rite of Christian Initiation of Adults* (RCIA) virtually requires that laypeople fill many roles to make it work. In addition, there is now the provision for a layperson to preside at the celebration of the "Sunday Liturgy in the Absence of a Priest."

The most dynamic spiritual renewal movements in the last four decades have been led and often initiated by laypeople: for example, *Cursillo*; the Charismatic Renewal; Marriage Encounter; Life Teen; *Focolare*; the *Sant' Egidio* Community; *Opus Dei*; Communion and Liberation; ministries to separated, divorced, and widowed Catholics, and other similar groups. In addition to their traditional involvement in the faith formation of children, adolescents, and young adults, laypeople are being challenged to expand their activity as evangelists.

In many parishes, dioceses, and church agencies, laypeople have the opportunity to contribute to policy formation and decision making through structures such as parish/pastoral councils, liturgy committees, finance boards, boards of education, boards of directors, Catholic conferences, and ecumenical or interfaith committees.

Laypeople are employed full-time on parish and diocesan staffs, especially in the areas of education, human services, pastoral care to people who are elderly or disabled, as well as in the areas of social action, liturgical music, and finance. In light of this, a growing number of laypeople have pursued graduate degrees in theology and ministry in preparation for full-time ministerial careers. Indeed, we have the newly defined category of lay ecclesial ministry to reflect this reality of full-time lay professionals in the church.

Finally, there are innumerable laypeople who now interpret their daily lives and responsibilities in family, business, civic community, neighborhood, school, interest groups, and culture as occasions for ministry, for Christian witness, and for extending their faith into the world.

The Development of the Role of the Laity

The emergence of this "age of the laity," as one might call it, is based upon two basic assumptions enshrined during Vatican II. First, all believers, through baptism and faith, are called to the mission and ministry of the church. Vatican II's constitution on the church puts it this way: ". . . the faithful who by Baptism are incorporated into Christ, are placed in the People of God, and in their own way share the priestly, prophetic and kingly office of Christ, and to the best of their ability carry on the mission of the whole Christian people in the Church and the world."[1] Second, God calls all believers to this mission and ministry. This call to ministry is not issued by a bishop or priest, but by God. Once again, the Vatican Council in its constitution on the church underscores this point. "The apostolate of the laity is a sharing in the salvific mission of the Church. Through Baptism and Confirmation all are appointed to this apostolate by the Lord Himself" (LG 33).

These basic premises about the role of the laity in the church, articulated at Vatican II and in their subsequent evolution, are the result of a century-long process of development. For example, in his 1906 encyclical, *Vehementer Nos* (On the French Law of Separation) Pius X wrote, "The Church is essentially an unequal society, that is, a society comprising two categories of persons, the Pastors and the flock, . . . the one duty of the multitude is to allow themselves be led."[2] We know that Pius X has been canonized by the church, but I suspect it was not for this particular statement. The image of a flock is a biblical and an important one. However, it seems misplaced in this context and interpretation. Whatever Pope Pius X's intent in *Vehementer Nos*, it is obvious that the official statements of the church concerning the role and the ministry of the laity have changed dramatically over the past century. Pope Pius XI, for example, encouraged the movement called Catholic Action, which was defined as "the participation of the laity in the apostolate of the hierarchy."[3] This movement had a very positive side and was a huge step forward in that it encouraged the active role of the laity and stressed their activity rather than their passivity. On the minus side, however, this definition seemed to imply that the laity were not involved in their own mission, but rather were permitted to share in the mission of someone else. Laypeople were portrayed as a tool or instrument to be used by bishops and pastors in those spheres of society into which the hierarchy themselves could not enter. In addition, the Catholic Action model seemed to suggest that, while the faithful were allowed to share in the mission and ministry of the church, they were called to such by delegation, not by God or by virtue of their membership in the church.

Pius XII, in his encyclical *Mystici Corporis Christi* (On the Mystical Body of Christ), began, at least tentatively, to recognize the weakness of the Catholic Action model, which held that any formal sharing of ministry by the laity was at the hierarchy's initiative and was a sharing in the hierarchy's apostolate. He pointed out that not only the hierarchy was called to service, but that the laity had a calling and mission which were properly their own. Pius XII still saw the calling and mission of the laity to be a participation, however, in the apostolate of the hierarchy. Prior to Vatican II, in other words, laypeople were defined in a negative way. Put most succinctly, those who were not ordained, by definition, were laypeople. This negative definition carried the further connotation that non-ordained meant inferior, or at least, subordinate. This inferiority or subordination was applied not only to the exercise of authority in the church but to the state of the laity's holiness as well. Inferiority in these areas suggested that the laity were dependent upon the clergy for the sacraments, correct doctrine, and other pastoral services. The clerical state was considered the normative model for Christian living to which the laity aspired as best they could, but they in no way were to compete with the clergy in holiness, prayerfulness, theology, spirituality and church leadership.

Vatican II, however, significantly shifted the ecclesiological ground for our understanding of laypeople. The council described the laity not just as instruments of the church, but they themselves comprise the church, the people of God. Furthermore, as result of the council's shift, the Catholic Action and lay apostolate model began to wane, and the notion of lay ministry began to evolve. This evolution has been developed and enhanced further by a rich and coherent body of postconcilliar documents: the *Rite of Christian Initiation of Adults* in 1972; Pope Paul VI's apostolic exhortation, *Evangelii Nuntiandi* (Evangelization in the Modern World) issued in 1976; and the teachings of Pope John Paul II articulated in *Christifideles Laici* (The Lay Members of Christ's Faithful People), *Catechesi Tradendae* (On Catechesis in Our Time), *Pastores Dabo Vobis* (To the Bishops, Clergy and Faithful On the Formation of Priests in the Circumstances of the Present Day), and *Redemptoris Missio* (On the Permanent Validity of the Church's Missionary Activity), as well as in the remarkable General Directory for Catechesis published in 1997 by the Congregation for the Clergy. Additionally, the documents of the American bishops, such as Called and Gifted, Called and Gifted for the Third Millennium, and Co-Workers in the Vineyard of the Lord: A Resource for Guiding the Development of Lay Ecclesial Ministry, have reinforced the teaching that all the baptized are given a share in the priestly ministry of Jesus, and that one and all are necessary for the fulfillment of the church's mission. These documents contribute to the development of *communio* which makes clear that these modes of participation in the priesthood of Christ are ordered to one another, so that the ministerial priesthood is at the service of the common priesthood and directed to the unfolding of the baptismal grace of all Christians (for example, *The Catechism of the Catholic Church*, 1547).[4] At the same time, the documents carefully draw the essential distinction between the common priesthood of the faithful and the ministerial or hierarchical priesthood that is rooted in apostolic succession and vested in the power and responsibility of the ordained to act in the person of Christ.

Lay ministry, then, is to be understood neither as a luxury nor concession brought about by some American desire to democratize the church or by the current shortage in vocations to the ordained and vowed life. Rather, it is the inevitable result of Vatican II's renewed appreciation of the laity, not only as mere instruments of the hierarchy, but as the people of God who possess personal gifts and charisms that empower them to contribute their part to the building up of the Kingdom of God in our time and in our place. The laity's responsibility is a necessary and perennial dimension of the church, exercised by those who are rooted in a living and loving relationship with Christ Jesus. Such a vision demands interdependence and partnership between bishops and priests; between clergy, religious, and laity; and between parishes and diocese.

In other words, Vatican II and subsequent papal and episcopal teaching emphasize that the church is not a stratified or clerically dominated society, but rather a community of persons, all sharing in the priesthood of Jesus Christ, and all called to be the people of God. These documents stress, furthermore, that the church is a community of collaborative ministers, that is, a community in which each member is challenged to see his or her baptism as a call to holiness and ministry. This community seeks to help its members discern the personal charisms given them by the Spirit, and seeks to enable them to employ their gifts in the mission of the church. This community has ordained and vowed ministers who see the fostering of greater lay participation in the work of the church and in the transformation of society as essential to their responsibility as leaders.

Two Theological Principles

For the vision of a church, in which all are called to ministry, to take root, I suggest that we must grasp and seek to reconcile two very important theological principles that coexist in our postconciliar church. On the one hand, Vatican II emphasizes the common dignity and equality that exists among all the members of God's people. All, therefore, are called to holiness of life, and all are entitled to become engaged actively in exercising the church's mission to the world. On the other hand, the council also highlights the hierarchical nature of the church. We live as believers within a church that has an appointed structure with predetermined ranks of authority.

These two notions—so evident in preconciliar and postconciliar documents and in the revised Code of Canon Law—are not contradictory, but they do create a tension when it comes to practical things such as how decisions get made in the church or to whom and how one is accountable. This tension is real at the level of the universal church, and it also affects the local church and our parish communities.

In the twenty-first century, then, we are faced with the challenge of living with this tension, with these two differing notions. One side stresses our unity with Christ Jesus and with one another; the other stresses the need for organization, structure and authority. One side acknowledges the gifts of God that exist within individual leaders; the other side stresses the diversity of functions that the Christian community must live. Somewhere in between, we are expected to govern and to be governed, to minister and to be ministered to. Hence, the challenge is to recognize the authority of those who hold pastoral office within the church, without diminishing the value of those lay ministers who recognize their call to shared leadership responsibility arising from baptism, confirmation, and the Eucharist.

As a diocesan bishop, I experience first-hand the living out of this tension. Take, for example, the problems that have arisen with our parish councils. From the pastor's perspective, and that of the parish staff, there are the problems of getting people who will be active, enthusiastic, and contributing members of the community. There are the problems of motivating council members to assume or to fulfill responsibilities without requiring the pastor or staff members to be present at every committee meeting or every parish function themselves. There is the ongoing problem of orienting the ever-rotating council members to an understanding of the parish community's history, its current situation, and its future. There is the problem of avoiding narrow parochialism, and of envisioning the parish community within the context of the diocesan, national, and universal church. In addition, there are the frustrating problems associated with collegial decision making when it might be easier, quicker, and perhaps more effective to do things oneself.

On the other hand, the laypeople often view parish councils as an exercise in futility. Some parishioners see councils as paper tigers that meet infrequently, if at all and then only to ratify or to confirm what the pastor or parish staff has already decided. Others are perceived as debating societies where various factions air their complaints and grievances, hoping to win a favorable hearing for their pet projects or their vision of the church, but with little interest in fostering authentic Christian community. Still others are viewed as dull, stodgy groups devoid of any purpose beyond ensuring that the parking lot is paved, the annual fundraising events are conducted, and the budget is balanced. There is also the problem created when a new pastor has an entirely different vision of church or differing expectations of council members than his predecessor. Moreover, for pastor, staff, and council members alike, there is often the tension over power, authority, and control, an experience that depletes people's energies and enthusiasm, and only creates frustration, cynicism, bitterness, and disillusionment.

However, with all these challenging problems, I also observe great progress being made as more and more councils move from strictly business boards to a community of servant leaders; transform from decision-making groups that happen to pray to prayerful communities that make decisions; from crisis management to long-range planning and stewardship of gifts and resources; and change from parochialism to outreach. Councils have moved away from rule by an elite group to become bodies in which many parishioners participate and feel a sense of ownership: progressing from "we have always done it that way" to groups who re-center themselves creatively; from merely managing conflict situations to recognizing the need for healing; leaving behind a dualistic worldview that assigns spiritual matters to the priests, deacons, and religious, and temporalities to the laity, toward an understanding of shared responsibility for the total mission of the church by all.

Two Challenges for the Laity

In this section, I cite two challenging issues to which I believe our laypeople have a unique contribution to make in our contemporary church and society. The first is the secularization of our culture. The United States of America remains a religious society, but, increasingly, religion is being relegated to our private lives. Our aggressively secular culture systematically seeks to exclude religion from all public space. Religion may be acceptable for private life, but, when its adherents seek to gain admittance to the public arena, they are told, "to check their bags at the door." Under the guise of enforcing an exaggerated notion of official "neutrality," the contemporary secular milieu actually promotes its own secular outlook, giving it a privileged position in shaping public opinion and public policy. Under the guise of promoting tolerance, the secularist outlook fosters the very intolerance it claims to abhor.

In other words, a phenomenon has developed in our national life that would seek to rule religiously based values "out of order" in the public arena simply because their roots are religious. In this view, pluralism means a public square purged of intolerance—which secularists define as the belief in exclusive truth claims that define right and wrong. They believe that any religious voice in a pluralistic society either will infect the body politic with unhealthy doses of fanaticism and ill will, or will contribute to the type of extremism and polarization along religious lines that have plagued Europe and the Mideast for centuries. Their fears are fueled further by these trends: the growing political voice of evangelical Christians; the efforts of some Catholic bishops to use the threat of excommunication to dictate to political leaders how to govern or to Catholics how to vote; and the omnipresent threat of Islamic extremism.

Hence, we have the anomaly in this country that in private, religion enjoys an overwhelming majority status (over 90 percent of people profess belief in God, and over 80 percent claim adherence to some religion),[5] but in public, religion has a definite minority status or no status at all. Either religion is eliminated from our public space, or, if it does exist at all, it exists uneasily in our public affairs, our entertainment, and our intellectual and artistic endeavors, disguised and on its very best and blandest behavior, preferably as a vague form of non-denominationalism. Consequently, we in the faith community are struggling with the challenge of how best to engage the public debate in a way that combats an elite secularism that is fundamentally antithetical to a spiritual message.

I believe it is especially important that there be such a voice, given the nature of the issues that now confront American society. There are all types of questions, from embryonic stem cell research to the Iraq War about which the public debate is not purely technical or practical, but is filled with moral content. On an increasing number of issues, it is impossible to formulate wise policy without asking what constitutes good policy in a morally normative sense.

Every day, technology produces choices for us that previous generations could not have imagined. In the past two generations, for example, we have cracked the genetic code and smashed the atom. Neither these nor the revolution they symbolize can be understood apart from moral analysis. Increasingly, then, this is a key public policy question: When we can do almost anything, how shall we decide what we ought to do? Or to put it more sharply still, when we can do almost anything, how do we decide what we ought never to do? It is precisely, I believe, because this question is intertwined in so many public policy issues today that it is critical that people of faith, rooted in religious traditions, be able to enter the public policy debate.

In doing this, I believe, we may need to relearn some of the lessons of the Catholic Action model of the pre–Vatican II church, in the sense that it is the laity's prime responsibility to fulfill the mission and ministry of the church to transform society by bringing the Christian message to bear in the realm of politics, economics, culture, and entertainment. It is not true that the laity can only act by participating in the ministry of the hierarchy in those places where the hierarchy cannot go. More of our laypeople must become aware of the social teaching of the church on cutting-edge issues, and seek to articulate this teaching in the public arena. Catholic social justice flows from the exhortations of the scriptures, papal encyclicals, and bishop's pastoral letters. However, Catholic social justice advocacy and ministry remain a secret for most laity. Knowledge of Catholic social teaching remains extremely low among most Catholic laypersons. Many fail to realize that this teaching is an integral part of our faith heritage—as much a part of our tradition as the proclamation of the word and the celebration of the sacraments.[6]

We then must make Catholic social teaching part of the credenda (the things to be believed), which, then, becomes for the believer a basis for the agenda (the things to be done). As chairperson for the Public Policy Committee of the New York State Catholic Conference who has to meet with the governor and testify before the legislature, I am aware that when we bishops advocate on behalf of social and moral issues with those in state government, our elected representatives often feel free to dismiss our concerns because they know that, in most instances, we bishops are like generals without armies, and, thus to ignore our pleadings will not cost them at the polls.

If, therefore, our Catholic Christian vision and philosophy of life, especially as it pertains to the poor, is to be translated into reality, then, it is imperative that the laity become aware of the issues confronting our society. Laypeople must be educated on the moral and social teaching of the Church as it applies to these issues, and be willing to let our elected officials know of their support of or opposition to particular public-policy concerns. I believe that the more credible the laity's witness becomes in this regard, the more credible and attractive our ministry of Word and sacrament will be.

In sum, if the voice of the church is to be heard in our very secularized and pluralistic society, the laity must fulfill this role and do it with vision, knowledge, civility, sensitivity, and integrity.

The second challenging issue that, I believe, is imperative for the laity to address in our contemporary church, is evangelization. In February 2008, *The Pew Forum on Religion and Public Life* released the results of a comprehensive study about religious practice in the United States. The data revealed that more than a quarter of Americans (28 percent) have left the faith of their childhoods for another religious denomination, or claim no faith tradition at all. Sadly, Roman Catholicism is the religious group with the largest loss of adherents, with former Catholics making up almost 10 percent of the United States population. The Pew research showed that while 31percent of United States citizens indicate they were raised Catholic, only 24 percent identified themselves as current Catholics. Some have joined other religious denominations, mainly evangelical churches. Some say they are spiritual but unaffiliated with any specific religious tradition, and others describe themselves as atheists or agnostics.[7] The editors of *America* suggested that the number of atheists or agnostics might reflect more apathy or indifference than an exodus from the church because of anger at the institution, or for a more emotional experience of faith. They note, "Suddenly Catholicism in the United States finds itself assailed not by the bigotry of ages past, but by the indifference of our current milieu."[8]

On a more positive note, the Pew data indicates that the Catholic Church has retained 68 percent of those who grew up Catholic—more than any other faith group in the United States except members of the Church of Jesus Christ of Latter Day Saints (Mormons) and Jewish communities. Certainly, this study reinforces anecdotal observations that many of our Catholic people are either not practicing their faith regularly (only about 25-30 percent of Catholics worship weekly) or are joining other churches. Indeed, it has been noted that the largest Christian denomination in the United States is Roman Catholicism and the second largest is made up of lapsed Roman Catholics.

How do we account for this hemorrhaging, and what do we do about it? Speculation about why our numbers are dropping is widespread. These are some of the cited causes: growing secularization; anti-authoritarianism; individualism; moral relativism; failure to assimilate new immigrants who do not feel comfortable with the more formal structure of our liturgies; the declining number of priests and religious; the clergy sex abuse scandal; the alienation of women; dissatisfaction with church teachings, especially regarding human sexuality; and poor efforts at evangelization. I have no doubt that all these factors as well as others have contributed to the phenomenon. However, I would hope that we will be prompted by this Pew study to make evangelization a priority, both to retain current membership and to recapture lapsed Catholics, as well as to reach out to the estimated ninety million Americans who are un-churched.

There is probably nothing that is more urgent in today's church than the need to respond to the gospel mandate to "Go, therefore, and make disciples of all nations" (Matt 28:19). Yet, despite the clear mandate and the exhortations of Popes Paul VI, John Paul II, and Benedict XVI, and the American bishops in our pastoral letter *Go Make Disciples,* most Catholics find the whole idea of sharing faith with others to be traumatic. There are various reasons for this. First, we American Catholics tend to be very private in our approach to religious belief and practice. The old saying that one should, "never talk about religion or politics in polite company" is very much ingrained in our Catholic psyche. It is acceptable to profess belief in a liturgical setting or in a faith formation program, but not in everyday life encounters. Second, the catechism format, experienced by an older generation of Catholics, tended to identify faith-sharing with knowledge. Consequently, many Catholic are reluctant to discuss matters of religion with others, and especially to invite them to join with us because of the fear they might not have "the right answers" to questions people may have or to observations they may make. Third, many Catholics today tend to identify faith-sharing with the pushy tactics of the Jehovah Witnesses, "the God on my sleeve" approach of some "born again Christians" or the blatant "hucksterism" of some of the televangelists. Thus, they in no way want to be associated with this type of coercive proselytism. Fourth, in the pluralistic society in which we find ourselves, many Catholics are hesitant to share their faith with others because they may be perceived as intolerant, paternalistic, judgmental, or condescending; they may also feel apprehensive that they themselves will be rejected.

I would suggest, then, that it is not so much the lack of programs, resources, or direction that is the primary cause of our reluctance as Catholics to evangelize, but a combination of historical, cultural, and social factors which have created an awkwardness or discomfort with the very idea of evangelizing. On the other hand, if our laity are equipped with the pragmatic and spiritual resources they need to undertake this venture of evangelization through "a peer approach on a friendship basis," then, I believe the church can unleash a dynamic new approach to evangelization in the twenty-first century: one that is not coercive, hysterical, paternalistic, condescending, nor engages in "spiritual mugging," if you will. Rather this approach can emanate from the love of God and the movement of the Spirit within us, that is respectful of the dignity of others, and that is responsive to the call to discipleship that each of us has received through our baptism and confirmation.

By addressing these two challenges of secularization and evangelization, the laity can make an enormous contribution to fulfilling their twofold mission of building up the faith community and being about the transformation of society. Granted, this mission is a tall order and the battle against cynicism, discouragement, disillusionment, apathy and indifference is a constant one, but the hopeful mystery of the death and resurrection of Jesus and the future of the church require nothing less.

Reflection Questions

1. How can we balance our belief in our unity with one another in Christ Jesus and our sharing in the one call to holiness of life with the need for structures of authority within the church?
2. How can Catholic laity bring a distinctively Catholic perspective to efforts to address issues of public morality (such as stem cell research and the wars in Iraq and Afghanistan) while, at the same time, showing respect for the diverse moral perspective within the Catholic Church and in our increasingly pluralistic and religiously diverse society?
3. How can Catholic laity take a leading role in developing an approach to evangelization that is not coercive but "that emanates from the love of God and the movement of the Spirit within us, that is respectful of the dignity of others, and that is responsive to the call to discipleship that each of us has received through our baptism and confirmation" (83)?

Notes

1. *Lumen Gentium* (Dogmatic Constitution on the Church) in *Vatican Council II: the Conciliar and Post Conciliar Documents,* ed. Austin Flannery, 350-440 (Northport, NY: Costello Publishing Company, 1987), 31.

2. Pius X, *Vehementer Nos* (On the French Law of Separation), Section 8, 1906. http://www.vatican.va/holy_father/pius_x/encyclicals/documents/hf_p-x_enc_11021906_vehementer-nos_en.html (accessed February 24, 2011).

3. Pius XI, "Discourse to Italian Catholic Young Women," *L'Osservatore Romano* (March 21, 1927), 14.

4. *Catechism of the Catholic Church: with modification from the editio typica* (New York: Doubleday, 1994), 430-431.

5. Pew Forum on Religion and Public Life, "U.S. Religious Landscape Survey"; http://religions.pewforum.org/reports (February 28, 2008), accessed May 9, 2011).

6. Paul Sullins, "Catholic Social Teaching; What Do Catholics Know, and What Do They Believe?" *Catholic Social Science Review* 7 (2003): 243–64. See also part one, section one of Edward P. DeBerri, James E. Hug, with Peter J. Henriot and Michael J. Schultheis, *Catholic Social Teaching: Our Best Kept Secret*, 4th rev. and exp. ed. (Maryknoll, NY: Orbis, 2003).

7. Pew Forum on Religion and Public Life, "U.S. Religious Landscape Survey," (February 28, 2008).

8. "Lost Sheep," *America* 198, no. 9 (March 17, 2008): 5.

CHAPTER SEVEN

Being a Minister and Doing Ministry
A Psychological Approach

Lisa M. Cataldo

Opening Exercise

Before reading this essay, try this short exercise: divide a piece of paper into two columns, labeled, "Who I am" and "What I do." Take a moment to write down what comes to mind regarding these two ways of thinking about yourself.

- *How do you see the relationship between the words you have written in the two columns?*
- *More specifically, how would you order the priority of these self-definitions? Does who you are determine or direct what you do? Or does what you do shape or determine who you are?*

Introduction

When I engaged in this exercise with a group of lay and ordained ministers participating in a conference organized around the Unites States bishops' document, Co-Workers in the Vineyard of the Lord, nearly every person initially affirmed the former choice, stating, essentially: "Who I am is foundational. What I do grows out of who I am." This is, as I told the participants, the response of the good Catholic person grounded in a sense of *Imago Dei*. First we *are* (created in the image of God), and then we *do*. It is also a "vocational" attitude. In thinking about vocation, or calling, many people, lay and ordained, take seriously the idea that there is a person we are "called to be." What we choose to do, for work or otherwise, ideally is consistent with and supportive of this sense of call—the call to be fully "ourselves." In the workshop, most participants were comfortable with the notion that there is the person they *are*, and that the vocation of each person is to become, grow into, or grow towards being that unique self they were "created to be." Moreover, in the case of those in the room, what they were created to be was a minister, and what they were called to do was to minister to the people of God in one capacity or another.

I propose that how we think about being and doing can make a significant difference in our understanding of how we operate in the world, and it can make a particular difference when we are talking about our understanding of ministry. Does one do ministry because one *is* a minister? Alternatively, does one become a minister by doing ministry? Of course, many of us will likely, and with good reason, protest that this is an arbitrary distinction: that who we are and what we do are, or at least ought to be, inextricably linked. I also suggest that the way we think about these questions has had a significant influence, consciously or unconsciously, on the way we think about lay and ordained ministry in the Catholic Church. If we are willing to examine closely our often-unconscious assumptions about these ways of framing identity and behavior, we may find new ways to approach questions about vocation and ministry.

On Adopting a Psychoanalytic Approach

Before exploring the above-mentioned questions any further, the reader should know that the approach I take in addressing them is not primarily a theological one, but rather a psychological one, and specifically a psychoanalytic one. My interest and training is in the psychology of religious experience: the ways our theologies and religious practices are connected to conscious and unconscious psychological dynamics. Within the psychoanalytic framework, my training and clinical practice are heavily influenced by contemporary relational psychoanalytic thought, which I will explain more fully below. To begin, however, it is important to state why a psychoanalytic approach might be relevant when considering the questions regarding our understanding of ministry as it relates to the issues of *being* and *doing*.

The relationship between psychoanalysis and religion has often been an uneasy one. Psychoanalysis, particularly of the classical Freudian variety, has been used to show that religion is an "illusion," a defense against anxiety and uncertainty that would be "cured" if only we could see the psychological dynamics that underlie it.[1] Alternatively, religious circles have sometimes appropriated Jungian theories of the psyche with a kind of fervor, as if Jung's insistence on the recognition of a numinous or transcendent dimension of the psyche is "proof" of the legitimacy of religion, and even of particular beliefs and practices. However, either dismissing psychoanalysis as an enemy, or valorizing it as an unequivocal ally of religion and faith, without critical examination, can limit the real contribution that psychoanalytic thought can make to our understanding of the multiple dimensions of religious experience and practice, including theology and the life of faith communities.

My own work in psychology and religion comes from the perspective that reductionism in any form is unhelpful. To paraphrase David Tracy, purveyors of certainty, whether they are from a psychological or religious perspective, are totalizing, and therefore, "boring."[2] To reduce our theologies or religious practices to underlying psychological dynamics does not honor the real and transformative power of faith. Yet to sequester our theologies and practices from our psychologies—to believe that they are somehow independent of psychological dynamics—creates a kind of anti-incarnational faith, one that floats "out there" in some disembodied sphere where our personal and communal psychologies, and therefore our bodies, are bypassed in the search for some unconditioned and unconditional truth. As I will discuss further later on, this is the kind of dichotomous thinking that can create problems when we are considering the questions of being a minister and doing ministry.

As Edward Hahnenberg states so aptly in his essay "From Communion to Mission," "the best theology is a theology rooted in reality."[3] What psychoanalysis *can* contribute to our thinking about theology and religious life and practice is an important piece of reality testing, as we therapists say. It can remind us that no idea, belief, or practice, religious or otherwise, can be understood independently of our embodied and conditioned selves. We can accept that religious longing or faith is a "psychic fact," as Jung says, and that it has real transformative power in the lives of individuals and communities, while we also acknowledge that it cannot be separated from the psychological histories and processes of those individuals and communities. What humans experience, they experience through the body, the brain, the senses, the psyche; we cannot separate our way of speaking about and relating to God (theology and practice) from our psychology any more than we can separate our mind from our body.

Further, psychoanalytic thought is grounded first and foremost in the acknowledgment of the unconscious. The recognition that not all our thinking is conscious, that there are desires, wishes, conflicts, and fantasies that influence our conscious thinking and behavior, is both humbling and freeing. It is humbling to the part of us that likes to believe our rational, conscious minds are always in charge. It is freeing in that it allows us access to a fount of creative energy and the possibility of deeper and more profound understanding of the ways we relate to others and ourselves. It allows for the recognition of "not knowing" as a vital and potentially fruitful aspect of experience.

Contemporary relational psychoanalysis goes beyond Freud and Jung to consider that every person *becomes* a person in and through relationship. An individual is not a closed system who is isolated from, or exists outside of, a relational environment. There *is* no person except a person in relation to others. Far from being a "warm and fuzzy" concept,[4] relationality in contemporary psychoanalytic thought entails a rigorous examination of the dynamics of relationship, including the importance of acknowledging aggression and loss as integral aspects of all intersubjective relating.

From a relational psychoanalytic standpoint, we are all mutually and continually created by and with each other. Our sense of individuality, our subjectivity, is at once an authentic center of our being and doing, and a center that exists only because—paradoxically—it is not ultimately autonomous. From the earliest moments of our lives, we begin to develop a sense of being and doing only because we are in relationship to a "good enough" caretaking other. Without such a relationship, as I will discuss, we cannot develop a sense of "I"—we cannot *be* a person with a sense of agency, someone who recognizes others and acts (does) in relation to others who are also agents with their own subjectivity.

This is a long introduction to the idea of psychoanalysis and relationality, but one that I hope will frame the following discussion of what it means to draw certain distinctions around the categories "lay ministry" and "ordained ministry," particularly in terms of their situation in relation to the ideas of *being* and *doing*. In the remainder of this essay, I will have three main dialogue partners: Edward Hahnenberg and two foundational figures in relational approaches to psychoanalysis: Donald Winnicott and Heinz Kohut.[5]

Ontology vs. Functionality

Edward Hahnenberg, whose essay is contained in this volume, reflects that as a teacher of graduate courses made up of both seminarians and future lay ecclesial ministers, he found that his students who were seminarians were most interested in questions of being and identity; they wanted to explore what it means to *be* a priest. His lay students were interested in questions of function and professional work; they wanted to explore what it means to *do* ministry. Hahnenberg ascribed a certain cross talk among his students due to this difference in priorities. Once this difference was identified, the students were able to listen to and learn from each other's experience in a more effective way.

Hahnenberg then reflects upon the meaning of these different priorities in light of historical understandings of the priesthood and lay ministry. In summing up post–Vatican II approaches, Hahnenberg notes that there are two conversations going on:

> One conversation revolves around the theology of priesthood. It is heavily christological (Christ-centered) and ontological ("being"-centered), emphasizing the priest's ability to act "in the person of Christ" and represent Christ to the community. This is the conversation taking place primarily in seminaries, bishops' committees, and Vatican offices. A different conversation revolves around the theology of lay ministry. It is heavily pneumatological (Spirit-centered) and functional ("doing"-centered), emphasizing the charisms of the Spirit flowing out of baptism and toward an individual's ministry. This is the conversation taking place primarily in universities, formation programs, and national ministry associations.[6]

Hahnenberg proposes that this distinction between being (assigned to priests) and doing (assigned to lay ministers) creates a separation between priests and laity.[7] He proposes a relational theology of ministry that recognizes that both lay and ordained ministers exist always in relation to each other and to the people they serve; keeping such relationship at the center can help to overcome the sense of separateness between priesthood and laity without erasing the distinctions between them.[8] Hahnenberg's theological insights, placed in his clear presentation of historical context, reflect a thoughtful corrective to the dichotomous thinking that has often resulted in the kind of cross talk his students experienced, as well as in more problematic and sometimes destructive dynamics. It is in dialogue with Hahnenberg's ideas that I want to introduce some psychoanalytic reflections on being and doing in relation to ministry.

Being and Doing in Psychological Perspective

Donald Winnicott, a British pediatrician turned psychoanalyst, was one of the foundational writers whose ideas have helped shape relational theory, and his writing on *being* and *doing* can help to illuminate further the potential psychological dangers that can accrue in maintaining the dichotomy of "ontological vs. functional" views of ministry. Winnicott is famous for the phrase, "there is no such thing as a baby." He elaborated this idea in the following words: "the unit is not the individual, the unit is an environmental-individual set-up. The centre of gravity of the being does not start off in the individual."[9] What Winnicott means is that the newborn child cannot exist without the mother, and so the nascent subjectivity of the baby is a subjectivity only in relation to the caretaker (whether or not that person is the biological mother, is female, or is actually breast-feeding the baby). Without this relationship to some "good enough" caretaking other, the child cannot *be*. Specifically, it is the relationship with a caring other who is physically and emotionally "good enough" that gives the child a sense of "going on being" in the world.[10]

This sense of being—we might say the feeling of being a person who is recognized as a person—is the foundation of our sense of agency, our sense of being an "I" who acts. The sense of "going on being" is the foundation of our lives as subjects. It is because we have a sense of going on being that we have memory, that we feel like our mind resides in our body, and that we can say the word "I" in reference to ourselves in past, present, and future tenses. Without a sense of going on being, the infant will never, in Winnicott's view, become a person. In today's language, we might say that the infant will not become a subject in the sense that he or she will not develop a feeling of authentic agency or a clear recognition of the boundary between self and world, and will therefore not recognize the separate but interdependent subjectivity of the other. It is possible, in this schema, to be alive, to have life in the physical sense, without actually having a sense of *being*. This is because our sense of being (being someone, being a self) arises not out of the physical body alone, but out of our earliest experiences in relationship with a significant caretaking other.

In order to go on being, we must have a secure relationship to a significant other who recognizes us as a person, and who welcomes our authentic subjective thought and action. As Winnicott states it, the "spontaneous gesture" of the infant must be received by the mother, without undue impingement. In other words, children must be able to experiment and express themselves, without having to produce only "correct" responses (physical, emotional, or verbal) that are expected by the parent. The mutual recognition of mother and infant that grows from this secure relationship affirms the subjectivity of both parties; the child develops what Winnicott calls "True Self" feeling—a center that is experienced as the authentic source of action.[11] "After being—doing and being done to," Winnicott says, "But first, being."[12]

Being is not a philosophical or theological category for Winnicott—it is a psychological experience, where "psychological" implicates not only the mind, but also the body. Being, in this sense is an experience of the "psyche-soma," a fully embodied self-feeling that recognizes the boundaries between me and not-me, and yet also the interdependence of my feeling of "me" on your feeling of "you," and our mutual recognition of each other.[13] For Winnicott, *all* authentic doing arises out of a secure sense of being. The definition of authentic doing is that action in relation to the world that feels resonant with what one experiences as the True Self.

It is important to note that for Winnicott, the True Self is not defined in terms of content or ontology—it is not a theological term ("the self God created me to be") nor is it an existential term ("I relate, therefore I am"). It is rather an experiential term—True Self is a feeling of "tissue aliveness" *in the body*, the place from which "we see everything afresh all the time."[14] True Self is not a thing or a fixed content—it is a *feeling of authenticity in our words and actions.* We know we are acting from our True Self when we feel that our actions belong to us, arise from our own (relational) desire, and represent our true personal gesture.

In contrast, the False Self, as Winnicott depicts it, is a self that acts from a sense of deprivation or impingement. Acting from the False Self feels not quite "real," not quite "me." It carries a feeling of alienation or superficiality, where we do not have access to a sense of authenticity in our relations with others. While we all practice a degree of False Self relating, if only in observing social conventions, the experience of living in the False Self is a lonely one. It lacks that feeling of "tissue aliveness" and spontaneous, creative interaction with the world. Most of us know this feeling at some time or another, and maybe even more often than not, if we are governed by pressures to conform, to curtail or suppress emotional life, or to please others at the expense of personal well-being. If we are "sacrificing" ourselves in what I would call an unholy way, there is a sense of being cut off not only from others, but also from ourselves. We may feel stuck, emotionally dry, or dead inside, while doing all the "correct" things on the outside. In False Self living, our doing is disconnected from our being—we are not acting from a center that feels real and alive.

Being a Priest vs. Doing Ministry: A Dangerous Road

Winnicott's ideas of True and False Self, and his proposition that authentic doing arises out of a secure sense of being, can be helpful in thinking about our visions of lay and ordained ministry. Remember how

Hahnenberg's students reflected this divide in their questions surrounding work in various ordained and lay ministries. The seminarians were concerned with what it means to *be* a minister, while the laypeople were concerned with questions of action or role—what it means to *do* ministry. When we create a dichotomy between the priesthood and the laity that is based on an idea of ontology vs. function, we are creating a separation between being and doing. We are, in short, creating categories of people who are in some way not quite fully *people.* When one group of people is designated (by themselves and others) in terms of who they are, and another group of people is designated (by themselves and others) in terms of what they do, we are facing a slippery psychological slope that has potential negative consequences for both groups of people and the community in which they minister.

Before I go further in exploring these consequences, I want to state clearly that I am not proposing to eliminate all distinction between clergy and lay ministers; what I am doing is considering the psychological implications of the division of persons by the categories of being and doing, and the real life consequences that can result. If we recognize that theology is an enterprise of the human mind and heart (even if in dialogue with a sacred reality), we must also recognize that it is imbued with both conscious and unconscious desire. Taking these desires seriously need not undermine or threaten the validity or power of the theological enterprise. I believe, rather, that an acknowledgment of the psychological dynamics that fuel our thinking, our *being* theological and our *doing* theology, is a step toward liberation and creativity. Again calling on Winnicott, we can see theology and religious practice as "real" in the sense that they grow out of our capacity to play—to interact with religion so as to "see everything afresh all the time." This capacity for play is the result of good enough recognition within a context of mutual relating; it results in an ability to interact creatively with what we find in the environment, including the religious and theological traditions we encounter in our families and communities.[15]

So what then might be the psychological consequences of classifying ministerial people based on the idea of ontology vs. function? First, if we consider Winnicott's approach as outlined above, it is clear that creating a dichotomy between being (ontology) and doing (function) is an impossible undertaking. All people *are* (assuming they had good-enough caretaking); all people *do.* All our doing is grounded in our sense of being; otherwise, we could not do at all. The more our doing is grounded in being (True Self feeling, a sense of agency and relatedness), the more authentic our doing will be. However, it is also true that our *being*, our feeling of living authentically and creatively, is ideally fueled and enhanced through our *doing*. The more we act authentically, the more secure our sense of living in a True Self way will be supported. It is in many ways not surprising that Hahnenberg's students found themselves with communication problems. Each group of students—the seminarians and the laypeople—had been educated to an idea of themselves and their vocational identity that was based in a psychologically impossible premise. Being and doing are mutually dependent and inextricable aspects of human identity.

Second, creating such a false divide places both clergy and lay ministers in an unrealistically narrow and ultimately unstable, psychological position. This instability shows itself in different ways in each group of ministers, each with its own dangers. To illustrate what I mean, let me share a classroom story of my own.

I have taught Professional Ethics for Pastoral Counseling and Ministry for several years. The class is invariably made up of ordained Catholic clergy (many from outside the United States) with many years' experience in ministry, along with lay Catholics and some lay and ordained Protestant students. In the first session, I ask for a show of hands as to who believes that priests are morally superior beings, or more inherently ethical than other people. Of course, the students recognize it as a trick question, and it generally gets a laugh from the class. However, in the final exam, in response to the multiple-choice question, "what unique qualification does the ordained minister bring to professional work?" about a quarter of the priests chose "moral superiority" as the answer (the correct answer was "specialized theological and sacramental knowledge and training").[16]

While I am ready to admit that this is at least partly a reflection of my own failure as a teacher, I was most distressed to imagine that these men imagined themselves to be morally superior to their congregations and lay minister colleagues. This self-classification reflects not only a failure in formation, but suggests an interior psychological pressure to *be* and therefore *act as if* they are morally superior. It is exactly this kind of pressure that creates the need for splitting off the "inferior" aspects of the self—those desires, longings, needs, and wishes, that would indicate a less than perfect state of being. As a result, those split-off and disparaged aspects of self have two main outlets: they are projected onto the laity, who are seen as the "morally inferior" other, in need of guidance, correction, and supervision; they are acted out unconsciously or secretly in acts of control, domination, and in the worst cases, exploitation and abuse of vulnerable others. Such *doing* (splitting, denial, projection, acting out) reflects an insecurity of being that is almost inevitable if one has been told he is ontologically different from other humans. How can anyone live well under the pressure of having to be a morally superior order of person? It seems that by emphasizing ontology, we are, at the very least, setting our priests up for a lifetime of psychological struggle, even if they espouse no sense of moral superiority.

For lay ministers, working in a church where the priestly class is designated to be ontologically different, the other side of the psychological coin is revealed. Even if their clergy colleagues would not consciously and intentionally classify themselves as morally superior (and I believe most would not), lay ministers are often trained to see themselves, as Hahnenberg's students did, as people vocationally identified by function. They are concerned with what it means to *do* ministry in a church that continues to identify them, at least in part, by who they *are not* (priests, ontologically differentiated). Even if they are officially and publicly commissioned, lay ministers are commissioned to *do* something; they are not recognized as *being* something different from who they were before the commissioning. In some ways, the lay minister's psychological lot is easier—she or he is not under the pressure of living up to a new ontological status. However, to the extent that there is an emphasis on the ontological difference between those who are ordained and those who do lay ministry, the lay minister's sense of being can be circumscribed by her or his functional designation. There need not be any conscious claim of moral superiority on the part of clergy for lay ministers to be seen (and to see themselves) as somehow lacking, in need of guidance, correction, and supervision by those whose being is perhaps just that much closer to the divine.

Of course, if my students are any indication, many people entering lay ministry today do not accept that they are ontologically inferior to the clergy, and most clergy would not accept this either. However, therein lies the rub. The expertise and gifts of lay ministers, who often take on substantial responsibility for the pastoral, liturgical, educational, and administrative life of a parish or diocese, become means of doing for the church, and even doing for their ordained supervisors. They themselves might feel that these gifts are reflections of and contributors toward their *being* as persons, and their clergy colleagues might feel the same, but there is something in the way that we classify ministers that can leave one dimension unacknowledged for both groups. Perhaps neither group is comfortable with this ostensible division between being and doing, nor perhaps happily accepts the circumscription of their identity or the concomitant expectations of their behavior.

Ministry and Narcissism: Health and Unhealth

To expand upon and deepen this examination of the psychological issues at stake in the division between being and doing in the vision of ministry, I want to invoke another foundational voice in the relational psychoanalytic conversation: Heinz Kohut, the founder of the psychoanalytic school known as Self Psychology.[17] Finding fault with Freud's view of all narcissism as pathological, Kohut proposed the idea of "healthy narcissistic development," the process by which we develop a coherent, realistic, sense of self.[18] Kohut suggests that the infant has three important needs that must be met in order to develop healthy narcissism, and that these needs, which continue throughout life, constitute the parameters of healthy intersubjective relationships. The first of these needs is mirroring—the child must see itself as the "gleam in the other's eye." That is, we must experience ourselves being recognized in an approving way by another person. Second is the need for idealization: the infant needs to be able to look up to someone who represents an ideal of perfection. While this idealization will gradually be modified by assimilation of the other's imperfections, the need for an object of admiration remains as a motivating energy that pulls us toward growth and self-improvement. Finally, there is the need for "twinship," or as Kohut puts it, the need to feel like "a human among humans."[19]

The experience of good-enough mirroring, idealization and twinship allows the child, and later the adult, to develop healthy and realistic self-esteem, which, Kohut claims, is intimately related to our sense of vocation and fulfillment. Specifically, we will be drawn to ways of working and living in which our innate talents and gifts are put in the service of realistic and motivating ideals. In such a healthy narcissistic life, we have a sense of both uniqueness and belonging. We feel like a human among humans, uniquely gifted and realistically humble, able to weather our failings with only passing embarrassment, and to celebrate our successes without undue inflation.[20]

Healthy narcissistic development can be inhibited or prevented in two significant ways. First, there may be a lack of mirroring of the child's natural grandiosity (for instance, a failure to say "wow—that drawing you made is really great!"), a loss or unavailability of an idealizable parent figure, or a lack of recognition of "likeness." Paradoxically, the other danger to narcissistic development occurs when these needs are met "too well." Part of becoming secure and realistic in our self-esteem depends upon the parent or significant other's "optimal failures" to meet the child's narcissistic needs. Such failures (which are optimal when they are in small doses, at age appropriate times, and tolerable in intensity) will gradually modify the child's infantile grandiosity, will allow the child to tolerate the beloved other's flaws, and will allow for the recognition of both sameness and difference.

Whether because of inadequate mirroring, idealization and twinship, or because of lack of optimal, gradual failures, healthy narcissistic development can be arrested, resulting in what we can call narcissistic pathology or damage. In this case, the person may exhibit notable outward grandiosity, but it will cover over a split-off sense of worthlessness and damaged self-esteem. The narcissistically wounded person will constantly seek idealizable figures ("hero-worship"), and may over-identify with others in an attempt to feel a sense of belonging. The normal ups and downs of life, particularly events of personal failure, insult, or revelation of flaws in an idealized other, will be met with intense shame and rage. The narcissistically wounded person lives a life divided: internally, he or she is in a constant battle to suppress feelings of shame, envy, worthlessness, and alienation that can only be combated by attempting to maintain a conscious sense of power, goodness, or superiority over others. The fact is that most of us have narcissistic vulnerabilities that remain from less than perfect childhoods. After all, who had perfect parents?

The good news is that narcissistic wounds can be repaired; our areas of arrested development can be addressed and healed by encountering others in our lives who can supply the experiences of mirroring, idealization, and twinship we may have lacked. At its best, religious or spiritual life itself can contribute to the healing of our narcissistic wounds. As I have written elsewhere,[21] if our sacred other (God) can be experienced at times as (tolerably) "failing" to mirror us, if our religious leaders can be seen as both idealizable and flawed, and if we can imagine ourselves enough "like" the sacred other (the human Jesus, for example), religious faith becomes an instrument of growth and resumed narcissistic development.

The bad news is that the opposite can also happen. When our theologies or our religious leadership fail to mirror the subjective, creative being, when theology, church, or leadership cannot tolerate the recognition of flaws and failings, or when there is a too-rigid denial of twinship (an emphasis on difference at the expense of likeness), religion reinforces narcissistic woundedness. In such a situation, religious believers, whether leaders or followers, are not given an opportunity to deal with narcissistic vulnerabilities. Rather, they are encouraged to split off their vulnerabilities and then to compensate for the resulting instability in the self by overidentifying with authority figures or idealized others or by persisting in an unmodified grandiosity. At the extreme, this kind of religion gives rise to the oppressive or dictatorial leadership and shame-filled submission seen in fanatical religious sects or cults.[22]

When we consider Kohut's picture of healthy narcissism in conversation with Winnicott's metaphor of True Self living and the dangers of separating being from doing, we can see in greater depth the potential psychological difficulties in emphasizing an ontological vs. functional view of ministry. If we are delineating a *being* group and a *doing* group, it seems we are setting up an environment that can be, at the least, narcissistically challenging for both. There is the potential for the creation of a system that maintains feelings of inadequacy, shame, and unstable self-esteem in all parties, thereby inhibiting the possibilities for true, intersubjective relating that foster creativity and reality in the Winnicottian sense. How, specifically might this occur?

First, the designation of the lay minister as a person whose vocational worth is established by function, by what she or he *does*, counters Kohut's insistence that healthy narcissism is based first and foremost in a recognition of our unique and valuable being. A significant other must see us as valuable and worthy for who we are. Of course, in Christian theological anthropology, this is exactly the claim: the person is created *in imago Dei*, and is therefore inherently valuable and recognized as such by God. But if our ecclesial theologies or behaviors somehow refute this, however unintentionally or subtly, a kind of narcissistic cognitive dissonance—perhaps an unconscious one—can result. Lay ministers can get the feeling that their doing of ministry is somehow subordinate to the ministry of the clergy, who are inducted into a different order of being at ordination.

Second, I would suggest that the ordained person is in even a more precarious narcissistic position by virtue of his induction into an ostensibly different order of personhood. As I stated earlier, it is not easy to grapple with the idea that one is ontologically different from others. Whether consciously acknowledged or not, there is a pressure to *be* and *act as if* one is just that much closer to perfection. For the ordained person who has been formed in an atmosphere of priestly privilege or superiority, the infantile sense of grandiosity may not be sufficiently modified. There may be an attitude that "the rules that apply to others do not apply to me."

Personal weaknesses or flaws may be split off and relegated to "not me" status, where they can act as unconscious stimuli to projection or abusive acting out against self or others. In the realm of idealization, there may be an ongoing sense of failure to live up to the priestly ideal (or the ideal of Jesus), and a concomitant and pervasive sense of underlying shame at this failure. Finally, given his ontological distinction, the priest may have trouble feeling like a human among humans. The priest, having the sense that he is not (or is not supposed to be) quite the same kind of human as others, can feel alien and alienated among the laity. I imagine this would be particularly true among those secular parish priests who often live without the support of resident communities.

By designating classes of ministers as either *being-centered* or *doing-centered*, we are creating a situation in which unmodified grandiosity, pervasive shame, and a sense of alienation are real dangers for every ordained person. Such situations foster unhealthy narcissism and create an internal and external environment ripe for abuses of power, secrecy about failings or weaknesses, and pervasive feelings of shame and alienation. We do not have to look further than the recent church sexual abuse crisis to see the concrete damage and suffering that such an environment can cause for both clergy and laity. A realistic assessment of our narcissistic vulnerabilities as lay people and clergy, and a willingness to consider the psychological ramifications of systems that encourage splitting and projection, may go a long way towards healing.

Conclusion: The Shared Vocation of Becoming Human

I began this essay by asking you, the reader, to consider the ways you think of yourself in terms of *being* and *doing*. Perhaps after reading through this chapter, you have found some ideas that have been useful in thinking about the relational nature of all our being and doing, and the grounding of our psychological health in this relational foundation. In terms of lay and ordained ministry, as Edward Hahnenberg states, "we need to attend to the ecclesial relationships at play in the ministerial work of the church."[23]

Whether we are lay ministers, clergy, or congregants, we all have a stake in the psychological and spiritual health of our relationships in the church. In addition, the stakes are high. They are high because the way we think about lay and ordained ministry has real effects on the real lives of priests, deacons, lay ministers, and congregants. Real people, lay and ordained, can experience their work as empowering, authentic, and affirming of their own lives and the life of the community, or they can experience it as limiting, alienating, or deadening, and sometimes destructive. Creating relationships that foster True Self living, where being and doing are inextricable aspects of authentic living, and where no person is required to engage in splitting off parts of self, is the task of all of us who are concerned with healthy religious life.

For myself, as a Catholic person, a psychoanalyst, and a teacher of lay and ordained ministers, the most helpful vision of such relationships that I have found comes from one of my own idealized (and flawed) mentors, Jean Vanier, the founder of the L'Arche communities.[24] Vanier calls for creating relationships that recognize and welcome difference, as well as celebrate our shared humanness. We can create these relationships, Vanier claims, by talking and listening deeply to one another's stories. He recognizes that the barriers we create to healthy and peaceful relationships often stem from fear, perhaps most often from the fear of being vulnerable if we reveal our pain or weakness. We also fear change, Vanier says, because it evokes the same feelings of vulnerability, especially if it means giving up a position of power or privilege (even an imagined one). Such fears can operate on both the individual and communal level, and it is possible to recognize the presence of these fears in our struggle to create healthy relating in the ministerial context. Authentic relating between ordained and lay ministers, and between all ministers and the people they serve, requires acknowledgment and sharing of the ways in which we have each been limited or hurt by our traditional ways of doing things. Vanier writes, "Let's try to understand each other. Tell me your story, the story of your pain, the story of your failures and I can tell you my story, and somewhere we will be coming together. Forgiveness is a long road. It is based on the knowledge that each person is important . . . that each person can change, that I can change and you can change."[25]

Vanier is a devout Catholic with a deep respect for the sacramental role of the priesthood as well as the indispensable ministry of the laity, always with an eye toward questioning structures and practices of power.[26] For those of us who are concerned with relationships in the church, Vanier's message is powerful in its simplicity. It challenges all of us, lay and ordained people alike, to be willing to let go of artificial and hurtful dichotomies that keep us from understanding each other. It calls for recognition that lay and ordained people *are* human beings called to *do* ministry, together, in the service of the people of God. In our humanness, we are all vulnerable to the dynamics of splitting, shame, fear, and False Self relating, and we have all experienced the consequences of these to a greater or lesser extent in our professional and personal lives. Our shared vocation, Vanier claims, is "becoming human." When we are willing to share our stories with one another, to recognize others and ourselves as authentic subjects, being and doing, we will create the possibility for us to respond to that call.

Reflection Questions

1. How did you answer the question posed by the author in the first paragraph of this essay? How do you see the relationship between who you are and what you do? What is your own experience of the emphasis on *being* and *doing* in lay and ordained ministries?
2. What do you make of the author's claim that psychology and psychoanalysis can provide an important lens through which to view religious experience and theological understanding?
3. What practical implications can you see for the idea that clergy and lay people share the vocation of "becoming human?" How might clergy and lay ministers help each other in this task?

Notes

1. Freud's works on religion reflect various views on the psychic function of religion as a defense. In *Future of an Illusion* (*The Standard Edition* Vol. XXI, ed. and trans. James Strachey [New York: W.W. Norton, 1961], Freud emphasizes the desire to feel a sense of control over the power of Nature or Fate; in *Totem and Taboo* (*Standard Edition* Vol. XIII), and *Moses and Monotheism* (*Standard Edition* Vol. XXIII), he emphasizes the role of the archetypal Oedipal conflict; and in *Civilization and Its Discontents* (*Standard Edition* Vol. XXI), he stresses the need for a Father's protection which is projected onto an illusory God.

2. David Tracy, *Plurality and Ambiguity: Hermeneutics, Religion, Hope*. (San Francisco: Harper & Row, 1987), 101. The statement by Tracy claims that totalization is an effort "to explain away religion by ignoring its distinctiveness and insisting that it is really something else, preferably something more familiar and manageable." And further, "patrons of certainty and control in the interpretation of religion are boring. And whatever else religion is, it is not boring."

3. Edward P. Hahnenberg, "From Communion to Mission: The Theology of Co-Workers in the Vineyard of the Lord," chapter three in this collection.

4. Hahnenberg, "From Communion to Mission," 25 is concerned about the "warm fuzzies" that can get attached to the term "relational," and points out that not all relationships are harmonious. In psychoanalysis, relationality is rec-

ognized as encompassing not only feelings of love or connection, but aggression, sexuality, loss, and mourning.

5. The writings of Winnicott and Kohut date from the 1950s through the early 1990s, and thus are not "contemporary" in terms of publication date. Yet both of these psychoanalysts were profoundly influential on later developments in relational theory, and their original writings are particularly apt for the issues under discussion here.

6. Hahnenberg, "From Communion to Mission," 22.

7. Ibid., 22-23.

8. Ibid., 25-27.

9. See Donald W. Winnicott, "Anxiety Associated with Insecurity" in *Through Pediatrics to Psycho-Analysis: Collected Papers* (New York: Bruner/Mazel, 1992), 99.

10. See Winnicott, "Primary Maternal Preoccupation," in *Through Pediatrics to Psycho-Analysis: Collected Papers*, 300-305.

11. See Winnicott, "Ego Distortion in Terms of True and False Self," in *The Maturational Process and the Facilitating Environment: Studies in the Theory of Emotional Development* (New York: International Universities Press, 1965).

12. See Winnicott, "Creativity and Its Origins," in *Playing and Reality* (New York: Routledge, 1971), 85. It is important to place Winnicott in his historical context. He was writing from the late 1940s to the early 1970s in England, and worked extensively with children who had been separated from their families during the London bombings in World War II, as well as with adults. Winnicott placed great (almost exclusive) emphasis on the mother-child relationship, and his views of women, mothering, masculinity, and femininity reflect some of the stereotypes prevalent at the time. However, while Winnicott assumed that female mothers were generally responsible for childcare, he actually recognized, more than any psychoanalyst before him, the subjectivity of the mother.

13. See Winnicott, "Mind and Its Relation to the Psyche-Soma" (243-254) in *Through Pediatrics to Psycho-Analysis*.

14. See Winnicott, "Living Creatively" (35-54) in *Home is Where We Start From: Essays By a Psychoanalyst* (New York: W. W. Norton & Company, 1986), 38.

15. See Winnicott, "Transitional Objects and Transitional Phenomena," and "The Location of Cultural Experience," in *Playing and Reality* (New York: Routledge, 1971). Winnicott describes religion and the arts as natural and creative outgrowths of the "transitional experiences" of childhood. These experiences are facilitated by the good-enough relationship with the caregiver, which allows the child to both "create" and "find" reality. Winnicott acknowledges the importance of recognizing external, "objective," reality (that which is "found" outside our own minds), but insists that this reality only *becomes* real through the creative use of "illusion"—that is, the child's imaginative "creation" of the world. Thus, for Winnicott, religious ideas at their best are both "created and found." To the extent that theological propositions or religious practices become reified or rigid (only "found"), the creative element is lost, and they become forces of deadness—they inhibit True Self living.

16. It can certainly be argued that many lay ministers have similar, if not identical, training in theology and professional pastoral arts, at least in the United States. One of the texts we use in the class is Richard Gula, *Ethics in Pastoral Ministry* (New York: Paulist Press, 1996), which acknowledges the particular training of ordained clergy. It is also important to note that the priests who chose "moral superiority" as a response in any given class were all international students, trained in West Africa, Asia, or the Caribbean. These students generally had a different priestly formation experience from their American counterparts. For example, none of them had had exposure to the idea that ordained ministry might be considered "a profession" in the sense we use the word in the United States.

17. Self Psychology is a school of psychoanalysis in its own right. While many of the ideas from Self Psychology have informed and shaped contemporary Relational Psychoanalysis, the two schools of thought are not equivalent. One prevalent "argument" between contemporary (post-Kohutian) Self Psychologists and Relational analysts has to do with the role of aggression in the human psyche. Many Self Psychologists see aggression as a byproduct of deprivation in childhood, while Relational analysis would be more inclined to include aggression as an innate capacity and natural tendency of the psyche, alongside other relational motivations.

18. Heinz Kohut, *The Search for the Self* (New York: International Universities Press, 1991).

19. Kohut, *The Analysis of the Self: A Systematic Approach to the Psychoanalytic Treatment of Narcissistic Personality Disorders* (New York: International Universities Press, 1971).

20. Kohut, "Forms and Transformations of Narcissism," *Journal of the American Psychoanalytic Association* 14 (1966): 243-272. See also: Kohut, *The Restoration of the Self* (Madison, CT: International Universities Press, 1977).

21. See Lisa Cataldo, "Jesus as Transforming Selfobject: Kohutian Theory and the Life of St. Francis of Assisi," *Journal of Religion and Health*, 46, no.4 (2007):527-540.

22. For an excellent discussion of the relationship between religious fanaticism and narcissism, see James W. Jones, *Terror and Transformation: The Ambiguity of Religion in Psychoanalytic Perspective* (New York: Brunner-Routledge, 2002).

23. Hahnenberg, "From Communion to Mission," 26.

24. Jean Vanier, a native of Canada and a world-renowned advocate for peace, founded the first L'Arche community in Trosly, France in 1965. In L'Arche people with and without developmental disabilities share homes together, grounded in the principles of welcome, forgiveness, and celebration. There are now 131 L'Arche communities in 40 countries around the world. While each is unique, all share a commitment to recognizing the value and giftedness of each person. I lived in the L'Arche Daybreak community in Toronto for brief periods in 1995 and 1996.

25. Jean Vanier, *Encountering the Other* (New York: Paulist Press, 2005), 37.

26. See Vanier, *Community and Growth*, rev. ed. (New York: Paulist Press, 1989).

CHAPTER EIGHT

A Latino/a Perspective on Co-Workers in the Vineyard of the Lord

Claudio M. Burgaleta, SJ

Introduction

I have been invited to write some reflections on Co-Workers in the Vineyard of the Lord: A Resource for Guiding the Development of Lay Ecclesial Ministry from the perspective of the Latino/a or Hispanic[1] pastoral reality in the United States. I do so as a Cuban-American professor of theology; a Jesuit priest who regularly ministers to the Latino/a community at St. Jean Frances de Chantal Parish in the Bronx, New York; and a co-worker in the vineyard of adult pastoral formation with the Latino/a communities of Southern California, the New York Metropolitan area, and Las Vegas since the early 1990s. I have organized my reflections in two principal parts: the echoes of the Latino/a reality in Co-Workers and lacunae of that reality in the document. In the echoes section, I highlight how the Co-Workers document adequately addresses the current situation of Latino/a lay ministry in the United States, while in the lacunae section, I suggest ways in which Co-Workers fails to engage that reality. I offer these reflections as a constructive critique; I support what Co-Workers has achieved and am desirous of fine-tuning its contribution for the second decade of the third millennium, that for the church in the United States will have a decidedly Latino/a flavor.

Before moving to address the echoes and lacunae of the document, a snapshot of the Latino/a pastoral reality in the United States is in order. According to recent United States government data, the Hispanic population of the United States on April 1, 2010, was estimated to be 50,478,000, up from 35,300,000 in 2000.[2] In 2007, the Pew Hispanic Center estimated that more than two-thirds of Hispanics (68 percent) identify themselves as Roman Catholics, approximately 33 percent of the total Roman Catholic population of the United States. However, the Pew Hispanic Center study estimates that by 2030, the number of Latinos/as who identify themselves as Catholics will decline from 68 percent to 61 percent, even while their numbers within the overall Catholic population will increase from 33 percent to 41 percent. The percentage of US Hispanic Catholics in 2007 among different national groups of origin were as follows: Mexico (74 percent), South America (71 percent), Dominican Republic (68 percent), Cuba (60 percent), Central America (60 percent), and Puerto Rico (49 percent). If they are not Catholic, Hispanics are most likely to be born-again or evangelical Protestants (15 percent). Nearly one-in-ten (8 percent) Latinos/as do not identify with any religion.[3]

The Hispanic Catholic population has certain demographic characteristics that distinguish it from other groups: 68 percent are foreign born; 55 percent say their primary language is Spanish; 42 percent did not graduate from high school, 46 percent have a household income of less than thirty-thousand dollars per year.[4] In 2003, *Instituto Fe y Vida,* a Hispanic Catholic youth and young adult ministry, estimated that Hispanics account for more that 45 percent of all Catholics under the age of thirty in the United States, and that more than half of all Hispanics are less than twenty-six years old.[5]

According to the 2007 Pew Hispanic Center study of Latinos/as and religion,[6] two interesting aspects of the Latino/a Catholic community in the United States are both its traditional and charismatic character:

- Three in four Latinos/as believe that miracles occur today: 45 percent of Latino/a Catholics and 50 percent of Latinos/as who are charismatic say they have witnessed or received a divine healing of an illness or injury.
- Eighty-eight percent of Hispanics believe Mary watches over them.
- Latino/a Catholics pray the rosary more frequently, and believe in doctrines such as transubstantiation and going to the sacrament of reconciliation more than the majority of non-Hispanic US Catholics.
- Forty-four percent of Latino/a Catholics favor the ordination of married men and women compared with 76 percent of non-Hispanic Catholics who favor the ordination of married men and 6 percent who favor the ordination of women.
- Fifty-four percent of Latino/a Catholics identify themselves as being charismatic.
- Latinos/as who are charismatic are unfamiliar with core renewalist tenets such as "second baptism," and participate more in smaller charismatic prayer groups than in larger charismatic movements that emphasize prayer for healings and other miracles.

- Sixty-seven percent of Latinos/as who are charismatics are "biblical literalists."
- Sixty-two percent of Latino/a Catholics report attending Masses where enthusiastic displays such as hand clapping, waving, and speaking in tongues characterize the worship of the congregation.

The snapshot that emerges from these statistics is of a rapidly growing Catholic population that is significantly, if not exclusively, traditionalist yet charismatic in its Catholicism; young; financially poor; poorly educated; and predominantly Mexican in origin. Ministry among Latino/a Catholics poses a unique set of challenges and opportunities that Hispanic ministers enumerated in the 2001 consultation by the United States bishops before they issued *Encuentro and Mission* in 2002, their renewed framework for Latino/a ministry.[7] These challenges include a ministerial environment characterized by proselytism of Hispanic Catholics by fundamentalist groups. Hispanic Catholic defections to other religious groups are increased by such unwelcoming factors in the Catholic Church as excessive administrative tasks and rules in Catholic parishes, as well as a lack of clergy and lay ecclesial members prepared and willing to minister to Latinos/as.

The numerous national groups that constitute the Latino/a Catholic population of the United States pose the further challenge of finding a common ministerial framework that will further the work of evangelization and pastoral care. Different groups have different traditions and require different pastoral approaches. The danger is to default to a one-size-fits-all approach to ministry that glosses over real differences and misses pastoral opportunities that those differences provide. Unfortunately, a least common denominator or multicultural approach to ministry is prevalent in many United States dioceses with diverse ethnic populations.

At the same time, there is a need for a common ministerial framework that takes into account the efforts of the United States bishops and the Hispanic ministry community in the United States during the last forty years. Many new Latino/a Catholic immigrants are unaware of such national initiatives that have formed a common history of cooperation and understanding about ministry. Examples include the four national Encuentros, or national pastoral gatherings of bishops, clergy, religious, and laity ministering in Hispanic ministry from the 1970s through 2000; as well as the 1987 *National Hispanic Pastoral Plan for Hispanic Ministry*. And in many cases, new Latino/a immigrants disparage and disregard this *memoria histórica* (historical memory) in favor of approaches from Latin America that do not do justice to the particularities of the context in the United States. And while the rich historical memory of Hispanic ministry in the United States provides roots for our ministerial efforts, a further challenge lies in preparing, with limited financial resources, new generations of leaders of the young Hispanic population, characterized by low educational attainment, to rejuvenate and bolster the efforts of veteran pastoral agents.

Echoes of the Latino/a Reality in Co-Workers

In writing Co-Workers, the United States bishops did not seek to promulgate laws or norms to govern lay ecclesial ministry in this country.[8] Rather, they sought to gather what they had learned about the experience of lay ecclesial ministry in the last many years, and to compile a statement of best practices that would serve as a common framework to guide the future growth of that ministry. Insofar as a significant portion of laymen and laywomen engaged in lay ministry in the United States are Latinos/as, their experiences are echoed in this document in a number of ways. This is the case even while the document recognizes that Latinos/as and other groups, that in many dioceses are already the majority of Catholics, are under-represented nationally among full-time lay ecclesial ministers.[9] Perhaps the most important way that the document echoes the incredibly varied Latino/a presence in the United States is its sensitivity to diversity and the need for adaptation.

The document's language on this crucial point for the Hispanic communities of this country is worthy of direct citation: "It [the Co-Workers document] invites local adaptation, application, and implementation to achieve consistency where possible and to encourage diversity where appropriate."[10] As Hispanic ministers have underscored, there is a tendency among United States dioceses to adopt a one-size-fits-all approach to ministry that does not do justice to the pastoral reality of Latino/a Catholics. The sensitivity that this document demonstrates by its frequent calls[11] to creativity, flexibility, and adaptation, particularly on behalf of immigrant communities in less affluent areas of dioceses and with regards to certification requirements,[12] is a welcome corrective to the one-size-fits-all approach to ministry.

Another welcome aspect of the Co-Workers document for the Latino/a community is the call it makes to lay ecclesial ministers (LEMs) to form themselves for ministry in an already multicultural Church. The document's call for an awareness and experience of different spiritualities and cultural expressions of Catholicism;[13] learning the language of those to whom one ministers,[14] and achieving this, when feasible, through immersion experiences;[15] augurs well for the pastoral care that Latinos/as will receive from LEMs who heed its injunction.

Before writing Co-Workers, the bishops consulted extensively, listened to the experience of LEMs,[16] and employed the results of David DeLambo's social-scientific survey of lay parish ministers[17] to describe the reality of LEM in the United States. This inductive methodology resembles the see-judge-act methodology or pastoral circle, developed by Cardinal Joseph Cardijn of Belgium and the Jeunesse Ouvrière Chrétienne (JOC) during the 1920s, that is very familiar to Hispanic ministers in the United States and throughout Latin America,[18] and which played a central role in the pastoral planning of the Encuentros of the 1970s and 1980s and the *National Pastoral Plan for Hispanic Ministry* of 1987.[19]

Latino/a Catholics will recognize a number of the core aspects of their lived Catholicism in the document's emphasis on a solid theological and devotional appreciation of Mary[20] and on the Eucharist, particularly adoration.[21] At the same time, the theological formation recommended by Co-Workers will challenge many Latinos/as to more fully appropriate the contemporary teaching of the Catholic Church. In particular, the call for a solid formation in the historical-critical method of biblical hermeneutics[22] and ecumenism[23] will help rectify the biblical fundamentalism found among many Latino/a charismatic Catholics, as well as a certain ignorance, disdain, and suspicion of different Protestant traditions.

Lacunae of the Latino/a Reality in Co-Workers

Our snapshot of the Latino/a religious landscape that emerges from recent surveys reveals a community where the "both/and" characteristic of the Catholic sacramental imagination is alive and well. Latinos/as are at the same time traditionalist in their theology and charismatic in their spirituality. The Co-Workers document recognizes that the call to serve as LEMs often emerges from small faith-communities such as charismatic prayer groups and the basic cells of New Ecclesial Movements.[24] The document also recognizes the role of the Holy Spirit mediated through the sacraments of initiation in that call,[25] even calling the Holy Spirit, "the principal agent of formation."[26] However, the richness, nuance, and particularity of the Latino/a charismatic experience are not captured in this document.

While no one document can do all things, the Co-Workers document does not address the complexity that characterizes Latinos/as in the United States. This absence is a particularly glaring lacuna because of the large number of men and women involved in LEM who come from this ecclesial reality, and because of the otherwise laudatory goal of Co-Workers to offer a common framework for LEM that begins with the existing pastoral reality. It will be crucial that future mandated revisions of the document[27] seek to give voice to the unique and different ecclesial and pastoral experience of LEMs from the Latino/a charismatic perspective so as to remedy this gap.

Two examples of where the Latino/a charismatic experience of LEMs have not influenced the document's recommendations include the paucity of references to pneumatology and apologetics in the theological formation suggested for LEMs, as well as treatment of the distinctive elements of a charismatic spirituality that permeates and animates so many Hispanic LEMs. The need for a solid grounding in pneumatology is obvious for men and women whose spirituality is shaped by the charismatic renewal as is the case with so many Latinos/as. However, in addition, given the importance of the renewal among all Latinos/as, pneumatology becomes a crucial area of study and formation for any LEM who is called to serve a church that is already demographically comprised of many Hispanics.

As I mentioned above, the ecumenical sensibilities of the formation program advocated by Co-Workers is to be praised and encouraged. However, the Latino/a pastoral experience, which is at times characterized by polemical encounters with the anti-Catholic bigotry of some Latino/a Evangelicals, Pentecostals, and members of non-Christian sects, requires an apologetic faith formation that is not often appreciated in ecclesial contexts where proselytism is not alive, well, and thriving. Both the Holy See[28] and the United States bishops[29] have in the past highlighted this unfortunate pastoral reality and have called for the theological formation of priests and laity that does not completely neglect a role for apologetics. In my pastoral experience, apologetics is often a popular characteristic of the formation received by members of the Hispanic Charismatic Renewal.

Co-Workers recommends that LEMs be formed in a spirituality that reflects the vocation to marriage that so many of them have chosen.[30] Given the large number of married women who are LEMs,[31] it is wise that the document should highlight this specific dimension of their spiritual formation. One wonders why, given the large number of Latino/a

LEMs who have a charismatic spirituality, the document did not also highlight this particular way of being a Catholic Christian in today's church, and move beyond its generic call[32] for an awareness of different spiritualities to a helpful and specific mention of Latino/a charismatic spirituality. Elsewhere too, Co-Workers' generic call for multicultural education[33] would profit from the specific mention of Latino/a cultures that now comprise a third of all Roman Catholics in the United States. This recognition is in keeping with the new fifth apostolic priority of the USCCB: "recognition of cultural diversity with a special emphasis on Hispanic ministry in the spirit of *Encuentro*."[34]

An important contribution of the Co-Workers' document is the well-founded communion ecclesiology it delineates and the theology of ministry that follows from it.[35] It overcomes divisions between the ordained and LEMs by highlighting the organic unity that emerges from the ordered communion: that is the church founded by Jesus Christ which mirrors the Trinitarian nature of God. All Christians, by virtue of the sacraments of initiation, share the common mission "to announce the reign of God and . . . [transform] the world in the light of Christ."[36] However, the specific ways that this mission is actualized will vary according to the different vocations and charisms that the Holy Spirit grants the church.

The document takes pains to address the tensions that sometimes arise between LEMs and ordained ministers[37] and other laity; the authors in particular exhort LEMs to avoid any appearance of elitism or of being in a caste set apart from other LEMs who are not full-time co-workers of the bishops.[38] Yet, despite these noble efforts, we are left with the concern and suspicion that the emphasis on professional graduate education and certification, as well as on the title "lay ecclesial minister," will perpetuate an unhelpful distinction in the church between different types of LEMs. Many part-time LEMs who are Latinos/as do not fit the bill presumed by the document. The particular contours of their lives and ecclesial reality (they are holding down several jobs to make ends meet, have a poor educational background, are living in areas of the country with few or no Catholic educational institutions, and belong to financially-strapped dioceses and parishes, for example) may prevent them from becoming part of the professional guild of LEMs that Co-Workers seems to presuppose.

Future revisions of the document should assess whether this distinction has come to pass and, if it has, articulate policies and structures that ensure that full-time LEMs do not continue to function as an elitist class of ministers, set apart from part-time and volunteer LEMs more characteristic of the Latino/a ecclesial experience. Perhaps one way of beginning to do this is to reconsider the name "lay ecclesial minister" which could abate a certain segregation and elitism, and borrow the title used throughout the Latino/a charismatic renewal for those of all capacities and responsibilities who exercise servant-leadership.

In Hispanic circles of the charismatic renewal, it is common to refer to participants at prayer meetings and other events as *hermano/a* (brother/sister). Those engaged in ministry—from the leaders of prayer, music ministers of all sorts, teachers, lay preachers, to those who cook and clean for retreats and other gatherings—are called *servidor/a* (server). The designation "server" within the context of a movement where members are called brother or sister, seems to us, to express better the communion theology of ministry that Co-Workers is after. Perhaps "server" or its equivalent can replace the more officious "lay ecclesial minister," and the spirit of "server-hood" can offset the dangers of polarization. A professionally educated, full-time, LEM-caste in the church could deleteriously contribute to a polarization between Anglos/as and Latinos/as; between professionally educated, full-time LEMs and movement-formed, part-time, *servidores/as.*

Conclusion

Co-Workers has much to recommend it to the Latino/a Catholic communities of the United States. Its inductive methodology, awareness of the under-representation of Latinos/as in the professional and full-time LEM community, flexible realism regarding the pastoral reality of the immigrant and the poor, and an emphasis on language and multicultural training for non-Latino/a LEMs, all augur well for the pastoral care of Latino/a Catholics in the United States.

The mandated assessment and refinement of this document should pay attention to certain *lacunae* that characterize the Hispanic Catholic experience in the United States. In particular, more specific attention needs to be paid to the culture, spirituality, and experience of Latino/a Catholics who are more traditional and charismatic than most Catholics in the United States. Furthermore, policies and structures should be instituted to prevent the growth and emergence of a two-tiered structure of LEM that disparages those LEMs who are movement-formed and part-time, as is the case with most Latino/a LEMs.

Reflection Questions

1. Latino/a Catholicism is traditionalist, charismatic, and often marked by a literalist approach to Scripture. What models of theological education and pastoral formation should be adopted for ordained and lay ecclesial ministers who will serve Latino/a faith communities?
2. How can Hispanic Catholics and their faith communities be invited to contribute more fully to efforts to reflect upon and guide the ongoing development of lay ecclesial ministry? How can we ensure that the Hispanic charismatic experience of *servidores/as* is more thoroughly represented in such efforts?
3. Given that Latinos/as and other ethnic groups are under-represented in the national ranks of professionally-educated, full-time lay ecclesial ministers, how can we ensure that full-time lay ecclesial ministers do not become an elitist caste of ministers, set apart from the *servidores/as* who are found within many Latino/a faith communities?

Notes

1. The terms Latino/a and Hispanic are used interchangeably throughout this essay. The term Hispanic was used by the U.S. Census in 1970, and was adopted in many Church documents and is still in use today. The term Latino/a emerged later from the usage of community leaders and has also come to be used by many Church leaders. Both terms refer to men and women, some born in the United States and some not, who share common linguistic, religious, and other cultural values that emerged from the symbiosis of Spanish faith and culture and Amerindian, African, and Asian peoples who found their way, sometimes in slavery, to the Americas.

2. Pew Hispanic Center, "How Many Hispanics? Comparing New Census Counts with the Latest Census Estimates" (March 30, 2011): http://pewhispanic.org/files/reports/139.pdf (accessed May 10, 2011).

3. Pew Hispanic Center, "Changing Faiths: Latino/as and the Transformation of American Religion," Chapter One. http://pewhispanic.org/reports/report.php?ReportID=75 (accessed February 24, 2011).

4. Ibid.

5. Instituto Fe y Vida, "Latino/a Youth by U.S. Dioceses 2003, http://www.feyvida.org/research/researchpubs.html (accessed April 15, 2008).

6. Pew Hispanic Center, "Changing Faiths: Latino/as and the Transformation of American Religion," ch. 2, 3, and 4.

7. USCCB, Encuentro and Mission: a Renewed Pastoral Framework for Hispanic Ministry, Appendix. http://www.usccb.org/hispanicaffairs/encuentromission.shtml#7 (accessed February 25, 2010).

8. USCCB, Co-Workers in the Vineyard of the Lord: A Resource for Guiding the Development of Lay Ecclesial Ministry (Washington, D.C.: USCCB, 2005), 6.

9. Ibid., 28.

10. Ibid., 6.

11. Ibid., 19, 33, 36, 38, 42-43, 56.

12. Ibid., 56, 59-60.

13. Ibid., 38, 36.

14. Ibid., 49.

15. Ibid., 51.

16. Ibid., 7-15.

17. David DeLambo, *Lay Parish Ministers: A Study of Emerging Leadership* (New York: National Pastoral Life Center, 2005).

18. Joe Holland, "Roots of the Pastoral Circle in Personal Experiences and Catholic Social Tradition," in *The Pastoral Circle Revisited: A Critical Quest for Truth and Transformation*, eds. Frans Wijsen, Peter Henriot, and Rodrigo Meija (Maryknoll, NY: Orbis Books, 2005), 9.

19. USCCB, *National Pastoral Plan for Hispanic Ministry*, November 1987, in Secretariat for Hispanic Affairs, United States Catholic Conference, Inc., *Hispanic Ministry: Three Major Documents* (Washington, DC: USCCB, 1995), no.6.

20. USCCB, Co-Workers, 40.

21. Ibid., 41.

22. Ibid., 46.

23. Ibid., 41.

24. Ibid., 27.

25. Ibid., 8, 18.

26. Ibid., 52.

27. Ibid., 67.

28. See Benedict XVI, "Interview of His Holiness Benedict XVI During the Flight to Brazil," May 9, 2007, http://www.vatican.va/holy_father/benedict_xvi/speeches/2007/may/documents/hf_ben-xvi_spe_20070509_interview-brazil_en.html (accessed July 9, 2008) and S.G. John Paul II, *Ecclesia in America* (The Church in America), given January 22, 1999 in Mexico City, http://www.vatican.va/holy_father/john_paul_ii/apost_exhortations/documents/hf_ip-ii_exh_22011999_ecclesia-in-america_en.html (accessed February 24, 2011).

29. See National Conference of Catholic Bishops, Ad Hoc Committee on Biblical Fundamentalism, "Pastoral Statement for Catholics on Biblical Fundamentalism," March 26, 1987, http://www.shc.edu/theolibrary/resources/fundmntl.htm (accessed February 24, 2011) and NCCB, "National Pastoral Plan for Hispanic Ministry," November, 1987, in Secretariat for Hispanic Affairs, United States Catholic Conference, Inc., *Hispanic Ministry: Three Major Documents*, no. 11, 39, 83.

30. USCCB, Co-Workers, 35.

31. Ibid., 13.

32. Ibid., 38.

33. Ibid., 36.

34. See USCCB, "Strategic Plan 2008-2011," http://www.usccb.org/priorities/old/USCCBApprovedStrategicPlan.pdf (accessed March 2, 2011), and Jerry Filteau, CNS, 'Bishops Downsize Their National Conference, Reduce assessments," November 15, 2006, http://www.catholicnews.com/data/stories/cns/0606525.htm (accessed February 25, 2011).

35. USCCB, Co-Workers, 17-21.

36. Ibid., 20.

37. Ibid., 21-25.

38. Ibid., 11-12, 25-26.

CHAPTER NINE

The Sacraments of Initiation
A Guiding Theme for the Future of Lay Ecclesial Ministry

Donna Eschenauer

> Ministerial relationships are grounded first in what all members of Christ's Body have in common. Through their sacramental initiation all are established in a personal relationship with Christ and in a network of relationships within the communion of the People of God. The personal discipleship of each individual makes possible a community of disciples formed by and for the mission of Christ.
>
> —*Co-Workers in the Vineyard of the Lord*[1]

Introduction

This essay explores the connection between lay ecclesial ministry and the sacraments of Christian initiation as celebrated in the Roman Catholic Church. It uses a liturgical perspective that maintains the vision and theology of liturgy, while at the same time, unfolds a *mystagogical* point of view. In this way, the essay captures some essential implications for identity and responsibility acknowledged in and through baptism, confirmation, and Eucharist.

The sacraments of initiation have a profound impact upon the worldview of the Catholic faithful. Baptism, confirmation, and Eucharist direct us beyond the comforts of our lives and stir within us a deep reality, namely, the responsibility of sharing in the mission of the church for the life of the world. While infant baptism, first communion with children, and adolescent or young adult confirmation each has significant merit in our time, this chapter suggests that a more precise connection between sacramental initiation and lay ecclesial ministry can come from the *Rite of Christian Initiation of Adults* (RCIA), promulgated for use in the United States in 1988.

The RCIA revitalizes the meaning of Christian initiation. In over twenty years of experience with the RCIA, I am amazed at the reaction of the assembly at the Easter Vigil, as well as the response of sponsors and catechists who directly minister in the catechumenate process. Succinctly, those baptized in infancy frequently recognize a deeper meaning hidden within the ritual action of their baptism that was celebrated many years ago. That is, they recognize that our initiation into the church is not merely celebrated for our own benefit. It is celebrated on behalf of the Body of Christ. The RCIA exposes this brilliantly, while, at the same time, it holds the potential for strengthening the entire church community.

The purpose of this essay is to explore the sacraments of initiation from a liturgical perspective and show how they awaken the call to holiness, and, at the same time, the call to lay ecclesial ministry. At its most basic level, a Christian's response to God's call is discipleship. However, as disciples, God calls all to dedicate themselves to ministry: some as lay ecclesial ministers, others as vowed religious or ordained ministers. In discussing how ministry is based on biblical characteristics, Thomas O'Meara writes, "Christian ministry *is the public activity of a baptized follower of Jesus Christ flowing from the Spirit's charism and an individual personality on behalf of a Christian community to proclaim, serve, and realize the kingdom of God.*"[2] This awareness, heightened through the Second Vatican Council's retrieval of the dignity of the baptized, captures lay ecclesial ministry's solid foundation in the sacraments of initiation.

This essay explores the relationship of Christian initiation to lay ecclesial ministry in the following sections:

- Call to Participation: Serving the Mission of the Church
- Christian Initiation: Awakening the Mystical Imagination
- Baptism: Vested for Lay Ecclesial Ministry
- Confirmation: Anointed for Lay Ecclesial Ministry
- Eucharist: Nourishment for Lay Ecclesial Ministry

Call to Participation: Serving the Mission of the Church

The documents of the Vatican II, read in tandem, reflect the reality of the church as a community of believers, while at the same time, their authors call for active participation on many levels. Key passages in *Sacrosanctum Concilium* (Constitution on the Sacred Liturgy), *Lumen Gentium* (Dogmatic Constitution on the Church), and *Gaudium et Spes* (Pastoral Constitution on the Church in the Modern World) explore the nature and mission of the church. Each document validates that, as the baptized, we are children of God, united in the Body of Christ. Moreover, the documents note that active membership in the Body of Christ entails making a commitment to care for the whole Body. In other words, active membership invites ministry.

The authors of *Sacrosanctum Concilium* (Constitution on the Sacred Liturgy) imply that there are many levels and layers of participation beyond the visible ones. The document reads, "To promote active participation, the people should be encouraged to take part by means of acclamations, responses, psalmody, antiphons, and songs, as well as by actions, gestures, and bodily attitudes. And at the proper times all should observe a reverent silence."(SC 30).[3] The document suggests that visible involvement in liturgy leads to deep participation in a life of faith that changes our worldview, which, in turn, leads us to change the world. More fully, participation in liturgy leads us to participate in God's ongoing creative effort to make all things new and to restore hope to the fragmented areas of human life. Thus, active participation involves faith and openness to God's presence and initiative. A more inspired participation in the ritual prayer of the church is an expression of one's share in the life of the divine.

Participation in liturgy calls us to take part in the paschal mystery, the very action made present for us. Liturgy, the ritual prayer of the community, can only be experienced as wholesome when viewed from this perspective of a deeper level of active participation. To think otherwise can lead to passivity, reverberation, or a mere going through the motions. This may lead to discontent with liturgy rather than its preeminent linkage with life. Participation in the liturgy, at the deepest level, is participation in Jesus Christ's paschal mystery that consoles the inner cravings of the human spirit, mending the fabric of empty ritual expressions with whole expressions of life-altering events made present here and now. Full, conscious, and active participation in liturgy offers the awe-inspiring opportunity to meet the mystery of God and live the mystery of life with a disposition of impregnable hope. It is important to note that full, active, and conscious participation does not exist in a vacuum but permeates every aspect of life. Full, active, and conscious participation in liturgy serves to drive the development of the grace of a paschal imagination that enables us to reclaim other ways of knowing.

For the lay ecclesial minister, Bishop Matthew Clark suggests developing a paschal spirituality as a source of hope.[4] A paschal spirituality offers a way to thrive, freeing us from our own, often skewed, expectations. The foundation for cultivating a paschal spirituality is the re-appropriation of the sacraments of initiation.

Christian Initiation: Awakening the Mystical Imagination

Rooted in some of the leading documents of Vatican II, the *Rite of Christian Initiation of Adults* (RCIA) was revised in 1972. Mandated for use in the United States in 1988, the RCIA ritualizes the stages of conversion and is formative for a Gospel way of life. The RCIA impacts and deepens the religious imagination of the parish community and affirms the call to active participation on multiple levels. The structure of the rite places initiation within the community and insists that initiation is the responsibility of all the baptized.[5] The RCIA also expresses and strengthens the vision and biblical identity of the church as the Body of Christ. This vision and identity is expressed vividly at the Easter Vigil when the community affirms what it believes and professes.

The Easter Vigil provides a moment in time to look at one's life in relation to the newly initiated. Through immersion in water, anointing with oil, and feasting at the banquet, the whole church can see, hear, taste, touch, and smell what it means to be Christian. This is the night when Karl Rahner's words resound, "the devout Christian of the future will either be a 'mystic' one who has 'experienced' something, or he will cease to be anything at all."[6] The rites of Christian initiation, then, evoke the mystical imagination, summoning new and deeper ways of experiencing God. The initiation rites, celebrated at the Easter Vigil, bring into focus a willingness to let go of certainty and live with the uncertainty that comes with a faith-filled existence. Baptism, confirmation, and Eucharist enable us to "see" what is hidden, and call us to revel in profound mystery.

The call to lay ecclesial ministry is a call to live profoundly in the present and imagine a future filled with hope. The sacraments of initiation can help laypeople recognize and respond to this call. Such ritual language spells out ways of knowing vital for our time. New possibilities are uncovered, inviting us to see what cannot be seen, even if it is only in a "mirror, dimly" (1 Cor 13:12; NRSV). As Nathan Mitchell writes, "few of us fully appreciate one of the most original aspects of Jesus' life and work—namely, his conviction that the act of salvation begins with an act of imagination."[7] The RCIA awakens the mystical imagination.

Baptism: Vested for Lay Ecclesial Ministry

> . . . you have become a new creation and have clothed yourselves in Christ . . . .
>
> — RCIA 229

The threshold for all sacraments is baptism, and genuine Christian life exists within a broader understanding of baptismal spirituality. For too long, the meaning of baptism was reduced to a washing away of original sin. However, original sin is the human condition into which we are born. Baptism, then, offers life in Christ, the power to transcend the conflicts in our human experience. Recovery of a baptismal spirituality, as a vocation to be lived, recognizes the baptized as gifted and called. Immersion in the waters of baptism is entrance into communion with God and one another. Awareness of the depth and meaning of baptism opens us up to greater possibilities for living the Christian life. It is in and through the waters of baptism, then, that lay ecclesial ministers realize their identities.

Jesus' baptism in the Jordan River serves as the paradigm for the continued realization of a baptismal spirituality. As New Testament scholars point out, Jesus' public ministry began with his baptism.[8] Similarly, our baptism shapes Christian identity and vocation. Richard Fragomeni writes, "When we are baptized, the ultimate purpose for us is the same as it was for Jesus—to be beloved children of God. During Jesus' baptism, the heavens opened and the Spirit descended upon him and a voice proclaimed, 'You are the beloved son of God.' When we are baptized, it is because of our faith that a similar transformation takes place in us."[9]

All ministry flows from an identity inherent in baptism. Baptism reminds us that we are sons and daughters of God. At the same time, baptism changes our relationship with others, the church, and the world. At baptism, we are invited into a process of living out a vocation and we are vested with responsibility. In and through baptism we are called to the healing, saving mission of Christ in the church and in the world.[10] Baptism, understood as a vocation to be lived, strengthens the community's resolve to live as they worship, meaning working toward deeper concern for the dignity of all people.

For some, the idea that baptism is a vocation to be lived has taken root. Sadly, many do not yet fully comprehend the profound implications of baptism. Whether one is baptized as an infant or as an adult, has no bearing on the sacrament's implicit meaning for a way of being in the world. Baptism, our first entry into the church, clothes us with Christ. It strengthens and empowers us to take part in the mission of the church: the proclamation of God's presence and action in the world.

Co-Workers states this about the reality and practice of lay ecclesial ministry: "by their baptismal incorporation into the Body of Christ, lay persons are also equipped with gifts and graces to build up the Church from within . . ."[11] For all engaged in ministry, on any level, and particularly for those who have made lay ecclesial ministry their life's work, it is baptism that commissions them for their work. Moreover, to understand ministry, we must begin with baptism. It is in and through the waters of baptism that the identity of a person's ministry is realized.

Discernment of gifts takes on many forms in the church. For too many years, the call to service in the church meant a vocation to ordination or vowed religious life. Following Vatican II, the importance of baptism was recovered. The organic development of lay ministry began to be realized as a call integral to baptism. Laypeople not called to ordained ministry or vowed religious life, although called to full-time or part-time service in the church began to have the opportunity to fulfill their vocation within the church. In view of the significance of baptism for lay ecclesial ministry, it is worthwhile to consider the renewal of our baptismal promises at the Easter Vigil and the rich meaning of the entire Easter season. The Easter season provides a powerful opportunity for parish communities to cultivate deep baptismal awareness for all, especially those called to lay ecclesial ministry. Baptism and its renewal spark mysticism. Luke Timothy Johnson puts it this way, "Mystics pursue the inner reality of the relationship between humans and God: they long for true knowledge of what alone is ultimately real, and desire absolute love for what is alone infinitely desirable."[12] Baptism, then, is initiation into mysticism.

Confirmation: Anointed for Lay Ecclesial Ministry

> The promised strength of the Holy Spirit, which you are to receive, will make you more like Christ and help you to be witnesses to his suffering, death, and resurrection. It will strengthen you to be active members of the Church and to build up the Body of Christ in faith and love.
>
> —RCIA 233

RCIA restores the order of the sacraments of initiation: the newly baptized are confirmed before coming to communion. The union of baptism and confirmation signifies a most important connection—linking baptism, the outpouring of the Holy Spirit, and mission (RCIA 215). Chrismation signifies the promised strength of the Holy Spirit. The anointing with chrism strengthens the newly baptized for witness and full, active, and conscious participation in Christian life.

Today, a debate continues over when the celebration of confirmation should occur for Roman Catholics baptized as infants. For our purposes, the issue is not when confirmation is celebrated. Rather, it is the essential meaning of this sacrament in relation to Christian initiation that bears attention. However, the revised Rite of Confirmation (1971) for those baptized as infants, recovers the connection with baptism, and, therefore, its connection to vocation and witness. Aidan Kavanagh writes that "the reform of confirmation which resulted from the Second Vatican Council cannot be grasped adequately except in view of a larger reform of which it is part. That larger reform was of Christian initiation itself . . . ."[13]

Theologically, confirmation ritualizes the gift and presence of the Holy Spirit inherent in baptism. Essentially, confirmation takes seriously, what happens at the baptismal font.[14] A person most effectively experiences this connection with the RCIA. However, good catechesis can create such awareness even when the rite of confirmation occurs separately from baptism.

Appropriately, the relation of baptism to confirmation impacts the identity of lay ecclesial ministers. The anointing with chrism, the seal of the gifts of the Holy Spirit, is the source behind the various charisms at the heart of lay ecclesial ministry. In *Christifideles Laici* (The Lay Members of Christ's Faithful People), John Paul II made this statement: "The Holy Spirit, while bestowing diverse ministries in Church communion, enriches it still further with particular gifts or promptings of grace, called *Charisms.*"[15] In Co-Workers, the bishops pick up on this theme. They write, "Charisms are those gifts or graces of the Spirit that have benefit, direct or indirect, for the community . . . .Thus, while there is a diversity of ministry in the Church, there is a unity of mission grounded in the one God, who is Father, Son, and Holy Spirit."[16] The call to lay ecclesial ministry takes seriously the action and presence of God: Father, Son, and Holy Spirit. God's innate presence, celebrated in and through the ritual of confirmation, animates the work of lay ecclesial ministry.

Eucharist: Nourishment for Lay Ecclesial Ministry

The context for lay ecclesial ministry is the church understood as the Body of Christ. While this image is not unanimously embraced, the Body of Christ provides a profound theological foundation for participation in the Eucharist.[17] A genuine understanding of Eucharist and the command to celebrate it in Jesus' memory is best disclosed in John's gospel. Jesus' gives this provocative testimony: "If I, therefore, the master and teacher, have washed your feet, you ought to wash one another's feet. I have given you a model to follow, so that as I have done for you, you should also do" (John 13: 14-15). Jesus' humble activity in this testimonial prompts and provides a paradigm for ministry.

The celebration of church as the Body of Christ, and the high point of initiation, is the Eucharist, the meal that gathers the community. The only repeatable initiation rite, Eucharist, feeds us through profound table companionship. Nathan Mitchell points out that Jesus' "table-centered vision" had the power to change the world.[18] Speaking of Jesus' table ministry, Mitchell continues:

> He sat at table not as the charming, congenial, ringleted centerpiece of a Rembrandt painting, but as a vulnerable vagrant willing to share potlock with a household of strangers. Normally, a table's prime function is to establish social ranking and hierarchy (by what one eats, how one eats, with whom one eats). Normally a meal is about social identification, status, and power. . . . But the very *randomness* of Jesus' table habits challenged the system of social relations modeled on meals and manners. . . . It wasn't simply that Jesus ate with objectionable persons—outcasts and sinners—but that he ate with anyone, indiscriminately.[19]

Jesus' ministry of table companionship announced the reign of God. Eucharist, the culmination of Christian initiation, provides a way for us to do the same. Undoubtedly, water, chrism, bread and wine bind us to community and commit us to seeking the fuller realization of God's reign, namely, God's inclusive love for all. They also offer a guiding theme for sustaining the development of lay ecclesial ministry.

Conclusion

This reflection on the sacraments of Christian initiation and their impact on identity and ministry prompt some relevant personal reflection. Three examples come to mind: First, I commute a long distance to the parish where I serve as a full-time pastoral staff member. My journey takes me past the church where I was baptized. In addition, in the not too far distance is the church where I completed my initiation into the Catholic Church as a youngster. As I view the weather-worn steeple through the trees, I cannot help thinking, "If it were not for that hot, July day, when I was brought to that church as an infant, I would not have the privilege and responsibility of serving the people of God as a laywoman." In a sense, I am renewing my initiation into the church every day.

Second, my youngest son was baptized on the feast of the Baptism of the Lord. Every year on that feast day, we remember the faith commitment of my husband and me, in addition to the profound impact of that day on our son's life. Finally, a liturgy program from a funeral I attended announced the date of the deceased's baptism. This was a statement not only of who this person was in life; it was also a proclamation of hope for the promise of everlasting life. These personal reflections show how memory and ritual bring us into the present and aid us in being open to God's guidance for the future.

The sacraments of initiation are the prelude for Christian discipleship and the foundation for lay ecclesial ministry. As stated at the beginning of this essay, the RCIA brings to the forefront the essence and impact of baptism, confirmation, and Eucharist for the life of the church. In *A Church for a New Generation: Sacraments in Transition,* Julia Upton anticipates the church in the twenty-first century. In relation to the RCIA she writes,

> Once we have experience the RCIA, however, either as sponsor or as members of the larger ecclesial community, the link between baptism and spirituality is no longer missing. Vicariously, through the journey of each new catechumen, every member of the community can enter once again into the mystery of salvation. It no longer matters at what age the commitment was made, for we see the profound need for conversion, personally, communally, and socially, played out before us through the rituals of the catechumenate. We do not have to search outside for a spirituality, for we recognize the response we gave to the call of Jesus by being incorporated into this community of faith. The character that was imprinted upon us at that time remains forever. The grace of baptism continues to strengthen us throughout our faith-life journey.[20]

To conclude, it is in and through the sacraments of initiation that lay ecclesial ministers can discover a paschal spirituality. A paschal spirituality makes it possible to experience the life, death, and resurrection of Jesus the Christ within the reality of our time and place. Through this way of being in the world, we can be ever open to transformation and hope. It makes real what the human heart longs for, namely, a paschal spirituality that shows us how to live and how to die.[21] Co-Workers affirms lay ecclesial ministry. In doing so, it acknowledges Christian initiation as the foundation and life-giving force behind the universal call to holiness and the recognition of diverse charisms for ministry within the church. As we build upon Co-Worker's grounding of ministry in the sacraments of initiation, we can seek to nurture a paschal spirituality to sustain lay ecclesial ministry.

Reflection Questions

1. What is your experience of liturgy? How might you deepen your participation in liturgical celebrations so that they become fuller experiences of the paschal mystery of Jesus Christ?
2. How can the renewal of our baptismal promises at the Easter Vigil provide an opportunity to deepen our baptismal awareness of the mystery of God present and active in our lives? How can this awareness heighten our sense of God's call to participate in the mission and ministries of the church?
3. How can our understanding of the theological significance of the anointing with chrism at confirmation, which serves as a seal of the gifts of the Holy Spirit, help us to appreciate and value the diverse charisms of lay ecclesial ministers?
4. How can the gathering of the Christian community for Eucharist nourish lay ecclesial ministers and help to sustain the development of lay ecclesial ministry?

Notes

1. USCCB, Co-Workers in the Vineyard of the Lord: A Resource for Guiding the Development of Lay Ecclesial Ministry (Washington, D.C.: USCCB, 2005), 21.

2. Thomas F. O'Meara, O.P., *Theology of Ministry* (Mahwah, NJ: Paulist Press, 1999), 150.

3. *Sacrosanctum Concilium* (Constitution on the Sacred Liturgy) in *Vatican Council II: The Conciliar and Post Conciliar Documents,* ed. Austin Flannery, 1-282 (Northport, New York: Costello Publishing Company, 1987).

4. Bishop Matthew Clark, "Fourth Annual Co-Workers Conference." Fordham University, September 17, 2010.

5. *Rite of Christian Initiation of Adults* (Chicago, IL: Liturgy Training Publications, 1988).

6. Karl Rahner, *Foundations of Christian Faith: An Introduction to the Idea of Christianity* (New York: Crossroads, 1978), 15.

7. Nathan Mitchell, *Forum Essays: Eucharist as Sacrament of Initiation* (Chicago, IL: Liturgy Training Publications, 1994), 5.

8. Maxwell E. Johnson, *The Rites of Christian Initiation: Their Evolution and Interpretation* (Collegeville, MN: Liturgical Press, 2007), 13.

9. Richard N. Fragomeni, *Come to the Light* (New York: Continuum, 2000), 8.

10. Barbara Searle and Anne Y. Koester, ed., *Called to Participate: Theological, Ritual, and Social Perspectives* (Collegeville, MN: Liturgical Press, 2006), 31-32.

11. Co-Workers, 12.

12. Luke Timothy Johnson, "Dry Bones: Why Religion Can't Live without Mysticism," *Commonweal* (February 26, 2010): 11.

13. Aidan Kavanagh, *Confirmation: Origins and Reform,* (New York: Pueblo Publishing Company, 1988), 81.

14. See Johnson, chapter 10.

15. John Paul II, *Christifideles Laici* (The Lay Members of Christ's Faithful People) (Boston: Pauline Books & Media, 1988), 24.

16. Co-Workers, 18-19.

17. See Keith Pecklers, *The Unread Vision: The Liturgical Movement in the United States of America: 1926-1955* (Collegeville, MN: Liturgical Press, 1998), 29-34.

18. Mitchell, 79.

19. Ibid., 89.

20. Julia Upton, *A Church for the Next Generation: Sacraments in Transition* (Collegeville, MN: Liturgical Press, 1990), 51.

21. Gabriel Moran, *Showing How: The Act of Teaching* (Valley Forge, PA: Trinity Press-International, 1997), 38.

CHAPTER TEN

Co-Workers in the Vineyard of the Lord and an Evolving Ministry

Zeni Fox

Introduction

In November of 2005, the United States Conference of Catholic Bishops approved Co-Workers in the Vineyard of the Lord: A Resource for Guiding the Development of Lay Ecclesial Ministry.[1] The following year, the Committee on the Laity of the Conference convened a number of persons who were involved in the development of the document, to assess the reception it received. By two measures, it was clear that Co-Workers already had a significant impact. First, participants reported that in dioceses throughout the country, ministry days and various workshops used the document as a central theme and that numerous articles about Co-Workers were solicited by and submitted to various journals. Second, participants, the bishops, and the invited guests alike, reported that those involved in ministry, especially lay ecclesial ministers, had expressed gratitude for and enthusiasm about the document. In the two years following this meeting, there were additional presentations and articles, a major symposium held at Saint John's in Collegeville, MN, a website posted on Co-Workers, and significant activity focused on implementation of the guidelines. Certainly, the document has been well received, theologically speaking, by the church in the United States.

A couple of years before the bishops approved the document, a major study was undertaken of pastoral leadership in Roman Catholic parishes in the United States. It was sponsored by six organizations (the National Association for Lay Ministry, the Conference for Pastoral Planning and Council Development, the National Association of Church Personnel Administrators, the National Association of Diaconate Directors, the National Catholic Young Adult Ministry Association, and the National Federation of Priests' Councils) and funded by a grant from the Lilly Endowment. Over the course of five years, the "Emerging Models of Pastoral Leadership Project" sought to understand the evolving ministry in this country.

Marti Jewell, director of the project, reported that for their research the team conducted eleven symposiums with nearly eight hundred people; thirty-one hundred online surveys; extensive written and phone surveys; focus groups of bishops; and diocesan consultations.[2] The report on the project was given at the National Ministry Summit, a gathering of thirteen hundred pastoral leaders, in Orlando, April 21–22, 2008. The first volume of the report has been published, and it profiles some of the leaders encountered through the research.[3] A primary finding of the research is that there is great diversity among pastoral leaders (age, gender, church status and role, ethnicity) and parish structures.

In many ways, Co-Workers was developed in response to a picture of ministry that began to emerge in the 1960s; the Emerging Models Project chronicles more recent developments. Viewing ministry in the light of these more recent developments raises the question, Can Co-Workers assist the ongoing evolution of ministry in the years ahead? In order to explore this question, I will first sketch some aspects of the story that preceded the development of Co-Workers, and then, using highlights from the Emerging Models research, explore how the document speaks to the unfolding reality of ministry in our American church today.

The Origins of Co-Workers

Where should I begin the story? We could begin with the theological developments in the early part of the twentieth century, including the renewal of the study of Scripture in Catholic circles, inviting understanding of our earliest stories, or the liturgical movement, with its emphasis on the role of the laity. Other starting points could be the movements that involved laity in new ways in the life of the church, for example, Young Catholic Workers and the Christian Family Movement or the shift in seminaries from a manual-based curriculum to one more focused on patristics and contemporary theology. All of these currents converged when the bishops of the world gathered in Rome for the Second Vatican Council. In their documents, the bishops included emphases on the centrality of baptism, the role of the laity in the church, and the mission of the entire church to the world. Not only that, but the same currents had prepared many in the church to receive these teachings with enthusiasm and to begin to act on them in varied ways.

The impact that these teachings had on parish ministry could be observed within a few years of the council's closing. A plethora of new programs for the preparation of laity for ministry was initiated, and pastors started hiring laypeople for roles on parish staffs. The impact, particularly in the area of religious education/catechesis, seemed almost immediate. In the decade after the council, one could note the quick expansion of persons employed in the role of director of religious education (DRE); the growth in the number and extensiveness of catechist preparation programs; and the convening of these catechists and DREs at spirited conferences and institutes, attended by large numbers of participants. Leadership in implementing a new vision was diverse, and included priests, vowed religious, laywomen and men, and bishops. People with responsibilities in dioceses, schools and universities, religious orders and parishes, undertook different initiatives. Within a few years, a similar pattern emerged in various other arenas of ministry. By 1980, commentators could speak of "an explosion of ministries."

The bishops' conference first officially noted these changes in the ministerial landscape in 1980. They said, "Since the Second Vatican Council new opportunities have developed for lay men and women to serve in the Church. . . . Growing numbers of lay women and men are also preparing themselves professionally to work in the Church. . . Ecclesial ministers, i.e., lay persons who have prepared for professional ministry in the Church, represent a new development."[4]

In 1989, the Committee on Pastoral Practices began to discuss these new ecclesial ministers, eventually deciding to commission a study to understand better who they were, the nature of their professional preparation, their theological self-understanding, and the manner in which they were being received by pastors and people in the parishes. Of course, the challenge was to determine how to delimit the study. They decided to include in the sample both vowed religious and laypeople employed in parishes at least twenty hours a week. The results of the study were presented to the Committee on the Laity whose members decided that further exploration was needed, particularly in order to provide leadership by the bishops relative to this new development. Hence, the bishops formed the Subcommittee on Lay Ministry, in 1994, whose work would culminate in the development of Co-Workers.

Ecclesial Context: Other Ministerial Developments

The twenty years after the council were marked by other significant developments in the church and in ministry. Because of a change in immigration policy and rising standards of living in Europe, the number of people emigrating from Europe dropped greatly, and the number of people coming from South America and Asia began to increase. Many immigrants were Catholics, especially those from South America and some areas of Asia, such as the Philippines. The result was an expansion of the American church toward the very multicultural church we know today.

In these same twenty years, the number of traditional ministers in Catholic parishes (priests, sisters, and brothers) began to diminish. The number of religious sisters and brothers declined after their peak in 1965. In the period from 1965 to 1975, the population of sisters decreased by 25 percent, and brothers by 30 percent. With priests, on the other hand, the peak number occurred in 1975, with less than a 15 percent decline in the next twenty years.[5] While the theological interpretation of these changes is varied, the practical result was that the ministerial context for the new lay ministers, professional and volunteer, was changing. Recognizing that there was a need for collaboration, the research study commissioned by the bishops in 1990 probed the kinds of relationships that employed lay ministers had with clergy on parish staffs.[6]

In the next twenty years, 1985-2005, further changes occurred. Vatican II had restored the permanent diaconate, but dioceses only gradually developed programs of preparation. Whereas there were fewer than a thousand permanent deacons in 1975, by 1985 there were over seven thousand permanent deacons serving in parishes; by 2005, this number would double. The 1983 Code of Canon Law permitted a parish to be entrusted to a deacon, brother, sister, layman or laywoman. Between the years 1985 and 2005, the number of such pastoral coordinators (there are various other names for this role) increased from 93 to 553.[7] In addition, the number of other persons involved in parish ministry continued to expand rapidly. Those employed as parish ministers increased from about twenty thousand in 1992 to about thirty thousand in 1997, an increase of 35 percent.[8] Their number has continued to rise. Furthermore, the number of laity involved as volunteers in a myriad of roles in parishes has continued to expand. One reason was noted in "The Notre Dame Study of Catholic Parish Life": "Our study findings as a whole show that since Vatican II, parish staffs (other than priests) have greatly increased, and they in turn have multiplied programs which involve more volunteer leaders."[9]

Research from the Emerging Models Project documents the shift from leadership in parishes being vested in pastors and associate priests to leadership by a diversity of pastoral leaders, and to the pastoring and leadership of multiple parishes by individuals and teams. *Shaping Catholic Parishes* tells the stories of men and women, ordained and laypeople, vowed religious and permanent deacons, pastors, parish council members, pastoral associates, pastoral administrators, and active parishioners—all of whom are serving as pastoral leaders. Furthermore, these leaders are of varied races and ethnicities, and serve in parishes that are multicultural. Often, leaders serve more than one parish; these parishes may be separate, linked, or merged, each structure with its own challenge for leaders.[10]

Does Co-Workers, with its focus on one group of ministers in our church today, address the present reality of parish life and leadership, which the Emerging Models Project presents? This question will be addressed by exploring each major section of Co-Workers.

An Assessment of Co-Workers in Light of the Emerging Models Research

Describing and Responding to New Realities

"God calls. We respond. This fundamental, essential pattern in the life of every believer appears throughout salvation history. . . . The Risen Lord calls everyone to labor in his vineyard."[11] In my experience, these opening words of the document have proven very meaningful to lay ecclesial ministers, grounding their personal stories in the Christian story. The theme of their call and response, as officially recognized here, gives validation to their ministry, and invites a deeper response. Second, this foundational understanding applies, as the document says, to all the followers of Christ, and therefore provides a framework adequate to embrace the diversity of pastoral leadership in the church today, of clergy and laypeople alike. The further specification of the call in this document, to the lay faithful,[12] is appropriate in considering lay ecclesial ministry—but it also provides a way of understanding, both self-understanding and ecclesial understanding, of all laity who serve as pastoral leaders. We do not have language adequate to name those leaders who volunteer in ministry, as a way of living out their baptismal commitment, but the Emerging Models research demonstrates their importance. Pastors surveyed said that what the future of the parish most needs is the formation of parishioners for leadership, especially as small faith-based communities continue to grow.[13]

The document explores the reality of lay ecclesial ministry, noting some relevant statistics. Co-Workers offers a listing of characteristics that describe lay ecclesial ministers, and vests responsibility for identifying roles that exemplify lay ecclesial ministry in each bishop, noting that, "Application of the term may vary from diocese to diocese."[14] Unfortunately, the result of this is that there is considerable ambiguity about who is a lay ecclesial minister. There are several aspects of this ambiguity. First, just as a few decades ago, laypersons began to claim the language of ministry, now they are claiming the name lay ecclesial minister. This claim is not surprising given that many of these ministers consider their choice to serve the church as a permanent commitment, flowing from their baptism and a call to ministry.[15] However, their bishops have not affirmed these decisions in most cases. Second, the application of the term has expanded considerably, beyond that which is outlined in the document. One diocesan leader explained, incorrectly, "Lay ecclesial ministry is the new name for lay ministry." Third, some dioceses have begun a process of certifying as lay ecclesial ministers those who complete the diocesan formation program, while many who have served in those dioceses for years are not similarly recognized. One can note that membership in one new group of ecclesial ministers, permanent deacons, is clearly delineated, to the point that there are carefully maintained lists of permanent deacons. There is little clarity relative to lay ecclesial ministers.

In Light of Theology and Church Teaching

As the bishops continued their reflection on lay ecclesial ministry, they turned to church teaching to understand this new reality further. Beginning with an emphasis on the Trinity, on trinitarian life as relational, they sketched the action of each Person relative to us and our world, emphasizing the ways in which Father, Son and Spirit work to bring all into relationship with them, into the communion they share with each other. They described the church as a communion for mission, and said that the purpose of ministry is service of the mission, for the sanctification of the whole world.[16] Once again, this vision encompasses all who are part of the church's mission, lay and ordained, in whatever role. This vision frames well the emerging models of pastoral leadership.

Further, this vision illumines the diverse ministries and ministers, and invites an exploration of the ordering of the relationships among ministers, the "ordering of right relationships among those called to public ministries."[17] The bishop has a primary role in this ordering; Co-Workers describes a variety of ways in which this can occur, from establishing standards for formation and evaluation, to supporting the resolution of conflict situations between lay ecclesial ministers and the ordained. The document also stresses the importance of collaboration and mutual respect between lay ecclesial ministers, priests, and deacons. In relationship with the lay faithful, lay ecclesial ministers are charged to equip "the community for every good work," and "strengthen it for its mission in the world."[18]

While the document sees oversight of lay ecclesial ministers on the practical level as the role of the bishop, it does not develop a theological response to the need for an ordering of ministry. In 2001, ten theologians worked together over a period of eight days to discuss position papers on lay and ordained ministry. Their discussion led to the articulation of seven convergence points, the last of which was: "These principles call us to an ongoing ecclesial discernment and a fresh articulation of an ordering of ministries (e.g., installation, commissioning) in the Church in order to recognize emerging ministries and changes in church practice."[19] The growing diversity of pastoral leadership makes such a need ever more evident, for the good of the community, and the effectiveness of the individual ministers.

Pathways to Lay Ecclesial Ministry

"The pathway to lay ecclesial ministry for any individual is as unique as that individual. No typical path exists, only a multitude of examples."[20] Since lay ecclesial ministry began as a grass roots dynamic, with no overall plan for calling forth and preparing persons for such service, this is not a surprising statement. However, the research about parishes today uncovers some limitations in this approach; two examples will demonstrate this. In exploring this issue, I will consider priests and deacons as well as lay ecclesial ministers, since this is the context of the Emerging Models research.

First, the research underlines the increasing multicultural nature of our parishes. Focusing on Hispanics alone, we can note the limitations of our present modalities for calling forth ministers to serve multi-cultural communities. The USCCB reports that about 39 percent of Catholics are Hispanic, and by the second decade of this century, the population is expected to rise to 50 percent.[21] However, Hispanics are significantly underrepresented among priests (3 percent),[22] deacons (15 percent)[23] and lay ecclesial ministers (paid, 8.1 percent, unpaid, 11.4 percent).[24] One might say that these statistics represent the many ministers called forth prior to the more recent Hispanic immigration. The statistics for those preparing for ministry are only somewhat better. Hispanics comprise 15 percent of those preparing for the priesthood; 16 percent of those preparing to be deacons; and 28 percent of those preparing to be lay ecclesial ministers.[25] Certainly, greater efforts to call forth Hispanic ministers are needed. (This is almost a truism in our day, but does need repeating.) One of the top ten recommendations from the Ministry Summit, which as noted earlier was a gathering of international pastoral leaders in Orlando in April 2008, calls for the creation of a structure for focusing this effort for lay ecclesial ministers: "Advocate for broadening the definition of Vocations Offices to include lay ecclesial ministers in addition to the ordained and religious life in order to share discernment resources, mentoring, support, etc."[26]

Second, the issue of the average age of those involved in ministry bears consideration. While the Ministry Summit focused on young adults, (except for the recommendation relative to an expansion of the role of Vocations Offices) as noted above, the top recommendations apply to drawing young adults into participation in parish life. Examining only the ages of those involved in ministry formation programs, we note the following trends: among seminarians, 31 percent are thirty-five or older, 50 percent over thirty; among those preparing to be permanent deacons (a statistic admittedly influenced by the minimum age of thirty-five requirement), 66 percent are over fifty; and among lay ecclesial ministers, 71 percent are over forty, 40 percent over fifty.[27]

Co-Workers reminds us that personal invitation to ministry is essential, and adds that this is "especially important in those communities that are still underrepresented among lay ecclesial ministers."[28] This admonition applies to both groups considered here: Hispanics, and by extension other underrepresented racial and ethnic groups; and young adults. The document also outlines various strategies that assist in the discernment process, and guidelines for judging the suitability of persons for ministry. These strategies and guidelines resemble those guiding the calling forth of deacons and priests, and represent a maturing intentionality in calling forth new ministers. However, the Emerging Models research underlines the need for a greater involvement of all in this effort. In his keynote address at the Ministry Summit, Bishop Cupich reminded those present that "we need to have a sense of corporate responsibility for vocations to the ordained ministry" [29]—as well, he said, as the calling forth of lay ecclesial ministers.

Formation for Lay Ecclesial Ministry

When the Subcommittee on Lay Ministry began its work, the members surveyed their fellow bishops to determine their central concerns relative to the committee's charge. The bishops ranked the formation of these new ministers first, along with an examination of a theology of lay ministry. Co-Workers addressed their concern with a comprehensive overview of formation, including a broad range of goals and methods, and of agents of formation. The framework follows the formation structure for priests and deacons, focused on four areas: human, spiritual, intellectual, and pastoral formation. This section is fully one-third of the total document.[30]

The section of Co-Workers most relevant to the agenda of the Emerging Models research is that of pastoral formation. The most important recommendation that pastoral leaders at the Ministry Summit made was "Develop a comprehensive training program and materials for ministry in a multiple-parish environment for diocesan staff, pastors, deacons, parish life coordinators, parish staffs, lay leaders, parishioners and seminarians."[31] Co-Workers does not have this focus. In light of our clearer understanding of the unfolding changes in pastoral leadership, changes that will continue, this goal will be increasingly important.

Another recommendation emerging from the research is, "A stronger program of forming all those involved in pastoral leadership into patterns of collaboration." In his concluding remarks at the Summit, Fr. Schreiter stressed that it is essential to give greater attention to collaboration.[32] Co-Workers states, ". . . we call both lay and ordained ministers to learn the skills of collaboration, to value the benefits it brings to Church life and ministry, and to commit themselves to practice it in their places of ministry."[33] To further this goal, seminaries, ministry preparation programs, and dioceses must seek ways to foster mutuality among those preparing for lay and ordained ministries, as well as teach skills for collaboration. Collaboration must also be addressed in continuing education programs. Progress toward this goal would be made if two recommendations from the Ministry Summit were implemented. "Develop measurable standards for forming collaborative ministers (clergy, religious, and lay ecclesial ministers) to be utilized in seminary and diocesan ministry formation programs" and "Develop pastoral planning processes which include greater consultation between lay leaders and pastors in area parishes with diocesan leadership when considering clustering, twinning, merging and closing parishes."[34]

The Ministerial Workplace

Co-Workers notes the importance of sound practices in human resources, consonant with Gospel values. At the same time, the bishops also acknowledge that the capacity for dioceses to manage human resources varies greatly. The Emerging Models research included the polling of over fifteen hundred people about the function of diocesan human resource departments. They found that, "More than 75 percent of those responding were well aware of the civil obligations of the church as employer. At the same time, however, less than 40 percent indicated adequate attention paid to the development of employees in terms of continuing education, evaluation, retirement, sabbaticals and so on."[35] The Summit responded to the research with one of its top ten recommendations: "Develop comprehensive human resource management systems at the diocesan level that integrate effective practices reflecting Gospel values, adaptable to local/parish needs, including just wage and benefit package."[36] This will be a formidable task. Mary Jo Moran, the executive director of NACPA (National Association of Church Personnel Administrators), notes that at the parish level, priests are not trained in this area, and at the diocesan level more human resource directors are part-time than before. As a result, they are usually able only to manage and to be reactive, rather than to provide leadership for the parishes.[37]

Rated even higher than the above in the top ten recommendations is: "Create a culture of accountability through performance reviews for all ministers—ordained, religious, and lay—that reflect the application of best practices of emerging models of parish leadership."[38] Co-Workers does not really develop the theme of accountability. Its mention surely is influenced by the clergy abuse crisis, and increasing numbers of financial scandals in parishes and dioceses; accountability can be expected to become more important in the years ahead. Developing accountability and transparency will be a difficult task, because it is counter to the culture of the church as an organization, at every level. This is a difficult task not because the church is unethical, but rather because its procedures are rooted in trust and interpersonal exchange. To develop the needed guidelines, structures, and skills, leaders should safeguard that which is best about the system as it is, even while seeking ways to improve it, in the light of human failure (which may be more prevalent because our systems today are larger, less familial and communal, more organizational and bureaucratic). The very models emerging in the church, with their emphasis on a rooting of all ministers in discipleship, and on collaboration among them, provide a helpful resource toward developing new models of accountability and transparency.

In its concluding section, Co-Workers quotes Pope John Paul II, and his reflections on the mission of the church. The pope said, "But it must be translated into pastoral initiatives adapted to the circumstances of each community. . . . It is in the local churches that the specific features of a detailed pastoral plan can be identified—goals and methods, formation and enrichment of the people involved, [and] the search for necessary resources."[39] Here, the guidelines presented in Co-Workers and the research and recommendations of the Emerging Models Project converge, offering an invitation, a mandate.

Conclusion

This essay began with the question, in light of the changes in ministry in the United States today, as described in the research from the Emerging Models Project, can Co-Workers assist the ongoing evolution in pastoral leadership we are experiencing? The assessment given above suggests ways in which it is already doing this, and identifies some areas that need further attention. Here is a brief summary:

The most important contribution that Co-Workers makes is the theological vision the document gives, one that embraces all pastoral leaders serving our churches today. Further explication of this vision, exploring its application to priests and deacons, will make what is here implicit, explicit. This can provide the impetus toward a more comprehensive ordering of ministry, one adequate to the new realities of our time. An aspect of this ordering would be work to bring greater clarity to the question, who is a lay ecclesial minister? which Co-Workers does not adequately answer.

The Emerging Models research gives a picture of parish life today, one that attests to the value of much of the document. However, it also suggests areas that need further reflection and response as reflected in these questions.

- What are effective ways for calling forth young adults and persons from varied cultures to serve as priests, deacons, and lay ecclesial ministers?
- How can pastoral leaders be prepared for the multiple parish environment which is ever more prevalent today?
- How can our communities foster the mutuality and teach the skills that are needed for collaboration?
- How can more adequate stewardship of human resources be developed?

- How can a culture of accountability be instituted in dioceses and parishes?

These are large tasks indeed. Co-Workers offers a final word, to energize and motivate us. "Let us go forward in hope! . . . The Son of God, who became incarnate two thousand years ago out of love for humanity is at work even today; we need discerning eyes to see this and, above all, a generous heart to become the instruments of his work."[40]

Reflection Questions

1. Fox explores how the development of lay ecclesial ministry is part of an ongoing evolution of ministry and pastoral leadership. In particular, she notes that there has been a "shift from leadership in parishes being vested in pastors and associate priests to leadership by a diversity of pastoral leaders, and to the pastoring and leadership of multiple parishes by individuals and teams" (128). How can the theological vision of relational ministry that is presented in Co-Workers guide efforts to develop viable structures of leadership in parishes today?
2. How can the theological vision of Co-Workers provide a guide for developing models of collaborative ministry?
3. How can Co-Workers serve as a resource for decisions within local churches about the stewardship of resources?
4. How can Co-Workers serve as a resource for efforts to create a culture of accountability in Catholic diocese and parishes throughout the country?

Notes

1. USCCB, Co-Workers in the Vineyard of the Lord: A Resource for Guiding the Development of Lay Ecclesial Ministry (Washington, DC: USCCB, 2005).

2. Jewell's presentation at the summit, "The Findings of the Emerging Models of Pastoral Leadership Project," is published in *Origins* 38 no. 1 (May 15, 2008):10-15.

3. Carole Ganim, ed., *Shaping Catholic Parishes: Pastoral Leaders in the 21st Century* (Chicago: Loyola Press, 2008).

4. USCC, Called and Gifted: The American Catholic Laity (Washington, DC: USCC, 1980), 4–5.

5. Center for Applied Research in the Apostolate (CARA), "Frequently Requested Church Statistics," www.Georgetown.edu (accessed September 16, 2008).

6. Philip J. Murnion, *New Parish Ministers: Laity and Religious on Parish Staffs* (New York: National Pastoral Life Center, 1992), 72-77.

7. CARA, "Frequently Requested Church Statistics."

8. Philip J. Murnion and David DeLambo, *Parishes and Parish Ministers: A Study of Parish Lay Ministry* (New York: National Pastoral Life Center, 1999), iii.

9. *The Notre Dame Study of Catholic Parish Life Report 15* (Notre Dame, IN: University of Notre Dame, 1989), 6.

10. Ganim, *Shaping Catholic Parishes.*

11. Co-Workers, 7.

12. Ibid., 7-10.

13. Marti Jewell, "The Findings of the Emerging Models of Pastoral Leadership Project," *Origins* 38, no. 1 (May 15, 2008): 13.

14. Co-Workers, 11.

15. David DeLambo, *Lay Parish Ministers: A Study of Emerging Leadership* (New York: National Pastoral Life Center, 2005), 71. ". . . better than two-thirds" of lay parish ministers (not including vowed religious) "believe they are pursuing a lifetime of service in the church."

16. Co-Workers, 17-21. In the concluding keynote at the Ministry Summit, "Pastoral Leadership: Moving into the Future," Robert Schreiter emphasized and expanded on the centrality of communion. *Origins* 38, no. 2 (May 22, 2008): 27.

17. Ibid., 21.

18. Ibid., 26.

19. Susan K. Wood, ed., *Ordering the Baptismal Priesthood: Theologies of Lay and Ordained Ministry* (Collegeville, MN: Liturgical Press, 2003), 264.

20. Co-Workers, 27.

21. "Factbox: America's Roman Catholic Population," www.rueters.com (accessed September 16, 2008).

22. USCCB, *The Study of the Impact of Fewer Priests on the Pastoral Ministry* (June 15-17, 2000) (Washington, DC: USCCB, 2003), 31.

23. CARA, "The Permanent Diaconate Today," www.cara.Georgetown.edu (accessed September 20, 2008).

24. DeLambo, *Lay Parish Ministers,* 48.

25. CARA, "Catholic Ministry Formation Directory Statistical Survey: 2007-2008," www.cara.Georgetown.edu (accessed September 23, 2008).

26. "Top Recommendations, National Ministry Summit," www.emergingmodels.org (accessed September 12, 2008).

27. CARA, "Catholic Ministry Formation Directory."

28. Co-Workers, 28.

29. Bishop Blase Cupich, "The Emerging Models of Pastoral Leadership Project: The Theological, Sacramental and Ecclesial Context," *Origins* 38, no. 1 (May 15, 2008): 7.

30. Co-Workers, 33-53.

31. "Top Recommendations, National Ministry Summit."

32. Robert Schreiter, "Pastoral Leadership: Moving into the Future," *Origins* 38, no. 2 (May 22, 2008): 27.

33. Co-Workers, 48.

34. "Top Recommendations, National Ministry Summit."

35. Jewell, 12.

36. "Top Recommendations, National Ministry Summit."

37. Mary Jo Moran, in discussion with the author, September 24, 2008.

38. "Top Recommendations, National Ministry Summit."

39. John Paul II, *Novo Millennio Ineute* (At the Beginning of the New Millennium), 29, quoted in USCCB, Co-Workers in the Vineyard of the Lord, 66.

40. Co-Workers, 58, 67.

CHAPTER ELEVEN

Formation of Lay Ecclesial Ministers
Rooted in a Genuinely Lay and Ecclesial Spirituality

Janet K. Ruffing, RSM

The stunning recognition of the emergence of the new vocation of lay ecclesial ministers over the last thirty years, as both a work of the Spirit and a development the United States bishops affirm and welcome with gratitude, is a cause for rejoicing.[1] This new Spirit-initiated development in our local churches leads to questions about how, as an ecclesial community, we might best nurture this expanding phenomenon with appropriate spiritual formation. This formation should assist ministry candidates in discerning their call and in developing an appropriate spirituality that will deepen and grow over time; that will help them integrate their distinctively lay spirituality with their new ministerial identity; and that will sustain them over time through disappointment, suffering, and conflict.

Zeni Fox reports that studies, prior to the release of Co-Workers in the Vineyard of the Lord: A Resource for Guiding the Development of Lay Ecclesial Ministry, discovered that spiritual formation within lay ministry programs varied significantly. She states, "twice as much time is given to spiritual formation of participants in non-degree programs as in degree programs." Spiritual formation components included eucharistic liturgies, prayer/reflection groups, prayer services, retreats or days of recollection, and spiritual advisors.[2] In a different study Fox cited, 50 to 80 percent of the participants rated opportunities for eucharistic liturgies, faith sharing, Scripture sharing, spiritual direction, and spiritual reading very highly.[3] Perhaps lay ecclesial ministry has grown primarily from the generous response of laypersons, predominately of women, to the interior nudging of the Spirit to extend their care and concern beyond their immediate families to their parish or diocesan communities. Paul Wilkes noted the striking difference in the reported prayerfulness of lay ecclesial ministers as compared to the priests with whom they serve.

They "are more solicitous about prayer. . . (46 percent versus 23 percent for priests), for days of reflection and retreats (31 percent versus 10 percent), and faith sharing (35 percent versus 18 percent)."[4] Is it possible that lay ecclesial ministers have a more personally developed relationship with God than some of their ordained partners in ministry? Is it their relationship with God that leads them into ministry because they want to share their experience of faith with others in their local parish community?

While Co-Workers espouses no single spirituality for lay ecclesial ministers other than "common grounding in God's word and the sacraments, in the pastoral life and communion of the Church, and in the one Spirit who has been given to all,"[5] more can be said about the developed lay spirituality many already bring to their ministries, and which they need to complement with an explicitly ministerial spirituality. Just as there have been developments in the theology of ministry and other areas of theology since the Second Vatican Council, so too has the understanding of lay spirituality and vocation developed. Vatican II dramatically affirmed the universal call to holiness within the Church in *Lumen Gentium* (Dogmatic Constitution on the Church): All in the church are called to the one holiness, and all ways of life within the church are schools of holiness for those called to them.[6]

For all Christians, vocational discernment is a major task throughout the adult years. To what is God calling each of us as our way of life and our mission in life?[7] Vatican II identified the transformation of the world as a task given specifically to lay men and women (LG 31). Although *Lumen Gentium* recognized that the laity are "called to participate actively in the whole life of the church" (LG 33), the Spirit's surprise was a vocation to church ministry for some laity.

With dramatically lengthened life spans, a call to ecclesial ministry may come later in life, enabling these ministers to enrich church communities with valuable life experience gained as spouses, parents, grandparents, adult children caring for parents. Ministers can bring valuable work experience in various careers from their vocations to single or married life. Youth ministers, who are typically much younger than their other partners in parish ministry, bring their unique understanding of the generation with whom they work, but may need something akin to initial formation in the spiritual life as well as in ministerial formation. Youth ministers frequently pursue a pastoral graduate ministry degree, but may have little experience of parishes and possess only an inchoate Catholic identity. Their spiritualities may be quite eclectic and less shaped by the traditional fonts of Christian spirituality. They will benefit most from deepening their appropriation of specifically Christian spiritual practices. It is important to keep in mind that lay ecclesial ministers differ from the many, many laypersons who serve in a variety of ministries on a part-time basis for varying periods of time. Lay ecclesial ministers also differ across ethnic communities. For instance, the overwhelming number of lay ecclesial ministers, who work twenty or more hours per week in paid ministry, is largely a phenomenon in parishes attended primarily by white Catholics, in diocesan offices, and in varying positions of leadership, which implies a certain level of education and professional expectations.

Lay ecclesial ministry is also taking place within the rapidly growing Hispanic community, now 30 percent of the American church, but in this community, the ministers are usually women who work on a volunteer basis, without having had the same access to prior general education[8] or access to Spanish language ministry programs. In the Hispanic communities and other ethnic communities, the spirituality and ecclesiology are deeply influenced by their countries of origin as well as their process of inculturation in the United States.

Lay Spirituality

There are many ways of describing lay spirituality at the present time. Both Ed Sellner and more recently Kees Waaijman go back to the New Testament and patristic periods of Christian life as the starting point of lay spirituality since the entire Jesus movement was a lay phenomenon. The first Christian churches were house churches, presided over by the leader who hosted the community. Waaijman writes, "In the first century, . . . the conviction prevailed that all the baptized formed the church: all took part in the life of the church, practiced theology as well as their personal charism. The people was the subject of the liturgy."[9] Sellner summarizes the results of consultations, prior to the Synod on the Laity in 1987, that revealed how deeply lay people had embraced the teachings of Vatican II. He described, "a universal reawakening among Roman Catholic laypeople to their gifts and responsibilities to serve wherever they are called, and they recognize that any dualism that splits body and soul, Church and world, ministry and work, laity and ordained is not true to their life experiences."[10] Co-Workers[11] and all other church documents assert that a common spirituality is lived by all members of the church in different ways; the primary sources for spiritual growth are sacramental life and Scripture; and the core spiritual dimension is a personal and growing relationship with Christ, from which flows one's life and actions in the world or in church ministries, according to the gifts of the Holy Spirit, for the good of the community.

However, what is distinctly lay in this spirituality? Waaijman puts it this way: "The unique profile of lay spirituality is defined by a number of structural elements: specific relational patterns (marriage partners, parents—children, family, neighbors, guests); a specific sense of time (generational consciousness, course of life, birth, death); a specific sense of space (the home), which mediates the connections with the immediate and more remote environment (world, church, labor, possessions); the personal life journey of the concrete individual is central."[12] Sellner offer descriptions and categories that further specify this distinction. "It is a spirituality of the family and the workplace, and is frequently expressed in the life of the local parish communities. Since there are many circumstances and types of lay people, there are a great variety of lay spiritualities related to personal vocations, choices, commitments, and life styles."[13] The ascetic dimension of lay spirituality arises from "the discipline and struggle to care for families, maintain careers and jobs," sustain extended family members, endure the sufferings of everyday life, make meaning of one's existence, and balance the demands between work or ministry outside the home and family life.[14] Fidelity to spiritual practices within this context is extremely important. Further, lay spirituality "is incarnational, enfleshed, and frequently expressed sexually."[15] Forgiveness and reconciliation is an integral aspect of family life before it is expressed in a liturgical ritual. While family life and its particular concern with human flourishing from birth to death shapes lay spirituality, it also includes openness to care for creation and concern for the poor, the abused, and the neglected. Waaijman goes so far as to identify the works of mercy as characteristic of lay spirituality. Finally, lay spirituality is not limited to the domestic sphere alone. It is also concerned with a faith that does justice and with vocations to political life, the professions, the arts, the sciences, agriculture, and so on. Family may or may not form the primary community for lay adults although it does for many. Families exist in and contribute to the larger communities in which they participate. Because there are few supportive structures for lay spirituality, many form some kind of small faith-sharing groups with other lay people, as well as make use of spiritual direction to support their on-going spiritual growth.

I have tried to create a "thick description" of lay spirituality, emphasizing the variety of contexts and factors that each layperson will incarnate uniquely, while at the same time expressing it within shared parish life or some other base Christian community. Lay ecclesial ministers bring their lived experiences of these realities, both their successes and their challenges, into their ministry. Because they share a similar "life-world" and experiences with those with whom they minister, they bring their graced wisdom and a deep understanding of the lives of the people they serve in ministry. In their public role of ministry, they exert a certain exemplary role in the community that in turn helps others to recognize their callings and gifts and live them more deeply both at home and in the community to which they are called.

Discipleship as the Shaping Influence

The spirituality common to all persons in the church, but absolutely essential for all ecclesial ministers, is characterized by a personal experience of "the love of the Father in Christ, through his Spirit."[16] This graced experience is central for all forms of Christian discipleship but is essential for grounding one's ministry. Candidates presenting themselves for lay ecclesial ministry may have had such an experience but may not necessarily be able to reflect on that experience and articulate it in explicitly theological terms. A goal for initial and on-going spiritual formation is an ever-deeper appropriation of one's Christian discipleship as the primary influence shaping how one relates and ministers within the community.

Cunningham and Egan[17] describe discipleship as the key category for Christian spirituality. They assert that from earliest times, converts to Christianity clearly understood that they were embracing a "way" of life, indicating that they were embarking on a journey that has a beginning and an end. Life is moving in a particular direction, but one is always "on the way"—the church is a pilgrim people. To embrace a way of life implies that there are practices and behaviors consonant with this way. As Egan and Cunningham develop this theme, they identify this way of life as a life of discipleship, and they further specify what is entailed in this richly evocative word.

The Spirit initiates discipleship. One becomes a disciple by being called by Jesus who calls his disciples across both social and sexual lines. Ritual purity and obedience (to the Law) are not the primary criteria Jesus used. Responding to Jesus' call demands a radically changed life: one that risks all kinds of securities in order to follow him, and one that ultimately could lead to the cross. Jesus relates to his disciples as a Teacher (Rabbi), making the disciples his students, yet following him means more than learning his teaching; it also means attaching oneself to him personally. This relationship is always ongoing and living. Becoming his disciple means not only relating to Jesus but also sharing his ministry. Finally, to be Jesus' disciple is to love one another as he did and to share with one another in the beloved community.

Lay ecclesial ministers are Jesus' disciples within the unique circumstances of their lives. Yet, there is more to a ministerial spirituality. A lived experience of Jesus develops into learning about his life and teachings at all stages of the life cycle. Jesus' birth, ministerial life, death and resurrection, through the power of the Holy Spirit, can become everyone's personal story. Continual meditation on the gospels throughout the liturgical cycle leads to deeper appropriation of Jesus' story in one's life over a lifetime, but also constantly challenges ministers to relate to others and minister as Jesus did. His teachings on the Kingdom of God, fullness of life, the character of God, the beatitudes and the works of mercy constantly inform pastoral practice. The Spirit of Jesus, dwelling within each person, gifts each disciple, through nature and grace, with specific gifts for the good of the whole church.

Life-long Ministerial Formation

The progressive reality of life-long formation and transformation, grounds an appreciation for on-going conversion. Ministers become ministers over a lifetime, just as everyone becomes a Christian over a lifetime. Ministry is grounded in the minister's ever-renewing experience of grace. Genuinely altruistic responses to the other, to the world, to the poor are rooted in the minister's affective experience of God's love that enables the person to put self-centered needs aside in ministry. This core relationship with the triune God may be expressed in an attitude of praise and gratitude for the abundance of the God revealed in Jesus. Faith, hope, and love grow and mature in this climate. As ministers grow in grace, they begin to recognize that they represent God, mediate God's grace, love, and compassion. They begin to recognize the symbolic and charismatic power of ministry. God/Jesus works through them, and as officially designated ministers, they represent the church and the Christian community. As they come to rely more and more on God, they discover that they do not need to compulsively over-work or neglect the self-care that insures professional, competent, and faith- enlivened ministry.

To live and minister this way requires sufficient personal prayer, corporate prayer, and reflection to enable discernment of interior movements within the minister that lead to a sense of abiding vocation and guidance in particular circumstances. By so doing, ministers grow to recognize God acting in and through pastoral relationships and activities such as teaching, preaching, facilitating, healing, organizing, counseling, and spiritual direction. This practice of prayer and the awareness of interior movements provide a contemplative sustenance for life and ministry. Ministry is relational and requires a developed capacity to live in the relational flow of God's triune love for oneself and for everyone, moving in and through the multiple interactions of the day, and of pastoral care with one another.

These relationships are multiple: self with God, self with oneself, self with the community, and self with the world beyond the church community. Ministry serves communion. Ministry is not authentic when it becomes self-serving. Ministers who are relational recognize a mutuality of interchange by offering competent and compassionate care to those who want the particular service offered. Ministers do not create dependency on their services. Rather, they strive to create a network of caring relationships within a community that can operate without the minister directing and controlling everything. They use their institutional and personal power for the up-building of the community and take responsibility for maintaining the safety and the boundaries for those who seek their care.

An intriguing issue around lay ecclesial ministry is whether or not the minister's call is to serve the church, the diocese, or the local parish. The most recent study of lay ministry published by the National Pastoral Life Center, done by David DeLambo, indicates that many lay ecclesial ministers are invited into ministry by their pastor or another local priest who knows them. Paul Wilkes states, "Lay workers do not consider themselves merely interchangeable contract laborers for hire. They are deeply and specifically committed to the parish in which they work, which is usually the parish in which they worship and in which their children may be educated."[18] This finding is somewhat troubling. Is perhaps the sense of call as encouraged or even initiated by a local pastor too dependent on a single parish community and on a personal relationship with a single priest or other local minister?

Women who may have been out of the work force while their children were young are more likely to lose their sense of competency beyond the home. The recognition of their gifts for ministry—through their volunteer work in the parish by serving on committees or participating in one program or another—can be very encouraging and affirming and draw women into ministry as they receive more preparation for and experience in the ministry. More than one lay ecclesial minister, however, has failed to survive a change of pastor when his or her ministry in the parish depended on a personal relationship with the previous pastor.

While it is understandable that lay ecclesial ministers may not wish to relocate to another part of the state or country, for example, can they be encouraged to grow into a sense of church that extends beyond their own parish? Some lay ecclesial ministers have earned a master's or doctoral degree, and have held leadership positions in diocesan offices. The experience they acquire in one church position (as chancellor, financial officer, canon lawyer, faith formation director, youth ministry director, and so on) is more easily transferable to another parish or diocese than for those who do not share the same level of education. One's level of professional experience and educational background profoundly affect ministerial identity and one's vision of whom one is called to serve within the church.

Professionalization

Because ministry is both professional as well as charismatic, it requires dedication to professional growth through theological and pastoral study beyond the period of initial formation. Contracts and compensation for lay ecclesial ministers should include church-funded opportunities for workshops, in-service education, and additional course work. Shared Scripture study in a supportive community is often a very helpful way of cultivating a deepening understanding of Scripture both personally and professionally. Such Scripture study can help the minister internalize a gospel vision of ministry.

Ministry Supervision

Formation programs need to include courses in the ethics of ministry, and church employers should encourage the use of a ministry supervisor. A ministry supervisor's role is not so much onsite mentoring or supervision of the minister's performance of assigned areas (although this is also very important). Instead, this supervision is a confidential, one-on-one relationship in which the pastoral minister can process challenging or troubling interactions with staff and people to whom they minister, so as to sort out the psychological issues from the minister's past that may get stirred up, or to help to interpret the transference and counter-transferential reactions in ways that support more competent ministry. This relationship with a supervisor is one way of coping with the unavoidable frustrations in ministry that are particularly difficult.

Spiritual Direction and Retreats

Finally, spiritual direction can assist the minister in a personalized way with growth in prayer, awareness of religious experience, reflection on interior movements, and the guidance offered by the Holy Spirit. Opportunity for an annual week-long retreat or two shorter periods of retreat should also be an employment benefit. Lay ministers may not be able to afford either the cost or the time for a retreat. If retreats are encouraged and expected for clergy and religious, they are needed just as much, if not more, by lay ministers. Extended retreat times often restore one's perspective, deepen one's relationship with God and sense of calling, and refresh one's body and spirit. Retreats allow time for discernment about particularly challenging situations and often help in restoring balance and reconnecting with God in a deeper way than may be possible in the midst of family and ministry.

Coping with Conflict

While the development and official recognition of lay ecclesial ministry is surely cause for rejoicing, lay ecclesial ministry is not universally accepted throughout the country in the same way. Power and authority within the church continues to be linked to ordination. Members of the clerical system today manifest differing ecclesiologies; differing liturgical preferences; differing attitudes about the role of laity, especially women, in ministry; and differing theologies of priesthood and ministry. As a result, many lay ecclesial ministers find themselves in conflict within the church.

The final issue I wish to address is preparing lay ministers for suffering and conflict within the church. Many who comment on Vatican II recognize that it takes a hundred years to implement an ecumenical council, and that we are only halfway there. Lay ministry and the affirmation of the women's contribution in the church were clearly significant theological and pastoral breakthroughs. These breakthroughs occurred within the larger paradigm shifts initiated by Vatican II and developments since the council, such as the preferential option for the poor from Medellin, a robust development in the social teachings of the church; and the need to reinterpret our understanding of the creation in response to the new cosmology. As Kenan Osborne so aptly describes in his book on lay ministry, when the laity who were depositioned gradually over many centuries in the church are rapidly repositioned, the clergy feel as if they are being depositioned.[19]

Jon Sobrino devotes an entire chapter in his *Spirituality of Liberation: Toward Political Holiness* to the topic of conflict in the church. His analysis is loving, courageous, and compassionate. He recognizes both the sinfulness of members within the church and the reality of conflict caused by "the newness willed by God for the church expressed in Vatican II and in Medellin."[20] We are still in the process of receiving and rejecting these developments and everything in between. These conflicting interpretations of Vatican II and subsequent developments are a major root of much conflict in the church today. All groups within the church—laity, clergy, hierarchy, and members of religious institutes—are on different sides of many issues. On the one hand, Sobrino suggests this is simply human nature. On the other hand, he acknowledges that "the most acute element of conflictuality is to be found in the difficulty of honestly maintaining the fundamental novelty of Vatican II and Medellin in the face of the ever present danger of involution that would put them both to a thousand kinds of death."[21] The conversion in thought and behavior required for the full implementation of the reform and renewal of the church is very hard for everyone.

In order to cope with such conflict gracefully, Sobrino proposes a spirituality of conflict which includes four basic principles encompassing both attitudes and behaviors of dealing with conflict and attempting to resolve conflicts in a way consonant with the Gospel. Without summarizing all of these principles, let me simply note that he sees conflict as a reality in the church and as inevitable. This reality requires a love for truth and neither denial of differences nor attempts to ignore it. At the same time, some members within a faith community may need to place their faith in God alone, and in the Spirit who is the ultimate norm and guide of the church, while living from a hope for church unity. A spirituality of conflict is opposed to the use of sheer force as the ultimate means of resolving conflict. Parties in conflict need to be willing to try to identify the issue correctly and engage in honest dialogue. Holiness is required as the ultimate means, but resolution from this approach historically takes a long time. Genuine humility and self-examination are appropriate dispositions. Ultimately, the criteria of verification are supplied by God's Spirit in the church's becoming more clearly a witness to the Gospel, appearing more like Jesus in his life and his death. And finally, conflict is reducible to love. "Within and without conflict, a member of the church should have great love for God and Jesus, for the poor, and for the reign of God."[22]

Conclusion

The advent of lay ecclesial ministry under the sway of God's Spirit is, indeed, cause for rejoicing. It is also one of the marks of novelty initiated by Vatican II. The bishops welcome it and affirm it, yet like all the developments heralded by Vatican II, this enthusiasm is not necessarily universal. Innovators and pioneers in lay ministry deserve the support and the formation that will enable them to serve communion in the church for the long haul. In turn, they will continue to deeply enrich the church by their particular expertise, their specifically lay spirituality, and their integrated ministerial identity.

Reflection Questions

1. Ruffing points out that *lay spiritualities* are often marked by concerns about family life and efforts to maintain jobs and careers. How can lay ecclesial ministers who are committed to the ongoing development of their spiritual lives bring a distinctive perspective to ministry, a perspective that enriches ecclesial ministry by complementing the spiritual and ministerial outlooks of vowed religious men and women and clergy?
2. From your perspective, what are the most important spiritual formation needs of those preparing to become lay ecclesial ministers? How can and should the church support the ongoing spiritual formation of lay ecclesial ministers?
3. How can lay ecclesial ministers be prepared spiritually to deal with conflicts about issues of power, authority, and ministerial responsibility? How might dealing with such conflicts in healthy ways contribute to the ongoing evolution of ministry in the church today?

Notes

1. USCCB, Co-Workers in the Vineyard of the Lord: A Resource for Guiding the Development of Lay Ecclesial Ministry (Washington, D.C.: USCCB Publishing, 2005), 9.

2. Zeni Fox, *New Ecclesial Ministry: Lay Professionals Serving the Church* (Franklin WI: Sheed and Ward, 2002), 32.

3. Ibid., 32.

4. David DeLambo, *Lay Parish Ministry: A Study of Emerging Leadership* (New York: National Pastoral Life Center, 2005), 73, quoted in Paul Wilkes, "A Prediction Fulfilled," *America* (February 27, 2006): 13.

5. USCCB, Co-Workers, 38.

6. *Lumen Gentium* (Dogmatic Constitution on the Church), in *Vatican Council II: The Conciliar and Postconciliar Documents,* ed. Austin Flannery, 350-440 (Northport, New York: Costello Publishing Company, 1987).

7. Since 1999, the Lilly Endowment's Programs for the Theological Exploration of Vocation has sponsored programs in eighty-eight U.S. colleges and universities. See John Neafsey, *A Sacred Voice is Calling: Personal Vocation and Social Conscience* (Maryknoll: Orbis, 2006) as representative of the recognition for the pressing need to development vocational awareness within the Christian community beyond specifically ecclesial vocations.

8. Thirty percent of white adults in the United States have at least a bachelor's degree, compared to 49 percent of Asians, 17 percent of blacks and 12 percent of Hispanics. Sisters of Mercy of the Americas, "Election 2008: A Practical Resource," http://www.sistersofmercy.org/images/stories/documents/resources/electionresource.pdf (accessed March 2, 2011):11.

9. Kees Waaijman, *Spirituality: Forms, Foundations, Methods* (Leuven: Peters, 2002), 21.

10. Edward C. Sellner, "Lay Spirituality," in *The New Dictionary of Catholic Spirituality,* in Michael Downey, ed. (Collegeville, MN: Liturgical Press, 1993), 593.

11. Co-Workers, 39.

12. Kees Waaijan, *Spirituality,* 23.

13. Sellner, 593-94.

14. Ibid., 594.

15. Ibid.

16. Co-Workers, 38.

17. The section that follows is based on Lawrence S. Cunningham and Keith J. Egan, *Christian Spirituality: Themes from the Tradition* (Mahwah, NJ: Paulist Press, 1996), 9-11

18. Wilkes, "A Prediction Fulfilled," 13.

19. Kenan Osborne, *Ministry: Lay Ministry in the Roman Catholic Church* (Mahwah, NJ: Paulist Press, 1993).

20. Jon Sobrino, *Spirituality of Liberation: Toward Political Holiness,* trans. Robert Barr (Maryknoll: Orbis, 1990), 145.

21. Ibid., 146.

22. Ibid., 149.

CHAPTER TWELVE

Ministry in Service to an Adult Church

How Lay Ministry Fosters Mature Faith in the Catholic Parish

Michael P. Horan

Introduction

Through official church documents in the past forty years, Catholic leaders have claimed that the goal of religious education/catechesis is the fostering of mature adult faith. Within that same period of time, the Catholic Church has witnessed an unprecedented flowering of lay ministries in Catholic parishes, expanding the role of laypeople in the leadership ministries that support parish life. Among these leadership ministries are "specialist" roles such as directors of religious education, youth ministers, and others who focus their service to a particular population or work. More recently, the emergence of new roles demands consideration of "generalist" ministers and their role in parish leadership. Parish life directors and pastoral associates are not specialists who focus their ministries on one activity or one age group; rather, they are generalists, who function as parish community leaders or as the associate leaders in promoting all the ministries and supporting all the volunteers who comprise the community's workforce. These groups of "generalists," who function as public professional leaders and who coordinate the general rhythm of parish life, receive particular treatment in this essay for two reasons. First, pastoral associates or parish life coordinators are gaining the attention of bishops and theologians. The attention is well deserved; the phenomenon of growing numbers of generalist ministers who collaborate with parish priests, or in some cases, function as the local leader in concert with a non-resident priest minister, has generated literature from the "official" leaders, the United States bishops. The rise in the number of parish generalist ministers also has led to increased numbers of students in graduate programs and ministry institutes who want to receive the level of professional education commensurate with their role.[1] The thinking of the United States bishops on this topic is best summarized in Co-Workers in the Vineyard of the Lord, a document that acknowledges the changes in the character of parish life and leadership roles.[2] In sum, these professional lay ministers have attracted the attention of the bishops and the academic theological community.

However, there is a second reason to focus on professional lay leaders at the parish level: These people strike the average parishioner as new, "different," and perhaps even strange. The specialist ministries are more established and better known to the average parishioner, who is neither surprised nor confused that the roles of director of religious education and school principal are assumed by single or married laypeople. By contrast, the average parishioner cannot help but notice that generalist ministers function in many (though certainly not all) of the leadership roles traditionally assumed by associate pastor priests or the pastor himself. Hence, their presence warrants attention and analysis.

Professional Leadership Ministry

An explanation of terms is in order here. Throughout this essay I use the term "professional leadership ministry" to describe what the United States bishops have termed "lay ecclesial ministry," because I believe the bishops' term has the disadvantage of being both vague and unfriendly to the lay parishioners, the very people who are served by these ministers. By contrast, the term "professional leadership ministry (and ministers)" is more intelligible in that the words are both familiar in sound and in content to the average parishioner. The term *professional* implies that the minister has preparation and competence, as well as dedication to pursue excellence. A *professional* is educated, otherwise prepared, certified, and compensated according to the standards of the profession; the other members of that profession have a role in the re-certification and assessment of the professionals. Nurses, attorneys, and teachers come to mind here as readily accessible examples of professionals well known to parishioners. All of them are well educated. All of them have to meet certain standards. All of them must continue their professional development and sharpen their skills if they wish to remain well regarded and officially certified members of that profession.

The second important adjective that modifies this type of ministry and ministers is *leadership*. A *leadership* ministry is distinct from a volunteer or membership ministry by virtue of the role of leading, a role common to the ministers I study in this essay. Volunteer ministries assumed by members of the parish are essential to the life of the parish, but they do not demand the work conditions, stable employment, serious preparation, and sustained education implied in the words *professional* or *leadership*. Still, the persons I seek to consider are the same ones described by the less helpful title "lay ecclesial ministers" in Co-Workers, with one notable difference. In Co-Workers, the bishops attend to ". . . those men and women whose ecclesial service is characterized by

- *Authorization* of the hierarchy to serve publicly in the local church
- *Leadership* in a particular area of ministry
- *Close mutual collaboration* with the pastoral ministry of bishops, priests, and deacons
- *Preparation and formation* appropriate to the level of responsibilities that are assigned to them."[3]

The writers of Co-Workers do not distinguish between the ministers who are full-time and salaried and those who volunteer their time and talent without compensation. This essay will focus on the full-time, professional, and salaried leaders rather than the volunteers.

The same body of bishops, who wrote about professional lay leaders as ecclesial lay ministers, also has produced the *National Directory for Catechesis* (NDC), the *Magna Carta* for faith formation in American parishes and diocesan venues. The NDC describes the general pastoral realities and challenges of catechesis/faith formation. It offers a description of the goals, context, personnel, methods, general content, and approaches that characterize successful practices of faith formation in parishes and dioceses today. Among its central claims is that effective catechesis fosters mature adult faith.[4] The NDC echoes the *General Catechetical Directory* (GCD), the original catechetical directory produced after the Second Vatican Council for the universal church. According to the GCD, the aim of catechesis is the fostering of mature faith.[5] The GCD based its claim on the conciliar document, *Christus Dominus* (Decree on the Pastoral Office of Bishops).[6] The writings by both the Vatican and the United States bishops, with their focus on mature faith, offer us various descriptors of maturity that can be summarized in this way: Mature faith is, first of all, a living, or vibrant faith; second, it is a conscious or intentional faith; third, mature faith is active/fruitful, exercising an effect in the life of the believer and in the world that the believer influences. How does the practice of professional leadership ministry promote mature faith? I pose this question as a pastoral theologian, eager to adopt the lens of religious education to analyze the situation of pastoral ministry today.

Pastoral Theology and Religious Education as Lenses

Pastoral theologians seek to observe, as clearly as possible, the actions (ministries) that build up the Body of Christ; to interpret these actions; and to consider the intentions, possible meanings, and consequence of the actions. The choice of a lens matters; the lens helps the pastoral theologian to see and interpret situations using both the tradition of theology and the related fields of pastoral care (such as religious education or pastoral counseling, for example), and to do so with clarity and depth.[7]

The lens used in this essay derives from the branch of pastoral theology known as religious education. I want to probe *how* the professional leaders contribute, perhaps unwittingly but effectively, to the goal of fostering mature faith among adults in the Catholic parish. Entering into the world of pastoral theology, I invite the reader to "try on" and to see through some lenses often employed by religious educators to consider this question from educational theory, biblical theology, and sociology of religion.

"Living Faith" Promoted By the Implicit Curriculum of Professional Lay Ministry

Professional leadership ministry contributes to the fostering of mature adult faith, as living faith, because it offers parishioners an implicit curriculum on a contemporary theology of ministry that is more effective than the official words, but also (usually) aligned with the words. The presence of lay professional ministers implicitly invites all lay people to consider the vibrancy of their own faith as that faith is lived, both within and beyond the walls of the parish church community.

The term *implicit curriculum* comes from the writings of educational theorist Eliot Eisner. Eisner proffered that the *explicit* curriculum never stands alone in any educational environment. For Eisner, the explicit curriculum is joined by two other curricula that operate beneath every learning environment; even as the explicit curriculum is articulated, the *implicit* curriculum, and the *null* curriculum are in the background or under the surface. (It should be noted that Eisner understood the learning environment in a very broad sense, not just the classroom.) The *implicit* curriculum pertains to the lessons communicated without explicit words, but no less effectively by the implicit actions, procedures, environments and structures that educators create in both the classroom and the larger learning environment. The implicit curriculum refers to those messages that the learners receive through body language, procedures, tone of voice, style of learning environment, and even by the seating arrangement. These messages murmur beneath the explicit curriculum stated in words. Eisner also drew educators' attention to the *null* curriculum, the material that is left out, unaccounted for, by virtue of either the conscious or the unconscious decisions made by the teacher in the creation and implementation of the "lesson" or educational experience.[8] Eisner's observation is valuable here if one accepts a supple definition for curriculum.

By *curriculum* I mean what religious educationist Maria Harris called the "course" (the meaning of the term *curriculum*, derived from the Latin), in the largest and most integrative sense possible.[9] Harris imagined that the curriculum of the church's life is that "course that we run" rather naturally through socialization into the general culture of Christian life, mostly by living it through family and community. In this sense curriculum is not simply the formal sessions, classes, and workshops that churches offer, but the gestalt, the full lesson that interaction in the culture of the church communicates. The curriculum includes prayer and worship, charity and justice, Word and sacrament, doctrine and right living. One of the teachers of Jewish Talmud remarked that the purpose of learning is not learning; the purpose of learning is living. I believe that Harris would agree with this assertion, and she would add that the curriculum of the church, then, is learned for the goal of living faith, and that it is learned *by* living faith. Harris writes:

> Widespread agreement exists today that although the meaning of curriculum from which the church works includes schooling and teaching—or *didache*—and involves printed, published resources, curriculum is a far broader reality. Necessarily, it includes the other forms through which the church educates, such as worship, proclamation, community and service. Today we are moving toward a refusal to limit curriculum as it has been limited in the past. Curriculum is more than materials and technique; it is intended for adults as well as children; and it is offered through more forms of education than what is called schooling. We are moving toward a creative vision that sees all the facets of the church's life as the church curriculum, with curricular materials named simply 'resources'.[10]

It seems clear that Eisner's theory sounds a caution to educators to pay attention. The implicit curriculum needs to align itself with the explicit curriculum; whenever they are not aligned, then the messages that the learner receives may not be the ones that the teacher intended. Education occurs with or without a clear plan, but the lesson planning that does not account for both the implicit and explicit curricula belongs to the naïve teacher.

Take the case of a Catholic school I visited some years ago, located in the center of an African American neighborhood in a large Unites States city. I visited the school as part of an assessment process of the religious education "curriculum" in the school. The school offered an oasis of hope to many youth in the neighborhood, as these teens had few choices for quality schools. The student body was 90 percent African American, while 90 percent of the teachers and administrators were Caucasian of western European descent. In that school, the explicit curriculum took into account the importance of celebrating African American heritage; black history month; and the leaders, politicians, and heroes from the local city, and other African American leaders who function as role models.

In many ways, it was a fine school that would bring pride to any observer. One day while observing a class, I looked up and noticed the crucifix. It was both familiar and jarring to see that wooden cross holding the corpus of a white Jesus with auburn hair. This same model hung in every classroom. Attentive to Eisner's theory, I asked myself, Why would a faculty and an administration dedicated to the religious education of African American teens display a white Jesus on the cross? Perhaps it was unconscious, and certainly left unnoticed by those who first installed the religious art. It was further left unnoticed each day by those who spent so much time in these rooms that they lost the gift to see afresh. Nevertheless, the implicit curriculum of the crucifix, a centerpiece of Catholic spirituality and the major piece of art in the school, was as clear as it was strong in informing the learning environment. Equally clear to me, a visitor who was seeing the school for the first time was the truth that the crucifix was at variance with the explicit curriculum of the school's life. The school's mission, activities, and course of studies proclaimed the beauty of African American culture, but the religious art offered an implicit curriculum, a mixed message, indeed a counter-message, about worshipping a white Jesus.

What is true of schools is also true for the "curriculum" broadly conceived in churches and congregations; the scenes in which professional ministry leaders find themselves illustrate as much or more about the "call of baptism" to do ministry, or the message of Co-Workers in the Vineyard of the Lord, than the words on the pages of church documents. The implicit message of ministry supports the theology of ministry found in Co-Workers and the wisdom about mature faith found in the NDC that seems now standard in most parishes today: Ministry is the logical outcome of baptism; everyone is called by the sacraments of initiation to conscious and active participation in the life of the church through *both* the church's internal ministries and its external mission.

The last four decades of Catholic parish life have witnessed a sea of change in thought about the responsibilities and even the rights that laypeople have to shape the internal life of their church communities. A theology of laypersons' role in the world—as leaven in the loaf of society, as players and prophets in the marketplace, and as shapers of the social and political order toward God's reign—this "witness in the world theology" cannot be forgotten or overlooked. This theology was the prevailing way that most lay Catholics imagined living their faith; that is, until recent years. But the role of laypeople in the internal works of the church, a role that was downplayed if not forgotten in the years before Vatican II, is both ancient and new, finding roots in the Pauline letters, and finding new wings in the thinking of the faith community today.

In the rise of professional lay ministries, and through the witness of individual professional lay ministers, one discerns an implicit message that coheres to the explicit one: Every Christian is called by baptism to ministry, not only in the world, but also in the church. Not all people are called to professional lay ministry; indeed few are. However, in professional lay ministers, other laypeople find role models who look and live like the majority of parishioners, and who struggle with the usual features of family and home life. Offering parishioners both a comfort and a challenge by their presence and example, lay professional ministers teach an implicit curriculum that enriches the imaginations of the parishioners about their own call, both in the world and inside the church, and empower them to express active faith lives in both arenas. The explicit message about the call to ministry carries weight when the implicit examples abound.

Whenever the explicit vision of Co-Workers and the theology that supports this vision exist in the implicit ways of parish life, then the people are learning the curriculum that the document intends. However, the opposite also is true. Whenever the implicit curriculum is violated, the message of the violation comes through. We are all aware of stories of arbitrary and even unjust treatment of lay ministers by pastors. There are many stories of talented lay people who were called, gifted, and pink slipped without due process or just cause, without consulting the people who are served and without much explanation to the minister. Such accounts tell the story of an implicit curriculum that chips away at the educational value claimed in the explicit message of Co-Workers.

Living Parables Awakening Conscious Faith

The stories do not stop with the pastors' resistance to lay leadership. There also are stories told tearfully by ministers of the resistance they encounter from some parishioners, who would rather not have lay people on the staff, wishing for the days when "their priests" were widely available to them. In such cases, lay leaders are regarded with either resentment or disrespect as second-tier substitutes rather than co-workers with both clergy and parishioners. What happens when people resent or resist the living witnesses who serve them as professional lay ministers? What happens in settings where parishioners encounter more challenge than comfort in seeing and interacting with a lay professional leader? What happens in those moments when the very thought of lay leadership gets a cold shoulder from the laity or their co-worker priests? If the task of pastoral theology is to interpret situations, how does one make sense of the resistance to lay ministers in some parishes? Two scenes from the document on ministry, As I Have Done for You: A Pastoral Letter on Ministry, from Cardinal Roger Mahoney and priests of the archdiocese of Los Angeles, may furnish an illustration of the kind of non-acceptance I seek to describe. While the scenarios are composites of experiences in Los Angeles, they ring true for many pastoral ministers across the nation.

> Scenario 1. A young couple is preparing for marriage. They expect to visit with a priest periodically in the course of the preparation. In the initial contact, the priest instructs the couple to work henceforward with the parish marriage preparation team, comprised of married couples and led by the lay pastoral associate. They express their disappointment at not having one-on-one contact with the priest and decide to go to another parish for 'personal attention.' If you were the lay pastoral associate, what would you say to the young couple?[11]
>
> Scenario 2. The pastor and priest associate of a large parish are both on the verge of burnout because of the weight of pastoral activity and, even more, because of the day-to-day maintenance of the parish. To meet the crisis head on, the pastor hires a parish business manager and asks the bishop for the appointment of a lay pastoral associate. The latter takes up several tasks often associated with the priesthood, among them: leading the prayers at the vigil service before a funeral Mass, conducting the prayers for the commendation of the dead at graveside, and visiting the seriously ill in home and hospital. But the parishioners want personal contact with a priest in such circumstances. Discuss various strategies for facing the ministerial challenges in this scenario.[12]

In these scenes, it is difficult to interpret the thinking or feeling beneath the actions, but one thing is clear and common to both scenes: The implicit curriculum functions to awaken and discomfort those learners who hear pretty words in church about the universal call to ministry, but they do not consciously receive them. This may be a sign of hope rather than discouragement, because the second marker of mature faith described in the NDC is *conscious* faith.

Conscious faith may be promoted in these scenes, provided that professional lay ministers can be not only living *witnesses*, but living *parables*, stirring people to conscious faith. Professional leadership ministry contributes to fostering conscious faith by virtue of its functioning like a parable, inciting confusion and reflection in the minds of the faith community's members. Jesus was fond of such ways of promoting learning. Here, biblical theology can help us to see how he did this, and to interpret the situations of resistance. Touching off the modern biblical study of parable more than forty year ago, Joachim Jeremias' classic description of a parable continues to be worthy of consideration. Jeremias described a parable as a simile or metaphor drawn from common experience that strikes us as strange and leaves us with the task of confronting its meaning in encountering God' reign.[13] Note that this description of a parable involves the collision of the familiar and comfortable on the one hand, with the strange and the challenging on the other. The simile or metaphor begins innocently enough, but quickly becomes strange or shocking to the hearer. Central to the understanding of a parable is the juxtaposition of the familiar with the strange. The gospels contain parables that both console the hearer in one perspective on the image, and cajole the hearer with another. When Jesus used parables, he shocked people awake and incited their attention by this juxtaposition: Samaritans who are *good*, a successful merchant searching for one fine pearl worthy of liquidating the entire stock, the smallest of seeds that becomes the largest of plants, a poor widow who spends lavishly on a party to celebrate the retrieval of one lost coin. One part is very familiar—a Samaritan, a merchant, small seeds, a poor widow—while another is quite strange and different, adding an upsetting twist.

Analogously, lay professional leaders function as visual parables, as their "stories" are not proclaimed but acted out in the arena of the parish, observed more than heard, but effective like Jesus' parables. Their observers are challenged by what they see, for they view active adult ministers who have found a way to give professional service and to do so, often from the context of their commitments to single or married life (though some lay leaders include vowed religious, that is, non-ordained religious sisters and brothers). All these professional leaders, no matter their state of life, assume roles that have been customarily associated with priests such as visiting patients in the hospital, leading prayer at the mortuary or graveside, presiding at liturgy of the hours in the parish church, leading communion services in the absence of a priest, or assuming leadership responsibilities for convening lay groups such as committees, parish councils or groups of volunteers. These leaders serve the church in new and exciting, albeit strange, ways. Professional lay ministers draw the familiar and unfamiliar together in an unlikely pairing that sparks questions and reflection.

The known and the unknown work in concert (and perhaps in some competition), to offer to the parish community an experience of both confusion and insight, sometimes uncomfortable, causing individual parishioners to embrace or reject what they regard as both familiar and strange, both known and jarring expressions of ministry. In those who can resolve the dissonance, there appear new ways to think about God's activity in the present moment and in the future of ministry that only God knows.

The familiar feature of the professional lay ministers' lives also offers new and strange questions previously left unconsidered in any sustained and public way. The familiar feature of the ministry is that it is, at the end of the day, much more than a job, but it also is real employment, with all the features of a job. Some of the questions that may arise are suggested in the concluding pages of Co-Workers, and these are questions of a very practical nature.[14] However, the questions remain largely unanswered either in official print or in coherent practices in parishes and dioceses:

- What emotional and financial support will lay leaders need to do their jobs and live their lives, not in a celibate context, not residing in a rectory?
- What resources from our tradition can inform us about just practices for all the church's ministers (ordained or not, celibate or married or single or religiously vowed) regarding work hours, job security, supervisors' demands, and the peoples' expectations of their ministers?
- How will the effectiveness of their ministry be assessed and rewarded? How will excellence in ministry translate into job security? How will lay leaders gain positions: By job interview, market competition, assignment by a central diocesan office or structure, or some other way? Will their certification be portable

to other parishes and dioceses (if they needed to relocate because of a spouse's job transfer, for example)?[15]

Beneath these procedural questions about employment lurk the questions that trump the others, questions that are more concerned with both the realm of the affect and the domain of ecclesiology, with emotional overtones:

- Will the people they seek to serve accept these lay professional ministers as credible?
- Will clergy respect them as peers?
- Is lay leadership ministry—as a movement—to be regarded as an action of the Holy Spirit, or is it merely a temporary measure to meet the church's many needs?
- Given their current experiences of job insecurity, stressful working conditions, and disrespect, are lay leaders actually the church's co-workers or the church's temps or temporary workers?

The bishops who wrote Co-Workers knew well that these questions comprise the next frontier for their reflection; in fact, they conclude Co-Workers with some of these questions. However, the official document barely acknowledges the growing pains that parables force upon all disciples, or the questions that parables put before us. The following scenarios, while not parables in the pure sense, come to us from the document *As I Have Done for You* cited earlier. They may be helpful discussion starters in any parish setting, and they will spark the kind of reflection that parables cause:

> Scenario 1: A laywoman feels called to lay ecclesial ministry but cannot afford to live on a "church salary." How to proceed?[16]
>
> Scenario 2: A 56-year-old Sister has been the Director of Religious Education in her parish for 13 years. Over the last year, tensions between herself and the pastor have been mounting. These tensions are brought to a head when a first-year seminarian, 30 years old, is assigned to help out in the parish as part of his seminary formation. He is introduced to the parish community during the Sunday Masses. The pastor is "all aglow with excitement and enthusiasm," referring to the seminarian as "the hope for the future of the Church." The DRE feels resentful because the pastor has made a "big scene," falling all over the seminarian. "The pastor acts like the only ones doing ministry are himself and this 'wet behind the ears' seminarian." She claims, "I cover for him day in and day out. So do all the other lay ministers on the staff. Each of us does

more than he does." The Sister, an appropriately trained minister, feels like hired help. She does not feel appreciated. Do you have any advice for her? For the pastor?[17]

Examples of Active Faith Inside the Church: Challenging Religious Consumerism

What was true in Jesus' time is true in ours: People who hear a parable and accept the challenge imbedded in it must not only decide; they must ACT. Active or fruitful faith is mature faith; it is faith that accounts for someone other than oneself, and benefits either another person or a group. Adulthood, according to the thinking of famous development psychologist Erik Erikson, is marked by generativity. "How shall we live on, and beyond ourselves? How will others benefit from our contribution?" Catholic laypeople have long answered these questions through theologies of family life and the laity. These theologies stress the idea of being faithful apostles in society, in the workplace, and through political action and ethical citizenship.

Nevertheless, this story of Catholic lay life has a shadow, as noted above. For many years Catholic laypeople understood their role in the world as active, and their role in the parish as either passive, or at best, auxiliary, as helpers to the ordained in indirect financial support of the parish. An unfortunate by-product of the former emphasis on laypeople's apostolate in the world was the lack of real emphasis on the ministry of the baptized, and on the limited number of practical ways for lay involvement in direct ministries within parish walls. The roles proceeded from an ecclesiology that did not emphasize ministry; indeed, the word "ministry" was not a word often used by Catholics prior to the Vatican II era. Until recent years, it certainly was not a word used to describe laypersons' activity.

I have already argued that lay leaders offer an implicit curriculum to reinforce a theology of ministry that proceeds from baptism. Pastoral associates, parish life directors, and other professional ministers provide all laypeople with examples of active faith carried out *inside the parish context*. While not all laypeople are called to, or should, become professional ministers, all laypeople can and should imagine the parish as a forum for service, and not only as the place where their needs are met. Parishes are places where people can find comfort, welcome, and educational and social services, to be sure. But parishes are not designed to endorse the popular cultural notion that religion is created for self-help and solace. Sociologists of religion observe that religion occupies a place in United States popular culture such that religion can become a commodity, and people can approach it like consumers.[18] In this mindset, parishes can come to be regarded as centers of experience, to be evaluated for their ability to help the consumer. Parishes that become islands of comfort lose their sense of the core Christian message of service. To the degree that lay leaders render a visual example of how to serve *within* the parish, they furnish role models for other laypeople. They teach the message that ministry, like charity, begins at home. For Catholics who call their parish their spiritual home, lay leaders offer an example of this message that is as stark as it is unavoidable. However, there is a second advantage in their presence. Lay leaders help parishioners to recognize a theology of parish that does not cave into the cultural pressure to make religion a narcissistic pursuit.

There is a pervasive tendency toward consumer religion in American culture.[19] Consumerist tendencies only reinforce the negative messages of a preconciliar theology of laity, that it is acceptable to be passive at the parish but active in society. Leaders challenge laypeople to regard parishes NOT as spiritual way stations that support people to live their faith only in the world. Rather, parishes gather the people and utilize the gifts, so that those in need are served, but also so that all parishioners use their gifts for others. For most Catholics, their service in the parish is volunteer service, demanding a modest commitment and amount of time, but it is service nonetheless. Such service is generative, giving new life to the community as a whole, even as various works benefit individuals. Lay service of every kind helps to promote the parish as a community for ministry and not as a place to shop in pursuit of meeting one's needs.

Conclusion

I have entitled this essay "Ministry in Service to an Adult Church." By that title, I do not mean to exclude the youthful generations of believers that comprise the parish community, but I *do* intend to draw attention to the features of mature faith that ought to characterize that community and its members: living, conscious, and fruitful faith.

In the first instance, I propose that living (or vibrant) faith is the kind of faith that calls spectators out of pews to become active agents of the gospel. Borrowing the lens of educational theory, we can see that these ministers furnish an implicit curriculum of the theology that every Christian is called by baptism to ministry, not only in the world, but also in the church. This understanding of ministry has been retrieved and reinvigorated in Catholic theology and practice in recent decades. Whenever that curriculum in aligned with the explicit one found in Co-Workers, the church fosters mature faith that is living or vibrant. In the second sense, borrowing the lens of biblical theology, we can observe that the presence of lay professional parish leaders fosters conscious faith because these lay leaders function as "living parables" in their work. Theologians and biblical scholars describe a *parable* as a simile or metaphor, drawn from common experience, which strikes the hearer as both familiar and strange, and incites in the hearer a deeper reflection. This deeper reflection is caused in part by the clash between comfort with the familiar and discomfort with the strangeness found in the parable. I argue that lay professional leaders (volunteers are another matter) offer parable-like familiarity and strangeness because, like parables, lay leaders are marked by the juxtaposition of the familiar and surprising—"lay" ministers function today like "good" Samaritans might have in Jesus' time. They defy the usual categories for *holiness* and *leadership* (formerly requiring *celibacy* and *ordination*), bringing faith to consciousness and summoning the newly confused to deeper reflection. "Lay minister" is a phrase in today's Catholic Church that functions much like the phrase "good Samaritans" did for some of Jesus' hearers, because the term marks the collision of a familiar idea with a strange one. Finally, borrowing the lens of the religious sociologist, we can observe that the popular cultural tendency to see parishes as "spiritual spas" can be both exposed and challenged by the example of very active lay people who have devoted their professional lives to serve in the parish.

For parishioners who are among "those who have ears to hear," the presence and implicit message of lay professional parish leaders resound like a clarion call to *all* lay people to assume responsibility for the internal works of the life of the church, whatever form (volunteer or professional) that ministry may take. Lay leaders function like "vocations recruiters" for those who may formerly have presumed themselves unworthy or merely uncalled, to become *active and conscious in living* their faith, not only in the world, but in the parish that many Catholics call their spiritual home.

Reflection Questions

1. To what extent do the lay ecclesial ministers you know, who are serving in what Horan calls professional leadership ministries, help to encourage the development of a *living and vibrant faith*? How do

they help people to recognize that "every Christian is called by baptism to ministry, not only in the world, but also in the church" (157)?

2. Based on your experience, to what extent do professional leadership ministers serve as living parables that can help to awaken or deepen a sense of *conscious faith* among the average layperson?
3. How might observing laypeople serving in professional leadership ministries challenge us to reflect more fully on what it means *to live according to our faith* and to integrate our faith into every dimension of our lives?
4. In your experience, how has the church supported laywomen and laymen serving in professional leadership ministries? How might we as church show greater support for professional leadership ministers and encourage them to model a mature faith for the people of our faith communities?

Notes

1. See Center for Applied Research in the Apostolate (CARA), http://www.cara.georgetowm.edu; National Association for Lay Ministry (NALM), http://www.nalm.org; and Association of Graduate Programs in Ministry (AGPIM). http://www.agpim.org (accessed January 11, 2011).

2. USCCB, Co-Workers in the Vineyard of the Lord: A Resource for Guiding the Development of Lay Ecclesial Ministry (Washington, DC: USCCB, 2005).

3. Co-Workers, 10.

4. USCCB, National Directory for Catechesis (Washington, DC: USCCB, 2005), 54-57.

5. USCCB, General Catechetical Directory in The Catechetical Documents: A Parish Resource (Chicago, IL: Liturgy Training Publications, 1996), 1-77.

6. *Christus Dominus* (Decree on the Pastoral Office of Bishops in the Church), in *Vatican Council II: The Conciliar and Post Conciliar Documents,* ed. Austin Flannery (Northport, NY: Costello Publishing Company, 1987) 564-610.

7. Lewis S. Mudge, *Formation and Reflection* (Philadelphia, PA: Fortress Press, 1989), 1-16.

8. Elliot Eisner, *The Educational Imagination: On Design and Evaluation of School Programs* (New York: Macmillan Company, 1979), 74-92.

9. Maria Harris, *Fashion Me a People: Curriculum in the Church* (Louisville, KY: Westminster: John Knox Press, 1989), 17.

10. Ibid., 17-18.

11. Roger Mahoney, *As I Have Done for You: A Pastoral Letter on Ministry* (Chicago, IL: Liturgy Training Publications, 2000), 31-32.

12. Ibid., 31.

13. Joachim Jeremias, *Rediscovering the Parables* (New York: Charles Scriber's Sons, 1966).

14. Co-Workers, 63-65.

15. Co-Workers, 62-63.

16. Mahoney, 32.

17. Ibid., 29.

18. Vincent J. Miller, *Consuming Religion: Christian Faith and Practice in a Consumer Culture* (New York: Continuum, 2003).

19. Ibid., 37-102.

CHAPTER THIRTEEN

A Cause for Rejoicing
Hopes and Horizons for Lay Ecclesial Ministry

Harold D. Horell

> The same God who called Prisca and Aquila to work with Paul in the first century calls thousands of men and women to minister in our Church in this twenty-first century. This call is a cause for rejoicing.
>
> —*Co-Workers in the Vineyard of the Lord*[1]

Catholics living in the United States today may sometimes be tempted by despair. Our church has been shaken by the crisis of sexual abuse. We suffer from an ongoing crisis of accountability, especially financial accountability, in many of our dioceses, parishes, and organizations. The sins of sexism and racism still plague our faith community. While we are gaining in membership (which is due mainly to immigration, especially in our Hispanic population), there are many people, particularly many of our young people, who have left the Catholic Church in recent times, and more are following. There is also a growing distrust of the church and other large institutions among many of our youth and young adults.[2] Furthermore, while we can affirm the beauty and goodness present in the world, most of us are also aware of the injustices, persistent poverty, human suffering, destructive materialism, and violence that we can find in contemporary societies. Many of us are also deeply concerned about the contemporary environmental crisis.

Yet, we have cause for rejoicing. We have a reason for hope. Despite our woes, there are many signs that the Spirit is moving within the church, energizing the community and calling forth new life. Some of the more viable signs of the stirrings of the Spirit are found in the Rite of Christian Initiation of Adults (RCIA) and the permanent diaconate. Many people have been welcomed into the Catholic Church through the RCIA since it was promulgated in the United States in 1988; because the RCIA involves the whole community in the initiation of new members, it has helped to renew many of our parishes. The RCIA has also become a model for the development of many fruitful faith formation programs. Similarly, the restoration of the permanent diaconate has widened the scope of ordained ministry and brought new energy into many of our parishes.

Another sign of hope is the commitment of many United States Catholics to social ministry. The United States Catholics bishops' 1983 pastoral letter on war and peace, *The Challenge of Peace,* and their 1986 pastoral letter on the economy, *Economic Justice for All*, expressed a growing awareness of the importance of addressing pressing social issues from a faith perspective.[3] Today, it is the norm for the bishops, individually and collectively, to address the pressing social issues of our day and to encourage Catholics to be involved in civic life.[4] Additionally, there are many Catholics committed to the social ministries of the church, including pro-life ministries that address abortion, capital punishment, and other practices that diminish respect for the dignity of persons.

Signs of hope are also found within the church in those places where ecumenical and interreligious dialogue and social action flourish. Despite different perspectives within the church, there have been notable efforts to seek common ground among Catholics and to encourage ecumenical and interreligious efforts to address issues of common concern.

One of the greatest causes for rejoicing, one of the clearest signs of hope in the Catholic Church, has been the renewal of the laity and what both Bishop Howard Hubbard and Michael Horan call a "flowering of lay ministries."[5] Laypeople's involvement in the life of faith and ministry has increased dramatically in the last half century, and as the essays in this collection attest, this has been accompanied by deep reflection on the meaning and significance of lay ministry and the roles of the laity in the church and world. As Ciorra notes, when we observe the radical character of the recent developments in lay ministry we can imagine the church engaging in a "*collective gasp* as something new is struggling to emerge from the ecclesial womb."[6]

As we attend to the movements of the Spirit in the church and world today, we can ask, how should we respond to God's presence in our midst? Toward what horizon are we being pointed? What path are we called to walk? How is God directing us from the present toward a better future?

As we strive to respond to the signs of the times, we must, if our efforts are to bear fruit, take into account the serious issues we face in both the church and broader world. At the same time, we must move toward the horizon, the future, with a realistic hope that we can discern what steps God calls us to take to welcome and to work to bring about the fuller realization of God's reign.

In order for the church to move forward today we need sustained and systematic efforts to explore each of the signs of hope found within the church and world. We need to attend to the movements of the Spirit and then test and refine our sense of the meaning and significance of the Spirit's promptings. In this chapter, I will explore only one of these promptings, and only in a limited manner. Specifically, drawing insight from Co-Workers in the Vineyard of the Lord, the insights found in the essays in this collection, other recent literature on the laity and lay ecclesial ministry, and my own pastoral experience, I offer four suggestions for naming and responding to the promptings of the Spirit in the development of lay ecclesial ministries.

As you explore each of the suggestions I offer, I invite you to keep a broad understanding of the contemporary Catholic Church in mind. Specifically, I invite you to consider how each suggestion (1) can help the church respond in the light of faith to the difficult issues it faces today, and (2) must be situated within the broader framework of a commitment to discern how God is calling the church as a whole to ongoing renewal.

First: Creating A Common Foundation for All Ministry

Throughout the development of lay ecclesial ministry, there has been a focus on baptism, confirmation, and Eucharist as providing the foundation for participation in the mission and ministry of the church. As we move toward the future, I suggest that we need to develop further our sense of the sacraments of initiation as the foundation for Christian living, and for both ordained and lay ecclesial ministry.

In Called and Gifted, Called and Gifted for the Third Millennium, Lay Ecclesial Ministry: The State of the Questions, and Co-Workers, the United States Catholic bishops affirm Christians' call to participate in the mission and ministries of the church through the sacraments of initiation. These documents discuss how our lives are transformed through initiation into the church. They explore how we as Christians are incorporated into the Body of Christ and made new through the sacraments of initiation, and how in the process we are empowered, first, with the eyes of faith to see and respond to the world and, second, with charisms and calls to ministries in which we are to use these charisms.[7]

It is important to note that in the process of initiation into the church, *being* precedes *doing*. First, our lives are transformed (being). Subsequently, we are called to action (doing). We must first learn to recognize and welcome the in-breaking reign of God in our midst. Then we are able to discern how we are called to be co-creators with God and to explore how the Creator is guiding us to help bring about the fuller realization of God's reign in the world.

Even though the bishops insist in their discussions of lay ministry that personal transformation (in the depths of our personhood or *being*) through incorporation into the Body of Christ in initiation is the foundation for all ministry, many—although certainly not all—of us who are involved in lay ecclesial ministries have and continue to define our roles functionally. That is, we tend to focus primarily on *doing*. We are, first and foremost, religious educators, pastoral associates, campus ministers, youth ministers, or people whose ministries are marked by a commitment to some other specific ministerial role or activity.

This focus on function is certainly due in part to the fact that we have had to prove our worth. For instance, while I no longer remember the details of the many lay ministry conferences and workshops I attended in the 1980s and 1990s, the one memory that stands out vividly is of nods and murmurs of assent as a speaker at one of these conferences proclaimed, "As lay ministers we must be confident and competent in our abilities as we strive to establish lay ministry as a new way of doing ministry in the church." There are, of course, many other reasons why lay ecclesial ministers have focused on a functional, "doing-centered" understanding of ministry, including the fact that many of us were drawn to ministry because we had learned to excel in care-giving and roles of service. Additionally, within many diocesan formation and graduate ministry education programs, there is more of a focus on learning to use the gifts or charisms of the Spirit from the sacraments of initiation than on the personal transformation and new being in Christ that is brought about and sustained by the sacraments of initiation.

However, drawing insight from Edward Hahnenberg's chapter in this collection, I suggest that if we are to embody theologically sound understandings of ministry, we must focus on what it means *to be a minister* and only then consider what it means to *do ministry*.[8] We must begin with an understanding of transformation by Christ, and then explore our call to participate in Christ Jesus' ongoing mission to transform the world.

Moreover, as Lisa Cataldo argues in her chapter, our psychological health also depends upon establishing a solid sense of ministerial identity as a foundation for doing ministry. Citing the psychologist Donald Winnicott, Cataldo points out that "all authentic doing arises out of a secure sense of being. Authentic doing is defined as that action in relation to the world that feels resonant with what one experiences as the True Self."[9] We will be able to sustain our involvement in ministry and serve others well only if our ministry connects to our sense of personal identity and sustains us as persons.

Ordained ministers also need to root their ministries in a healthy sense of being and doing to solidly ground ordained ministry. However, as both Hahnenberg and Cataldo point out, this is not always the case with the ordained priesthood. Hahnenberg notes that the theology of priesthood taught in seminaries today is often "heavily christological (Christ-centered) and ontological ('being'-centered), emphasizing the priest's ability to act 'in the person of Christ' and represent Christ in the community."[10] While such a theology begins with a focus on being and grounds the doing of ministry in a sense of being a minister, the theology can be problematic. Specifically, insofar as it elevates the ordained priest above the other members of his community, it can undermine the essential relational dynamics of ministry. That is, it can undercut the ordained minister's ability to enter into ministerial relationships in which he is not just doing something for others but rather caring for them with the ultimate goal of helping them to discern how God is present in their lives and is calling them to participate in the mission and ministries of the church. Moreover, as Cataldo contends in her chapter, such a heavily christological theology of priesthood can make it difficult for an ordained priest to form life-giving and life-sustaining relationships with others in his community, which can consequently have a negative impact on his psychological health.[11]

My own experience and the insights of others who have researched the ordained priesthood suggest that present-day, ordained priestly ministry is even more problematic than Hahnenberg and Cataldo suggest.[12] In pastoral practice, many priests have come to focus heavily, if not exclusively, on doing—on being a servant and servant leader in a community of faith. Priests' days are often filled with one activity after another, including everything from celebrating masses and pastoral caregiving to overseeing parish administration and finances. In some faith communities, priests are expected to be fully available, day or night, for any pastoral needs. As Catholic parishes increase in size and the number of priests declines, the demands made on priests continue to increase. Moreover, when an ontological, being-centered theology of priesthood (in which the ordained priest is envisioned as an *alter Christus* or another Christ) is combined with demanding self and communal expectations, the pressures on ordained priests can be, and often are, overwhelming.

Given our awareness of the challenges in ministry, and our sense that it is important to have both a healthy sense of being a minister and a similarly healthy sense of doing ministry, where can we turn? In her chapter in this collection, Eschenauer argues that "in and through the sacraments of initiation . . . lay ecclesial ministers can discover a paschal spirituality" and "we can seek to nurture a paschal spirituality to sustain lay ecclesial ministry."[13] I suggest that Eschenauer's insight holds true for all ministry, not just lay ecclesial ministry. That is, I contend that as we attend to the movement of the Spirit in the flowering of lay ecclesial ministry, we can discern how striving to embrace more fully an understanding that all ministry is rooted in the sacraments of initiation, can support the ongoing development of all forms of ministry in three significant ways. I explore these three in the following subsections.

The Sacraments of Initiation as the Foundation for all Ministries

First, fully embracing the sacraments of initiation as the foundation for all ministries can allow us to nurture both a sense of new life in Christ (being) and a sense of the unique call of each person to ministry (doing). Through the sacraments of initiation, we are transformed in Christ. We are also given a name. We are baptized and confirmed, for instance, as Peter, Paul, Mary, or Elizabeth. Our Christian name is a sign of our uniqueness (being) and our unique gifts for (doing) ministry. We can empower all ecclesial ministers, lay and ordained, to establish a firm foundation for their ministries by encouraging them to ground their spiritual lives in a sense of being called by name, as persons with unique gifts, for specific ministries.

We can support all ecclesial ministers to nurture a healthy sense of ministerial identity and ministerial praxis by inviting them to focus first on themselves (on self-awareness, self-reflection, and self-care). We can subsequently invite them to reflect about how their sense of being called to specific (lay or ordained) ecclesial ministries flows from and enables them to more fully develop an understanding of who they are as unique persons. Furthermore, by emphasizing that our baptismal call to unique personhood is the origin of all calls to ministry, we can provide a common foundation for ministry, while also acknowledging the diversity of gifts among lay ecclesial ministers and the differences between those called to lay ecclesial ministries and those called to ordained ministry.

Christian Initiation and Christian Community

Second, a spirituality based on the sacraments of initiation can root our lives in a Christian community and communal relationships. We celebrate the fact that all Christians are called and gifted for ministry through the *communal* rites of baptism, confirmation, and Eucharist. To focus only on being a minister and doing ministry can lead to a ministerial individualism, that is, an over-concern with one's self as a minister and one's achievements in ministry. By encouraging all ministers, lay and ordained, to focus more fully on the way their calls to ministry are grounded in the sacraments of initiation, we can strengthen an awareness of the way all ministries are situated within a community of faith, how all ministries take place on behalf of a community of faith, and how all ministries are part of a communal effort to carry on the mission of Jesus within the world. Such a focus can lead us to develop a richer sense of the common foundation of lay and ordained ministries. Additionally, by stressing that it takes all members of a faith community to meet the ministerial needs within our faith communities and the broader world, we can help lay and ordained ministers to avoid overcommitting themselves as individuals.

Moreover, we can nurture spirituality for ministry by encouraging all ecclesial ministers, lay and ordained, to adopt the spiritual practice of reflecting on their call to ministry within community. This opportunity recurs as ministers renew their baptismal commitments throughout the liturgical year, such as during communal celebrations of baptisms at Sunday liturgies, and especially during the yearly celebration of the Triduum. We can also encourage all ecclesial ministers to reflect on the ways their spiritual lives are rooted within community every time they participate in the communal celebration of the Eucharist.

Christian Initiation and a Paschal Spirituality

Third, a focus on the sacraments of initiation can enable ecclesial ministers to nurture a paschal spirituality; that is, a spirituality that fosters a realistic hope for ongoing renewal within the church and broader world. We are incorporated into the Body of Christ through the sacraments of initiation, and through them, we can develop a relationship with Jesus Christ, and we can understand the meaning of the paschal mystery of Jesus' life, suffering, death, and resurrection. As we develop an understanding of the paschal mystery, we can come to grasp the significance of life, suffering, death and the possibility of resurrection as part of the human condition. At its core, a paschal spirituality can enable us to recognize how God calls us to fullness of life for both the here and hereafter, and to see how God is continually working to open up possibilities for new life where there is suffering and death.

If ecclesial ministers are to address the challenges in the church and world today, I suggest that a paschal spirituality rooted in the sacraments of initiation is essential. For example, while only a small percentage of ecclesial ministers have been involved in sexual abuse and the covering up of sexual abuse, many ecclesial ministers have had to lead efforts to address the effects of the recent crisis of sexual abuse. Being rooted in a paschal spirituality can help ecclesial ministers acknowledge and discuss how an evil that existed within the church has greatly harmed many people, families, faith communities, and society. At the same time, this spirituality can enable them to recognize how the Spirit remains at work in the church and world, guiding us to possibilities for new life and renewal. Similarly, a paschal spirituality is centered in an awareness of the realities of suffering and death and the belief that God continually opens up possibilities for new life that overcome suffering and death. Such a spirituality can enable those involved in social ministry to perceive clearly injustices, human misery, and the threats to society today and, yet, to avoid being overwhelmed by these harsh realities and to remain open to discerning how God calls us to respond to the socio-moral issues of our day.

In summary, recent developments in lay ecclesial ministry have implications for all ministries. Insofar as the development of lay ecclesial ministry is leading us to deepen and enrich our understanding of the call of all baptized believers to ministry, it has the potential to spark hope and help to sustain the church. As we develop further a theology of the laity and lay ecclesial ministry today, I suggest that our efforts will bear the most fruit if we are first open to recognizing how a spirituality rooted in the sacraments of initiation can guide us in exploring the common foundation of *all* ecclesial ministry. Then, it is possible to explore how *lay* ecclesial ministry is built upon this foundation.[14]

Second: Defining Ministry Roles

There have been numerous discussions about the need to define ministerial roles more clearly. I suggest that the time has come to make it a priority, to find a more adequate way to discuss ministerial roles and functions within the church.

The formulation and use of the phrase *lay ecclesial ministry* has been a positive development. It has helped us to recognize that there is a broad-based movement within the church underlying the reality of greater lay involvement in specific ministries (such as parish catechesis, campus ministry, and youth and young adult ministries), and that this movement has begun to renew and even transform our understanding and practice of ministry. Yet, as many of the contributors in this collection have pointed out, the language of lay ecclesial ministry is problematic. The language is based on a distinction between laity and clergy that can prompt us to think of the laity (the *laos*) as being deficient in holiness or faith when compared to a chosen ordained few who are called to embrace fully the teachings of Jesus and a Christian way of life. Additionally, insofar as lay ecclesial ministers are laity, and the term *laity* has the connotation of lack or deficiency, doubts or suspicions about the legitimacy of lay ecclesial ministry are likely to breed. Lay ecclesial ministry will be seen as authentic only insofar as it is sharing or participating in the ministry of the ordained.[15]

The development of the term, lay ecclesial ministry, has also been problematic insofar as it has led us at times to define ministry too broadly. That is, there has been a temptation to define everything done by Christians as a ministry. Overall, the language of lay ecclesial ministry has been far too imprecise. On the one hand, we need a clearer sense of lay ecclesial ministry in relation to ordained ministry. On the other hand, we need a better understanding of the nature and scope of lay ecclesial ministry as one way of responding to the call of God.[16] In the following subsections, I discuss these issues more fully and present a way of defining ministry and making sense of various forms of ministry and ministerial roles.

Christian Social Responsibility, Ministry, Ministry in the World, and Ecclesial Ministry

In striving to define lay ecclesial ministry more clearly, it can be helpful to begin by distinguishing between Christian social responsibility and Christian ministry. It is the responsibility of all of us, as Christians, to respond to God's presence in our lives and in the world. In all we do, we are called to show respect for ourselves and others as a way of valuing all people as having been made in God's image. As beings made in the image of a Trinitarian, relational God, we are also social beings; as social beings, whose lives depend on social structures and supports, we are called to be concerned about the common good of society. Additionally, we are called to care for the natural world as God's creation. Ultimately, it is our responsibility as Christians to care for ourselves, others, society, and creation in order to welcome and work to bring about the fuller realization of God's reign in our midst.

Christian ministry builds upon yet goes beyond a sense of Christian social responsibility. To begin, ministry involves a more *intentional* response to God than Christian responsibility. While we as Christians are called to bring our faith into all aspects of our lives, we are also unique persons with specific talents and gifts. Our intentional effort to identify these gifts and to discern how God is calling us to use them is what guides us in our ministries. All Christians are called to be morally and socially responsible persons; we are also called as unique persons to develop and use our particular gifts in specific ministries.

Additionally, ministry is always on *behalf of and affirmed by the Christian community*. When we strive to act in socially responsible ways informed by our Christian faith, we may at times draw explicitly from our faith, while at other times our faith may remain in the background. In caring for a neighbor or participating in the civic life of our community, our focus is on our neighbor and the common good of our community rather than on showing how our faith motivates and guides our actions (although if asked we should be able to give an account of the relationship between our faith and our everyday lives). In contrast, a person involved in Christian ministry is always a *representative of a Christian faith community*. All Christian ministries are expressions of a faith community's intentional and public commitment to preach the gospel.

Once we have a clear sense of the difference between Christian social responsibility and Christian ministry, it is important to distinguish between the mission and ministry of the church within the world and ecclesial ministry. The Christian community is a community of mission. The church exists to carry on, through word and deed, Jesus' mission of preaching the reign of God within the world. Moreover, there are certain activities that are ministries within the world. Specifically, within the social spheres of human work and family life, Christians sometimes carve out spaces for ministry.[17] A paradigmatic example of ministry in daily life is parenting. Marriage is a primary social institution, and family life and the raising of children are essential activities for every society. Marriage is also a primary Christian vocational life choice. A Christian family is a domestic church, and parenting is a sacred calling. When couples embrace parenting as both an important social responsibility and as an intentional effort that is affirmed by the church to educate and form children in faith, parenting becomes a ministry within the world.

Christian parents are involved in ministry in their everyday lives as they educate their children for both citizenship and discipleship.[18]

Ecclesial ministries aim to enable people to *integrate their faith more fully into everyday life* or, in the case of social ministries, provide people with opportunities for *social outreach as representatives of a Christian community*. For instance, the ministry of ordained liturgical leadership involves leading a congregation in communal prayer and worship, and can lead us to center our lives more fully in God so that we are better able to bring a sense of God's guiding presence into our everyday lives. Religious educators nurture insights, practices, and abilities for reflection that can enable us to develop a fuller understanding of Christian faith, and be better able to integrate our faith into our lives. Christian social ministries are similar to secular social activism insofar as both involve outreach to those in need and efforts to address pressing social issues. Yet, social ministry differs from secular social activism because the former intentionally and explicitly includes a focus on revealing the public significance of our Christian beliefs. That is, social ministries help people to recognize the ways Christian beliefs can shape how we perceive everyday life issues and work for social change. In summary, all ecclesial ministries are, in the end, focused on enabling and supporting Christian social responsibility and Christian ministry in the world.

In current discussions, there is a tendency to define lay ecclesial ministry functionally, that is, to focus on how lay ecclesial ministers are serving as liturgical ministers, catechists, pastoral care givers, and in other ministerial roles. When this emphasis on function is pushed to an extreme, all activities taken on by Christians that are even remotely connected to their faith, could conceivably be defined as ministry. Therefore, for example, we might speak of people who shovel the sidewalks of their elderly neighbors or the walks around the church building after a winter storm as being engaged in the ministry of snow removal. However, I suggest that we think of shoveling snow and other acts of concern for our neighbor, our parish, and the common good of society that are motivated by Christian faith as acts rooted in Christian social responsibility. Christian social action becomes a ministry in the world only when it involves an intentional commitment to embrace specific vocational life commitments (such as marriage and parenting) in response to the call of God and with the affirmation of a community of Christian faith. Moreover, we can define the nature and scope of lay ecclesial ministry more clearly if we limit it to acts of service within or by a specific Christian faith community that prepare people to live their faith in their everyday lives. Lay ecclesial ministries are distinguishable from both Christian social responsibility and Christian ministry in the world because they involve intentional efforts to use our specific talents and gifts in specific ministries as representatives of a faith community as a way of preparing people to carry on the mission of the church in the world.

Various Forms of Ecclesial Ministry

We can further define the nature and scope of lay ecclesial ministries by distinguishing between the two primary types of lay ecclesial ministry (professional and volunteer) and by examining the relationship between lay ecclesial ministry and ordained ministry. With regard to the first distinction, Michael Horan, in chapter twelve, argues that the designation *professional leadership ministry* should replace lay ecclesial ministry when discussing laymen and laywomen who take on the generalist roles of pastoral associate or parish life coordinator/director. He argues that the adjectives *professional* and *leadership* are, essentially, more descriptive of the ministry of such generalists and can be more easily understood by the average parishioner.[19] I suggest that *professional ecclesial leadership ministry* can replace lay ecclesial ministry in discussing the work of all laypeople who serve in paid ministry positions; who have a graduate degree or equivalent in a pastoral theological area; who are involved in ongoing education and formation for ministry; and who have been publically affirmed, installed, or certified for ministry in a local church. Hence, I suggest that we can use the designation professional ecclesial leadership ministers for educated, prepared, compensated, and publically recognized ministry professionals in religious education, pastoral care and counseling, and other areas, as well as for ministry generalists serving as pastoral associates or parish life coordinators.

Second, we can distinguish *professional ecclesial leadership ministries* from *volunteer ministries* and *volunteer leadership ministries*. The core ministry workforce of many parishes consists of volunteers serving as catechists, youth ministers, family life ministers, and in other ministry roles. Sometimes such volunteers help to provide leadership for the ministries in which they are involved, and because of their added responsibilities, they merit being called volunteer leadership ministers. Volunteer ministers require training and formation for ministry but in most cases neither desire nor need the graduate education that is essential for professional ecclesial leadership ministry. Additionally, there is a movement to commission volunteers at Sunday liturgies. If this movement becomes more firmly rooted in the church, we could further develop lay ecclesial ministry by referring to volunteer ministers as commissioned ministers. This would reinforce the idea that all people involved in ministerial roles have responded to an intentional call to service within and on behalf of a faith community. However, we need a more fully developed theology of ministry, and we need to educate people about ministry before the designation *commissioned ecclesial ministry* would be understood clearly by most of the people in our parishes.[20]

Next, it is essential today that we define more clearly the relationship between lay ecclesial ministry and ordained ministry. In the previous section, I argued that we should think of all ministries as having a common foundation in the sacraments of initiation. When we then turn to ordained ministry, the most important question to ask is, if all ministries share a common foundation, what is distinctive about ordained ministry—especially in relation to lay ecclesial ministry? If we claim that the sacraments of initiation are the foundation of all ministry, then we must reject any theology of the priesthood that emphasizes how the priest is changed ontologically and set apart and, thus, becomes an *alter Christus* (another Christ) who stands above the average Christian. That is, Christ changes our lives, and we do become new persons in Christ. However, we acknowledge that this change occurs through the sacraments of initiation, not the sacrament of ordination. All baptized believers stand together because we are all called and gifted for ministry.

Still, we can speak of ordained priestly ministers as acting in the person of Christ in a unique way, in the way they relate to others in a community of faith. Specifically, it is the distinctive ministry of the ordained to represent the leadership of Christ in a community of faith by hierarchically ordering the calling forth and use of the gifts of the Spirit. More fully, Richard R. Gaillardetz argues, "the qualifier 'hierarchical' can serve an important purpose if we purge it of those pyramidal conceptions it gained in the thirteenth century."[21] Gaillardetz contends that in using the term hierarchical we should "return to its literal sense of 'sacred order' (the Gr. adjective 'hier,' meaning 'sacred' with the Greek noun 'arche,' meaning 'origin,' 'principle' or 'rule'). This leads to the key affirmation that the Church of Jesus Christ, animated by the Spirit, is now and has always been subject to church ordering as it received its life from the God who, in Christian faith, is ordered in eternal self-giving as a triune communion of persons."[22] Gaillardetz adds that the ways the church has ordered its ministers has changed throughout history.[23] As lay ecclesial ministries continue to develop, a reordering of the church's ministries is needed if we are to utilize the gifts of the increasing numbers of laypeople called to ecclesial ministry. Moreover, it remains the distinctive ministry of the ordained to do this ordering. Those called to ordained ministry must strive to bring a sense of sacred or holy order to the discernment and use of the Spirit's gifts in the communities of faith they serve. Of course, however, there needs to be sustained discussion about the extent to which clericalism has diminished the capacity for ordained ministers to bring a sense of holy order to the life of our faith communities today.

Drawing insight from Kieran Scott's discussion of ministry in chapter five, I suggest that ordained ministry, in relation to lay ecclesial ministry, be envisioned as being inclusively, rather than exclusively, unique.[24] That is, ordained ministry is not unique because ordained leaders have exclusive access to powers and privileges denied other member of the church. Rather, ordained ministry is unique because ordained ministers have a distinctive role to play within inclusive communities of baptized believers. This role, as already noted, is to bring holy order to all that the community does. Moreover, greater lay involvement in the life of faith and the burgeoning of lay ecclesial ministries in no way diminishes the importance of ordained ministry. Rather, as more people strive to embrace a sense of Christian social responsibility and become involved in ministry in daily life and the ministries of the church, the ministerial role of ordering the life of a community of faith becomes more, not less, important.

Overall, we can and should rejoice at the development of lay ecclesial ministry in the church today. Yet, as we attend to the ongoing unfolding of lay ministry, it is increasingly important to distinguish it from Christian social responsibility and ministry in the world, to recognize both the difference between and the differing needs of professional ecclesial leadership ministries and volunteer ecclesial ministries, and to situate lay ecclesial ministry within the ordered communion of the church. If we as church are to identify, order, and use the gifts of Spirit we have been given to address pressing needs both within and beyond the church and to witness to the gospel in the world today, we need a more clearly defined sense of ministerial roles.[25]

Third: Attending to the Secular Character of Everyday Life

As we strive to attend to the promptings of the Spirit in lay ecclesial ministry, our understanding of the mission and ministry of the church can be enriched if we attend to the secular character of everyday, and especially lay, life.

In discussing the call of the lay faithful, Co-Workers follows a thread of conversation that can be traced back to Vatican II that focuses on the roles of laymen and laywomen in secular society. As I noted previously, the church as a whole is called to carry on Jesus' mission of preaching the gospel and working to transform the world. However, laymen and laywomen are called to take the lead in showing how Christian faith can shed light and often new light, on all aspects of the secular, everyday life. As stated in Co-Workers, "Lay men and women hear and answer the universal call to holiness primarily and uniquely in the secular realm."[26] The United States Catholic bishops express this idea in Called and Gifted when they write, "It is characteristic that lay men and women hear the call to holiness in the very web of their existence (*Lumen Gentium*, 31), in and through the events of the world, the pluralism of modern living, the complex decisions and conflicting values they must struggle with, the richness and fragility of sexual relationships, the delicate balance between activity and stillness, presence and privacy, love and loss."[27]

As we strive to understand the leadership role of laywomen and laymen in secular society, it is helpful to note that the term secular, as used in recent ecclesial documents and discussions of lay ministry, is best understood as *secular* in contrast with *religious* rather than as *secular* in contrast with *sacred*. More fully, within our communities there are distinct yet always interrelated spheres of life, including the religious, civic/political, social, cultural, and economic spheres. One way of discussing the distinctiveness of the religious sphere of life is to contrast the religious with the secular, with the secular sphere including the civic/political, social, and other non-religious realms of human activity.

The secular realm of everyday life contains both profane and sacred aspects. More fully, the secular is the arena of the profane, the base; it is the realm of vice and sinfulness; it is the realm of the world when the term *world* is used with a pejorative connotation. It is also an arena of the sacred, a space within which God reveals God's self. Additionally, as the bishops suggest in the Called and Gifted, dealing with the complexities and even difficulties of daily secular life can lead us to discover more deeply the paschal nature of all human existence. Joy, suffering, life, death, the goodness yet limitedness of our lives here and now, and the ever-present signs of God's ongoing creation of the world are all part of the complex web of human living.

In Co-Workers and their other statements on lay ecclesial ministry, the United States Catholic bishops comment on the role of the laity in bringing Christian faith into all aspects of secular life. The bishops also acknowledge that some laymen and laywomen are also called to ministry within the church. However, the bishops have not discussed how laypeople called to ecclesial ministry bring insights from the secular realm into their work in the church. That is, the bishops have not explored how the wisdom gleened from everyday life experiences and expertise in secular careers and life pursuits can and in many cases already does inform and enrich lay ecclesial ministry. Nor have the bishops explored how lay ecclesial ministers' everyday, secular lives are enriched by their experiences of ministry. I contend that it would benefit the church if there were further study and reflection in these areas.

I also suggest that as lay ecclesial ministry continues to develop it will become increasingly evident that lay ecclesial ministers have taken a leading role in enriching and renewing the ministries of the church by showing how insights from secular spheres of life can inform the ministries of the church.[28] For instance, in my work in the areas of youth and young adult ministries and in the religious education of children, I have found that in many parishes and congregations, it is parents and grandparents serving as lay ecclesial ministers who have taken the lead in developing youth and young adult ministries and in renewing or redesigning programs for the religious education of children. These lay ecclesial ministers have led the effort to draw attention to the exodus of young people from our faith communities. They also often strive to find ways to invite today's Gen X, Millennial and Cyber generation children, youth, and young adults to learn more about their Christian faith and to attend to their own calls to Christian social responsibility and ministry. By drawing insight from their experiences in the secular world, these laymen and laywomen have helped their faith communities to understand and discern how we can respond to the sense of anxiety and "anomie" often found today in youth culture. At the same time, they have helped the people of their faith communities recognize how God is being revealed to young people in our globalized, technically advanced, postmodern age.

Similarly, whenever I meet people who are doing research in religious education and ministry with children, youth and young adults, I ask them about the origin of their interests and insights. Often times their responses include stories about their children, grandchildren, or other young people for whom they have cared. These researchers draw insight from their own life experiences to help them understand the everyday lives of young people and then to bring what they have learned about the secular lives of young people into discussions about educational and ministerial outreach with them.

Furthermore, if they are to bear fruit, ecclesial ministries must in many instances be adapted to take into account the socio-cultural, ethnic, racial, and economic factors that shape everyday, secular life in specific communities and local churches. For instance, there are distinctive life perspectives and patterns of life within the various Hispanic Catholic communities in the United States. These distinctive outlooks should be taken into account in the further development of lay ministries and the formation of ecclesial ministers for service within Hispanic communities.[29]

On a more general level, a greater openness within the church since Vatican II to draw insight from the secular spheres of life has contributed to the development of many areas of ecclesial ministry. For instance, many ecclesial ministers are better able to provide pastoral care today because their education and formation programs have been enriched by scholarship that brings insights from the secular discipline of psychology (the sub-discipline of mental health counseling in particular) into dialogue with theological explorations of human personhood and society. Similarly, the academic discipline of religious education developed as scholars brought a new level of professional competence to the educational ministries of the church with insights, approaches, and models from such secular educational sub-disciplines as educational psychology, curriculum and instruction, and the philosophy of education.

As already discussed, we face many challenges both within and beyond the church today. We are better able to understand and respond to these challenges because the ministries of the church have been enriched by a greater understanding of the secular world and the incorporation of insights from secular scholarship within our ministries. Moreover, lay ecclesial ministers have helped to foster and maintain a culture of openness within the church to learning from the secular spheres of life. Today, people working in the church are drawing insight from the secular sciences of management and leadership as they strive to create greater accountability in the ministries of the church. As we look to the future, it would benefit the church if we had a greater awareness of how the work of lay ecclesial ministers relates to their everyday, secular lives and how the ministries of the church can be enriched by insights from secular culture.

Fourth: Being Open to the Ongoing Movements of the Spirit

As we strive to contribute to the ongoing development of lay ecclesial ministry, I suggest that the most important guideline we can adopt is to be open to the ongoing movements of the Spirit, including being receptive to experiencing the presence of God in surprising ways

Many of the chapters in this collection, especially the opening chapters by H. Richard McCord and Amy Hoey, point out that lay ecclesial ministry grew organically. It was not planned. Its course was not charted in advance.[30] Moreover, McCord notes that the bishops have adopted "a methodology of response in guiding the development of lay ecclesial ministry."[31] He adds that the bishops have not tried to control lay ecclesial ministry; they have observed, assessed, and responded.[32]

If lay ecclesial ministry is to thrive, we need to explore its theological and pastoral foundations more fully, and we need to clarify the nature and scope of lay ecclesial ministry. However, we also need to recognize that we cannot chart or control the future of lay ecclesial ministry. We can observe the work of the Spirit in and through lay ecclesial ministry. Then, we can assess developments in ministry in terms of whether or not they enable us to address the needs of the church and broader world more fully and, in the process, contribute to the renewal of ministry currently underway in the church. In the end, however, our primary response should be to rejoice in seeing how the Spirit is renewing the church through developments in lay ecclesial ministry and be patiently attentive to whatever new and perhaps surprising developments lay ahead.

Reflection Questions

1. How does the ongoing development of lay ecclesial ministry contribute to the church's ability to meet the challenges it faces today, both internally and in its mission to the world?
2. Are there ways you may be called to contribute to the ongoing development of lay ecclesial ministry?
3. How can we remain open to the promptings of the Spirit as we strive to contribute to the ongoing development of lay ecclesial ministry?

Notes

1. USCCB, Co-Workers in the Vineyard of the Lord: A Resource for Guiding the Development of Lay Ecclesial Ministry (Washington, DC: USCCB, 2005), 66.

2. See "Chapter 1: State of the Church in the Twenty-first Century" in Dean R. Hoge and Marti Jewell, *The Next Generation of Pastoral Leaders* (Chicago: Loyola Press, 2010), 1-10. For a discussion of the crisis of accountability in the church

today see Paul Lakeland, "Understanding the Crisis in the Church," in *Church Ethics and Its Organizational Context: Learning from the Sex Abuse Scandal in the Catholic Church*, eds. Jean M. Bartunek, Mary Ann Hinsdale, and James F. Keenan (Lanham, MD: Rowman and Littlefield, 2006), 3-15.

3. NCCB, *The Challenge of Peace: God's Promise and our Response, A Pastoral Letter on War and Peace* (Washington, DC: USCC, 1983); and NCCB, *Economic Justice for All: Pastoral Letter on Catholic Social Teaching and the U.S. Economy* (Washington, DC: USCC, 1986).

4. See USCCB, Justice, Peace and Human Development, http://www.usccb.org/sdwp/ (accessed January 15, 2010).

5. Howard Hubbard, "Lay Ministry and the Challenges Facing the Church," chapter 6 of this collection, 73-74; and Michael P. Horan, "Ministry in Service to an Adult Church: How Lay Ministry Fosters Mature Faith in the Catholic Parish," chapter 12 of this collection, 151.

6. Anthony Ciorra, "Engaging in a Collective Gasp," chapter 4 in this collection, 36.

7. In Called and Gifted, the bishops state that "baptism and confirmation empower all believers to share in some form of ministry." USCC, Called and Gifted: The American Catholic Laity (Washington, DC: USCC, 2005), 3. Similarly, in exploring the theology of lay ecclesial ministry in Lay Ecclesial Ministry: The State of the Questions, the bishops claim that "lay ecclesial ministry is rooted in and flows from the sacraments of initiation, which incorporate individuals into the body of Christ and call them to mission." USCCB, Lay Ecclesial Ministry: The State of the Questions, http://www.usccb.org/laity/laymin/layecclesial.shtml (accessed March 2, 2011). See also Called and Gifted for the Third Millennium (Washington, DC: USCC, 1995), 15, and Co-Workers, 8 and 21.

8. Edward P. Hahnenberg, "From Communion to Mission: The Theology of Co-Workers in the Vineyard of the Lord," chapter 3 in this collection, 22.

9. Lisa Cataldo, "Being a Minister and Doing Ministry: A Psychological Approach," chapter 7 in this collection, 91.

10. Edward P. Hahnenberg, "From Communion to Mission: The Theology of Co-Workers in the Vineyard of the Lord," 22.

11. Lisa Cataldo, "Being a Minister and Doing Ministry: A Psychological Approach," 97-98.

12. See, for example, Donald Cozzens, *The Changing Face of the Priesthood: A Reflection on the Priest's Crisis of Soul* (Collegeville, MN: The Liturgical Press, 2000).

13. Donna Eschenauer, "The Sacraments of Initiation: A Guiding Theme for the Future of Lay Ecclesial Ministry," chapter 9 in this collection, 122.

14. As Bishop Gregory Aymond notes in his Foreword to this collection, "We live in a time when we must ask, 'How do we bring lay and ordained ministries together?'" I suggest that the key to addressing the challenges Bishop Aymond outlines is to begin with an understanding of the sacraments of initiation as the common foundation for all ministries (Aymond, "Foreword," in this collection, viii).

15. See Kieran Scott, "Swimming Against the Tide: Language and Political Design in Lay Ecclesial Ministry," chapter 5 in this collection, 57-58.

16. The discussion of ministry that follows is based on my pastoral experience and informed by Richard P. McBrien, *Ministry: A Theological - Pastoral Handbook* (San Francisco: Harper and Row, 1987); Thomas F. O'Meara, *Theology of Ministry* (New York: Paulist Press, 1999); and Edward P. Hahnenberg, *Ministries: A Relational Approach* (New York: Crossroads, 2003).

17. See Linda L. Grenz and J. Fletcher Lowe, Jr., eds. *Ministry in Daily Life* (New York: Episcopal Church Center, 1996).

18. See NCCB, A Family Perspective in Church and Society, 10th anniversary ed. (Washington, DC: USCC, 1998) and NCCB, Follow the Way of Love: A Pastoral Message of the United States Catholic Bishops to Families On the Occasion of the United Nations 1994 International Year of the Family (Washington, DC: USCC, 1984).

19. Michael P. Horan, "Ministry in Service to an Adult Church: How Lay Ministry Fosters Mature Faith in the Catholic Parish," chapter 12 in this collection, 152-153.

20. Both Richard Gaillardetz and Edward Hanhenberg endorse the use of the designation "commissioned minister" for those currently known primarily as volunteers. They both also prefer the designation "installed ministers" for what I, following Horan, have called professional ecclesial leadership ministers. I suggested that the term "professional" is far more likely to communicate the ministry role of full-time, paid, educated, and publicly recognized lay ecclesial ministers than the term "installed." Moreover, use of the term "installed" is too likely to give the impression that lay ecclesial ministers are a minor or lesser order of ordained ministers insofar as it would communicate the idea that some ecclesial ministers are ordained while others are *only* installed. See Hahnenberg, *Ministries: A Relational Approach*, 176-210; and Gaillardetz, "The Ecclesiological Foundations of Ministry within an Ordered Communion," in *Ordering the Baptismal Priesthood: Theologies of Lay and Ordained Ministry*, ed. by Susan K. Wood (Collegeville, MN: Liturgical Press, 2003), 44-47.

21. Gaillardetz, "The Ecclesiological Foundations of Ministry within an Ordered Communion," 34.

22. Ibid., 34-35.

23. Ibid., 35.

24. Kieran Scott, "Swimming Against the Tide: Language and Political Design in Lay Ecclesial Ministry, 63.

25. In her chapter in this collection, Fox explores how ministry is being reordered within our faith communities today because of the development of lay ecclesial ministry, and how this reordering is enabling the church to respond more fully to the ministerial needs of our times. See Zeni Fox, "*Co-Workers in the Vineyard of the Lord* and an Evolving Ministry," chapter 10 in this collection, 125-138.

26. Co-Workers, 8.

27. USCC, Called and Gifted: The American Catholic Laity (Washington, DC: USCC, 1980), 2-3. Howard Hubbard draws attention to the importance of attending to the primary role of the laity in secular society in his chapter in this collection. See Howard Hubbard, "Lay Ministry and the Challenges Facing the Future," 79-83.

28. I owe a debt of gratitude to Janet Ruffing for this insight. Additionally, between 2005 and 2009, I had several conversations with Janet about laity being involved in the ministries of the church that helped me to clarify my understanding of the issues raised in this subsection. See Ruffing's discussion in this collection of the importance of attending to the secular lives of lay men and women in their formation and education for lay ecclesial ministry—Janet Ruffing, "Formation of Lay Ecclesial Ministers: Rooted in a Genuinely Lay and Ecclesial Spirituality," chapter 11 in this collection, 139-150.

29. Claudio Burgaleta discusses the importance of attending to the "real difference" among the various groups and traditions within the church, especially the various Hispanic groups, and the "pastoral opportunities that those differences provide" (Claudio Burgaleta, "A Latino/a Perspective on Co-Workers," chapter 8 in this collection, 105).

30. See H. Richard McCord, "The Development of Lay Ecclesial Ministry in the United States" chapter 1 in this collection, 3-10); and Amy Hoey, "How Co-Workers Came to be Written," chapter 2 in this collection, 11-18.

31. H. Richard McCord, "The Development of Lay Ecclesial Ministry in the United States," 8.

32. Ibid.

Bibliography

Benedict XVI. "Interview of His Holiness Benedict XVI during the Flight to Brazil." May 9, 2007. http://www.vatican.va/holy_father/benedict_xvi/speeches/2007/may/documents/hf_ben-xvi_spe_20070509_interview-brazil_en.html (accessed February 24, 2011).

Boff, Leonardo. *Saint Francis: A Model for Human Liberation.* New York: Crossroads, 1982.

Brueggemann, Walter. "The Legitimacy of a Sectarian Hermeneutic: 1 Kings 18-19." In *Education for Citizenship and Discipleship*, edited by Mary C. Boys, 3-34. New York: Pilgrim Press, 1989.

———. *The Creative Word: Canon as a Model for Biblical Education.* Philadelphia, PA: Fortress Press, 1982.

Carroll, Lewis. *Through the Looking Glass.* New York: W.W. Norton, First Published 1872.

Cataldo, Lisa. "Jesus as Transforming Selfobject: Kohutian Theory and the Life of St. Francis of Assisi," *Journal of Religion and Health*, 46, no.4 (2007): 527-540.

Catechism of the Catholic Church: with modification from the editio typica. New York: Doubleday, 1994.

Center for Applied Research in the Apostate (CARA). "Catholic Ministry Formation Directory Statistical Survey: 2007-2008." http://www.georgetown.edu (accessed September 23, 2008).

———. "Frequently Requested Church Statistics." http://www.cara.georgetown.edu (accessed September 16, 2008).

———. "The Permanent Diaconate Today." http://www.georgetown.edu (accessed September 20, 2008).

Clark, Matthew H. *Forward in Hope: Saying Amen to Lay Ecclesial Ministry.* Notre Dame, IN: Ave Maria Press, 2009.

———. "Fourth Annual Co-Workers Conference." Fordham University, September 17, 2010.

Coday, Dennis. "Document Delivers on its Promises." *National Catholic Reporter.* (September 8, 2010): 1-2.

Code of Canon Law. Washington, DC: Canon Law Society, 1983.

Congar, Yves. *Lay People in the Church: A Study for a Theology of Laity.* Translated by Donald Attwater. Westminister, MD: Newman Press, 1959.

———. "My Path-Findings in the Theology of Laity and Ministries." *The Jurist* 32 (1972): 169-188.

Congregation for the Clergy, et al. "On Certain Questions Regarding the Collaboration of the Nonordained in the Sacred Ministry of Priests." *Origins* 27 (November 27, 1997): 397-409.

Cozzens, Donald. *The Changing Face of the Priesthood: A Reflection on the Priest's Crisis of Soul.* Collegeville, MN: Liturgical Press, 2000.

Cunningham, Lawrence S. and Keith J. Egan, *Christian Spirituality: Themes from the Tradition.* Mahwah, NJ: Paulist Press, 1996.

Cupich, Bishop Blase. "The Emerging Models of Pastoral Leadership Project: the Theological, Sacramental and Ecclesial Context." *Origins* 38, no. 1 (May 15, 2008): 1-10.

DeBerri, Edward P. and James E. Hug, with Peter L. Henriot and Michael L. Schultheis. *Catholic Social Teaching: Our Best Kept Secret.* 4th rev. and exp. ed. Maryknoll, NY: Orbis Books, 2003.

DeLambo, David. *Lay Parish Ministers: A Study of Emerging Leadership.* New York: National Pastoral Life Center, 2005.

Dulles, Cardinal Avery. *Models of the Church.* New York: Doubleday, 2002.

Eisner, Elliot W. *The Educational Imagination: On the Design and Evaluation of School Programs.* New York: Macmillan Co., 1979.

"Factbox: Americas Roman Catholic Population." http://www.reuter.com (accessed September 16, 2008).

Filteau, Jerry. "Bishops Downsize Their National Conference, Reduce Assessments." *Catholic News Service* November 15, 2006. http://www.catholicnews.com/data/stories/cns/0606525.htm (accessed February 25, 2011).

Finn, Daniel. "The Catholic Theological Society of America and the Bishops." *Origins* 37, no.6 (June 21, 2007): 88-95.

Flannery, Austin, ed. *Vatican Council II: The Conciliar and Post Conciliar Documents.* Northport, NY: Costello Publishing, 1996.

Fox, Zeni. New Ecclesial Ministry: Lay Professionals Serving the Church. Franklin, WI: Sheed & Ward, 2002.

———, ed. *Lay Ecclesial Ministry: Pathways toward the Future.* Lanham, MD: Rowman & Littlefield, 2010.

Fragomeni, Richard N. *Come to the Light.* New York: Continuum, 2000.

Freud, Sigmund, *Totem and Taboo (The Standard Edition)* and *Moses and Monotheism. (The Standard Edition)* can be found in Volume XIII. *The Future of an Illusion (Standard Edition)* and *Civilization and Its Discontents (Standard Edition)* can be found in Volume XXI. Both volumes come from *The Complete Psychological Works of Sigmund Freud.* Edited and translated by James Strachey. New York: W.W. Norton, 1961.

Gaillardetz, Richard. "The Ecclesiological Foundations of Ministry within an Ordered Communion." In *Ordering the Baptismal Priesthood: Theologies of Lay Ecclesial Ministry.* Edited by Susan K. Wood, 26-51. Collegeville, MN: Liturgical Press, 2003.

———. "Shifting Meanings in the Lay-Clergy Distinction." *Irish Theological Quarterly* 64: (1999): 115-139.

———. "The Theology Underlying Lay Ecclesial Ministry." *Origins* 36 no. 9 (July 2006): 138-143.

Ganim, Carole, ed. *Shaping Catholic Parishes: Pastoral Leaders in the 21st Century*. Chicago: Loyola Press, 2008.

Grenz, Linda L. and J. Fletcher Lowe, Jr., eds. *Ministry in Daily Life*. New York: Episcopal Church Center, 1996.

Groome, Thomas. "The Future of Catholic Ministry: Our Best Hope." In *Priests for the 21st Century*. Edited by Donald Dietrich. New York: Crossroads Publishing Co, 2006.

Gula, Richard. *Ethics in Pastoral Ministry*. New York: Paulist Press, 1996.

Habermas, Jurgen. *Knowledge and Human Interests*. Boston: Beacon Press, 1971.

Hahnenberg, Edward. *Ministries: A Relational Approach*. New York: Crossroads, 2003.

———. "Think Globally, Act Locally: Responding to Lay Ecclesial Ministry." *New Theology Review* 17 (2004): 52-65.

———. "Ordained and Lay Ministry: Restarting the Conversation." *Origins* 35 (June 23, 2005): 94-99.

———. "The Vocation to Lay Ecclesial Ministry." *Origins* 37 no.12 (2007): 177-182.

Haight, Rodger. "Lessons From an Extraordinary Era: Catholic Theology Since Vatican II." *America* (March 17, 2008).

Harris, Maria. "Questioning Lay Ministry." (pp. 97-110) In *Women and Religion: A Reader for the Clergy*. Edited by Regina Coll. New York: Paulist Press, 1982.

———. *Fashion Me a People: Curriculum in the Church*. Louisville, KY: Westminster/ John Knox Press, 1989.

Heidegger, Martin. *Being and Time*. New York: Harper and Row, 1962.

Himes, Michael. *Doing the Truth in Love: Conversations about God, Relationships, and Service*. New York: Paulist Press, 1995.

Hinze, Bradford. *Practices of Dialogue in the Roman Catholic Church*. New York: Continuum, 2006.

Hoge, Dean R. and Marti Jewell. *The Next Generation of Pastoral Leaders: What the Church Needs to Know*. Chicago, IL: Loyola Press, 2010.

Holland, Joe. "Roots of the Pastoral Circle in Personal Experiences and Catholic Social Teaching." (pp. 1-14) in the *Pastoral Circle Revisited: A Critical Quest for Truth and Transformation*. Edited by Frans Wijsen, Peter Henriot, and Rodrigo Mejia. Maryknoll, NY: Orbis, 2005.

Instituto Fe y Vida. "Latino/a Youth by U.S. Dioceses 2003." http://feyvida.org/research/reserchpubs.html (accessed April15, 2008).

Jeremias, Joachim. *Rediscovering the Parables*. New York: Charles Scribner's Sons, 1996.

Jewell, Marti. "The Findings of the Emerging Models of Pastoral Leadership Project." *Origins* 38 no. 1 (May 15, 2008): 10-15.

John Paul II. *Christifideles Laici* (The Lay Members of Christ's Faithful People). Washington, DC: USCCB Publishing, 1988.

———. *Ecclesia in America* (The Church in America). January 22, 1999 in Mexico City. http://www.vatican.va/holy_father/john_paul_ii/apost_exhortations/documents/hf_jp-ii_exh_22011999_ecclesia-in-america_en.html (accessed February 24, 2011).

———. *Novo Millennio Ineunte* (At the Beginning of a New Millennium). *Origins* 30 (January 18, 2001): 491-508.

———. *Pastores Dabo Vobis* (I Shall Give You Shepherds). Washington, DC: USCCB Publishing, 1992.

———. *Redemptor Hominis* (The Redeemer of Man). Boston: Pauline Books and Media, 1979.

———. *Vita Consecrata* (The Consecrated Life). Washington, DC: USCCB Publishing, 1996.

Johnson, Luke Timothy. "Dry Bones: Why Religion Can't Live without Mysticism." *Commonweal* (February 26, 2010): 11-14.

Johnson, Maxwell E. *The Rites of Christian Initiation: Their Evolution and Interpretation.* Collegeville, MN: Liturgical Press, 2007.

Jones, James W. *Terror and Transformation: The Ambiguity of Religion in Psychoanalytic Perspective.* New York: Brunner-Routledge: 2002.

Kasper, Walter. *The God of Jesus Christ.* Translated by Matthew J. O'Connell. New York: Crossroads Publishing, 1984.

Kavanagh, Aidan. *Confirmation: Origins and Reform.* New York: Pueblo Publishing Company, 1988.

Kohut, Heinz. "Forms and Transformations of Narcissism." *Journal of the American Psychoanalytic Association* 14 (1966): 243-272.

———. *The Analysis of the Self: A Systematic Approach to the Psychoanalytic Treatment of Narcissistic Personality Disorders.* New York: International Universities Press, 1971.

———. *The Restoration of the Self.* Madison, CT: International Universities Press, 1977.

———. *How Does Analysis Cure?* Edited by Arnold Goldberg with the collaboration of Paul E. Stepansky. Chicago: University of Chicago Press, 1984.

———. *The Search for the Self.* New York: International Universities Press, 1991.

Komonchak, Joseph A. "Clergy, Laity and the Church's Mission in the World." *The Jurist* 41 (1981): 422-47.

LaCugna, Catherine Mowry. *God For Us: The Trinity and Christian Life.* New York: HarperSanFrancisco, 1991.

Lakeland, Paul. *The Liberation of the Laity: In Search of an Accountable Church.* New York: Continuum, 2003.

———. "Understanding the Crises in the Church." (pp. 3-15) in *Church Ethics and Its Organizational Context: Learning from the Sex Abuse Scandal in the Catholic Church*, edited by Jean M. Bartunek, Mary Ann Hinsdale, and James F. Keenan. Lanham, MD: Rowman and Littlefield, 2006.

———. "Maturity and the Lay Vocation: From Ecclesiology to Ecclesiality" (pp. 241-259) in *Catholic Identity and the Laity*. Edited by Tim Muldoon, 241-259. Maryknoll, NY: Orbis Press, 2009.

"Lost Sheep." *America* 198 no. 9 (March 17, 2008): 5.

Mahoney, Cardinal Roger. *As I Have Done for You: A Pastoral Letter on Ministry.* Chicago, IL: Liturgy Training Publications, 2000.

McBrien, Richard P. *Ministry: A Theological—Pastoral Handbook.* San Francisco: Harper and Row, 1987.

McGeary, Sylvia. "A Critical Reflection: Naming Lay Ecclesial Ministry—the Political and Personal Narratives." *The Journal of Adult Education* 4 no.2 (2007) 165-179.

Mickens, Robert. "Pope Insists on Strict Demarcation Between Clergy and Laity." *The Tablet: The International Catholic Weekly* (September 26, 2009): 31.

Miller, Vincent. *Consuming Religion: Christian Faith and Practice in a Consumer Culture.* New York: Continuum, 2003.

Mitchell, Nathan. *Forum Essays: Eucharist as Sacrament of Initiation.* Chicago, IL: Liturgy Training Publications, 1994.

Moran, Gabriel. *Religious Body: Design for a New Reformation*. New York: Seabury Press, 1974.

——— *Uniqueness: Problem or Paradox in Jewish and Christian Traditions*. Maryknoll, NY: Orbis Books, 1992.

———. *Showing How: The Act of Teaching.* Valley Forge, PA: Trinity Press International, 1997.

———. *Fashioning A People Today: The Educational Insights of Maria Harris.* New London CT.: Twenty-Third Publishing, 2007.

———. *Believing in a Revealing God: The Basis of the Christian Life*. Collegeville, MN: Liturgical Press, 2009.

Moran, Mary Jo. Interview by Zeni Fox. September 24, 2008.

Mudge, Lewis S. *Formation and Reflection: The Promise of Practical Theology.* Philadelphia, PA: Fortress Press, 1989.

Murnion, Philip. *New Parish Ministers: Laity and Religious on Parish Staffs.* New York: National Pastoral Life Center, 1992.

Murnion, Philip and David DeLambo. *Parishes and Parish Ministry: A Study of Parish Lay Ministry,* New York: National Pastoral Life Center, 1999.

National Association for Lay Ministry, National Conference for Catechetical Leadership, and National Federation for Catholic Youth Ministry. *National Certification Standards for Lay Ecclesial Minsters Serving as Parish Catechetical Leaders, Youth Ministry Leaders, Pastoral Associates, and Parish Life Coordinators.* Washington, DC: NALM, NCCL, and NFCYM, 2003.

NCCB. *Economic Justice for All: Pastoral Letter on Catholic Social Teaching and the U.S. Economy.* Washington, DC: NCCB, 1986.

———. *A Family Perspective in Church and Society*, 10th anniversary edition. Washington, DC: NCCB, 1986.

———. *Follow the Way of Love: A Pastoral Message of the United States Catholic Bishops to Families: On the Occasion of the United Nations 1994 International Year of the Family.* Washington, DC: NCCB, 1986.

———. *Pastoral Statement for Catholics on Biblical Fundamentalism* (1987). http://www.shc.edu/theolibrary/resources/fundmntl.htm (accessed February 24, 2011).

Neafsey, John. *A Sacred Voice is Calling: Personal Vocation and Social Conscience.* Maryknoll, NY: Orbis, 2006.

Nicolás, Rev. Adolpho, SJ. "Companions in Mission: Pluralism in Action." Address given at Loyola Marymount University, February 2, 2009

Notre Dame Study of Catholic Parish Life, Report No. 15. Notre Dame, IN: University of Notre Dame, 1989.

O'Meara, Thomas, OP. *Theology of Ministry.* Mahwah, NJ: Paulist Press, 1999.

Osborne, Kenan B. *Ministry: Lay Ministry in the Roman Catholic Church.* New York: Paulist Press, 1993.

———. *Orders and Ministry: Leadership in the World Church.* Maryknoll, NY: Orbis Books, 2006.

Pecklers, Keith. *The Unread Vision: The Liturgical Movement in the United States of America: 1926-1955.* Collegeville, MN: Liturgical Press, 1998.

Pew Forum on Religion and Public Life. "U.S. Religious Landscape Survey." (February 28, 2008). http://religions.pewforum.org/reports. Accessed May 9, 2011.

Pew Hispanic Center, "Changing Faiths: Latino/as and the Transformation of American Religion," http://pewhispanic.org/reports/report.php?ReportID=75 (accessed April 15, 2008).

Pius X. *Vehementer Nos* (On the French Law of Separation). February 11, 1906. http://www.vatican.va/holy_father/pius_x/encyclicals/documents/hf_p-x_enc_11021906_vehementer-nos_en.html (accessed February 24, 2011).

Pius XI. *L'Osservatore Romano* (Discourse to Italian Catholic Young Women) (March 21, 1927).

Rahner, Karl. *The Trinity.* Translated by Joseph Donceel. New York: Herder and Herder, 1970.

———. *Foundations of Christian Faith: An Introduction to the Idea of Christianity.* New York: Crossroads, 1978.

Rite of Christian Initiation of Adults. Chicago, IL: Liturgy Training Publications, 1988.

Robinson, Geoffrey. *Confronting Power and Sex in the Church.* Collegeville, MN: Liturgical Press, 2008.

Schreiter, Robert. "Pastoral Leadership: Moving into the Future." *Origins* 38 no. 2 (May 22, 2008): 27.

Schuth, Katherine. "A View of the State of the Priesthood in the United States." *Louvain Studies* 30 (2005): 8-24.

Scott, Kieran. "Illness and the Paradox of Power: A Spirituality of Mortality." (pp. 101-112) In *Spiritual and Psychological Aspects of Illness,* edited by Beverly A. Musgrave and Neil J. McGettigan. Mahwah, NJ: Paulist Press, 2010.

Searle, Barbara and Anne Y. Koester, eds. *Called to Participate: Theological, Ritual, and Social Perspectives*. Collegeville, MN: Liturgical Press, 2006.

Sellner, Edward C. "Lay Spirituality." (589-595) In *The New Dictionary of Catholic Spirituality*. Edited by Michael Downey. Collegeville, MN: Liturgical Press, 1993.

Sisters of Mercy of the Americas, "Election 2008: A Practical Resource." http://www.sistersofmercy.org/images/stories/documents/resources/election resource.pdf (accessed March 2, 2011):11.

Sobrino, Jon. *Spirituality of Liberation: Toward Political Holiness*. Translated by Robert Barr. Maryknoll, NY: Orbis Press, 1990.

Steinfels, Peter. *A People Adrift: The Crisis of the Roman Catholic Church in America*. New York: Simon and Schuster, 2003.

Sullins, Paul. "Catholic Social Teaching: What Do Catholics Know, and What Do They Believe?" *Catholic Social Science Review* 7 (2003): 243–64.

Taylor, Charles. *A Secular Age*. Cambridge: Harvard University Press, 2008.

Teilhard de Chardin, Pierre. "Patient Trust." (pp. 102-103) in *Hearts on Fire: Praying with Jesuits*. Edited by Michael G. Harter. Chicago, IL: Loyola Press, 2005.

"Top Recommendations, National Ministry Summit." http://www.emerging models.org (accessed September 12, 2008).

Tracy, David. *Plurality and Ambiguity: Hermeneutics, Religion, Hope*. San Francisco: Harper & Row, 1987.

United States Census Bureau, http://www.census.gov/population/www/socdemo/hispanic/files/Internet_Hispanic_in_US_2006.pdf Slide 3 (accessed January 4, 2011).

Upton, Julia. *A Church for the Next Generation: Sacraments in Transition*. Collegeville, MN: Liturgical Press, 1990.

USCC. *Called and Gifted: The American Catholic Laity*. Washington, DC: USCC, 1980.

———. *The Challenge of Peace: God's Promise and our Response, A Pastoral Letter on War and Peace*. Washington, DC: USCC, 1983.

USCCB. *General Catechetical Directory*, 1971 (pp. 1-77) in *The Catechetical Documents: A Parish Resource*. Chicago, IL: Liturgy Training Publications.

———. *Called and Gifted for the Third Millennium*. Washington, DC: USCCB, 1995.

———. "National Pastoral Plan for Hispanic Ministry" (November, 1987). In Secretariat for Hispanic Affairs, United States Catholic Conference, Inc., *Hispanic Ministry: Three Major Documents* Washington, DC: USCCB, 1995.

———. *Study of the Impact of Fewer Priests on the Pastoral Ministry*. June 15–17, 2000. Washington, DC: USCCB, 2003.

———. *Lay Ecclesial Ministry: The State of the Questions* (1999). http://www.nccbuscc.org/laity/laymin/layecclesial.shtml (accessed January 15, 2011).

———. *Encuentro and Mission: a Renewed Pastoral Framework for Hispanic Ministry* (2002) http://www.usccb.org/hispanicaffairs/encuentromission.shtml#7 (accessed February 25, 2011).

———. *Program of Priestly Formation*. 5th ed. Washington, DC: USCCB, 2005.

———. *National Directory for Catechesis*. Washington, DC: USCCB, 2005.

———. *Co-Workers in the Vineyard of the Lord: A Resource for Guiding the Development of Lay Ecclesial Ministry*. Washington, DC: USCCB, 2005.

———. *National Directory for the Formation, Ministry, and Life of Permanent Deacons in the United States*. Washington, DC: USCCB, 2006.

———. "Strategic Plan 2008-2011." http://www.usccb.org/priorities/old/USCCBApprovedStrategicPlan.pdf (accessed March 2, 2011).

Vanier, Jean. *Encountering the Other*. New York: Paulist Press, 2005.

———. *Community and Growth*, revised edition. New York: Paulist Press, 1989.

Waaijman, Kees. *Spirituality: Forms, Foundations, Methods*. Leuven: Peters, 2002.

Wilkes, Paul. "A Prediction Fulfilled." *America* (February 27, 2006): 12–14.

Winnicott, Donald W. "Ego Distortion in Terms of True and False Self, in *The Maturational Process and the Facilitating Environment: Studies in the Theory of Emotional Development*. New York: International Universities Press, 1965.

———. "Creativity and Its Origin" (pp. 65-85) "Transitional Objects and Transitional Phenomena" (pp. 1-25) and "The Location of Cultural Experience Experience" (95-103), In *Playing and Reality*. New York: Routledge, 1971.

———. "Living Creatively" (pp. 35-54) In *Home is Where We Start From: Essays by a Psychoanalyst*. New York: W. W.Norton, 1986.

———. "Anxiety Associated with Insecurity," (pp. 97-100); "Primary Maternal Preoccupation," (pp. 300-305); and "Mind and Its Relation to the Psyche-Soma" (pp. 243-254) in *Through Pediatrics to Psycho-Analysis: Collected Papers*. New York: Bruner/Mazel, 1992.

Wittgenstein, Ludwig. *Tractatus Logico-Philosophicus*. London: Routledge and Kegan Paul. Original edition 1921, reprint 1961.

———. *Philosophical Investigations*. New York: MacMillan, 1953.

Wood, Susan K., ed. *Ordering the Baptismal Priesthood: Theologies of Lay and Ordained Ministry*. Collegeville, MN: Liturgical Press, 2003.

Contributors

Archbishop Gregory M. Aymond, DD, is archbishop of New Orleans. He has served the church on the national and international level. The archbishop holds an MDiv and was granted an honorary doctorate from Notre Dame Seminary in New Orleans, Louisiana where he was also a professor of pastoral theology and homiletics. He was a member of the USCCB Committee on Laity, Marriage, Family Life, and Youth and the USCCB Committee on Clergy, Consecrated Life and Vocations. His is the author of *Courageous Moral Leadership* (National Catholic Educational Association, 2004), and co-author of *Facing Forgiveness: A Catholic's Guide to Letting Go of Anger and Welcoming Reconciliation* (Ave Maria Press, 2007).

Claudio M. Burgaleta, SJ, PhD, is associate professor of theology and coordinator of Latino Studies at the Graduate School of Religion and Religious Education (GSSRE) of Fordham University. He holds a PhD from Boston College, an MDiv and an STL from the Jesuit School of Theology of Santa Clara University. In addition to his faculty appointment at the GSRRE, Fr. Burgaleta is a member of Fordham University's Latin American and Latino Studies Institute. His recent publications include *Manual de la teología para los católicos de hoy* (Liguori Publications, 2009), and *Manual de Cristología para los católicos de hoy* (Liguori Publications, 2010).

Lisa Cataldo, PhD, is an assistant professor of pastoral counseling at the Graduate School of Religion and Religious Education of Fordham University, and a licensed psychoanalyst in New York State. She holds a PhD and MDiv from Union Theological Seminary in New York. Her recent publications include "Multiple Selves, Multiple Gods? Functional Polytheism and the Postmodern Religious Patient" in *Pastoral Psychology* (2008) and "Mourning the Religious Self: An Experience of Multiplicity, Loss, and Religious Melancholia" in *Pastoral Psychology* (2010).

Anthony Ciorra, PhD, is associate vice-president for mission at Sacred Heart University, Fairfield, CT. He served as dean of the Graduate School of Religion and Religious Education of Fordham University from

2004–2011. He holds a PhD from Fordham University, an MDiv and MA in psychological counseling from Seton Hall University, and an MA in Theology from Saint Bonaventure University. He is the co-author, with James Keating, of *Moral Formation in the Parish: With All Your Heart Turn to God* (Alba House, 1995) and author of *Everyday Mysticism: Cherishing the Holy* (Crossroads, 1998).

Donna Eschenauer, PhD, is the director of religious education and the catecheumenate at the Cathedral Parish of St. Agnes, Rockville Centre, New York. She received her PhD from the Graduate School of Religion and Religious Education of Fordham University, and her MA in Theology from New York's Seminary of the Immaculate Conception, where she has also completed postgraduate studies in pastoral liturgy. Her recent publication, "A Second Look at the Directory for Masses with Children," was a featured article for Praytellblog.com (Liturgical Press, September 3, 2010). Her book on the Easter Triduum is forthcoming.

Zeni Fox, PhD, is a professor of pastoral theology at Immaculate Conception Seminary, Seton Hall University. She received her PhD and MA from Fordham University. She served as an advisor to the USCCB Subcommittee on Lay Ministry in its preparation of Co-Workers in the Vineyard of the Lord. Fox is widely published on the topic of lay ecclesial ministry. Her publications include: *New Ecclesial Ministry: Lay Professionals Serving the Church* (Sheed and Ward, 2002); *Called and Chosen: Toward a Spirituality for Lay Leaders* (Rowman and Littlefield, 2005), co-edited with Regina Bechtle, SC; and her most recent edited collection, *Lay Ecclesial Ministry: Pathways Toward the Future* (Sheed and Ward, 2010).

Edward P. Hahnenberg, PhD, holds the Jack and Mary Jane Breen Chair in Catholic Systematic Theology at John Carroll University in Cleveland, Ohio. He received his PhD from the University of Notre Dame and later served as a consultant to the USCCB Subcommittee on Lay Ministry in its preparation of Co-Workers in the Vineyard of the Lord. His publications include *Ministries: A Relational Approach* (Crossroads, 2003), *A Concise Guide to the Documents of Vatican II* (St. Anthony Messenger Press, 2007), and *Awakening Vocation: A Theology of Christian Call* (Liturgical Press, 2010).

Amy Hoey, RSM, PhD, is currently serving as a hospice volunteer. She received her MA from Boston College, and her PhD from the University of Connecticut. She served as project coordinator for the USCCB Subcommittee on Lay Ministry from 1996–2006. As project coordinator, she served as staff for the bishops in writing *Together in God's Service: Toward a Theology of Ecclesial Lay Ministry, Lay Ecclesial Ministry: The State of the Questions*, and *Co-Workers in the Vineyard of the Lord: A Resource for Guiding the Development of Lay Ecclesial Ministry.*

Michael P. Horan, PhD, is professor and chair of the Department of Theological Studies at Loyola Marymount University, Los Angeles. He holds a PhD from the Catholic University of America. He has chaired the Advisory Board for the Office of Pastoral Associates for the Archdiocese of Los Angeles. His publications include various works on religious education and pastoral ministry including "Egeria Revisited: Adult Catechesis in a New Time" in *Catechumenate: Inspiration for Catechesis,* edited by Joseph P. Sinwell (National Catholic Educational Association, 2002), and "The Participants in Catechesis" in *Empowering Catechetical Leaders,* edited by Thomas Groome and Michael Corso (National Catholic Educational Association,1999). He is a contributing author of *Blest Are We,* the parish and school religious education series published by RCL-Benziger.

Harold D. Horell, PhD, is assistant professor of religious education at the Graduate School of Religion and Religious Education of Fordham University. He holds a PhD from Boston College, an MTS from Harvard Divinity School, and an MA in Philosophy from the University of Dayton. His recent publications include *Human Sexuality in the Catholic Tradition,* edited with Kieran Scott (Rowman and Littlefield, 2007); *Horizons and Hopes: The Future of Religious Education*, edited with Thomas Groome (Paulist Press, 2003); and "Moral Catechesis," in *Catechetical Scholars IV*, edited by Diana Dudoit Raiche (National Catholic Educational Association, 2011).

Bishop Howard J. Hubbard, DD, is bishop of the Diocese of Albany, New York. He holds degrees in philosophy and theology and did postgraduate studies in social services. He has been a leader in ecumenical and interfaith relationships, as well as an advocate for the importance of religious education / catechesis and the development of lay ministry. His publications include *Fulfilling the Vision: Collaborative Ministry in the Parish* (Crossroads, 1998), and *I Am Bread Broken: A Spirituality for the Catechists* (Crossroads, 1999).

H. Richard McCord, EdD, is executive director of the USCCB Secretariat for Laity, Marriage, Family Life, and Youth. He directed the project that produced Co-Workers in the Vineyard of the Lord. He holds a EdD from the University of Maryland, an MA from Princeton Theological Seminary, and a MDiv from Mary Immaculate Seminary in Pennsylvania. He is the author of numerous articles on church issues and a contributing author of *Lay Ecclesial Ministry: Pathways Toward the Future*, edited by Zeni Fox (Sheed and Ward, 2010).

Janet K. Ruffing, RSM, PhD, is professor of the Practice of Spirituality and Ministerial Leadership at Yale Divinity School, New Haven, Connecticut. She is professor emerita of Spirituality and Spiritual Direction at Fordham University, where she chaired the program in spirituality and spiritual direction from 1986 to 2009 in the Graduate School of Religion and Religious Education. She holds a PhD from the Graduate Theological Union, Berkeley, California, and a STL from the Jesuit School of Theology, Berkeley. Her recent publications include *Elizabeth Leseur: Selected Writings* (Paulist Press, 2005), and *To Tell the Sacred Tale: Spiritual Direction and Narrative,* forthcoming.

Kieran Scott, EdD, is associate professor of theology and religious education at the Graduate School of Religion and Religious Education of Fordham University. He holds an EdD from Columbia University, New York, and a MA in Theology from New York Theological Seminary. His publications include a series of essays in *Critical Issues in Religious Education*, edited by Oliver Brennan (Veritas, 2005); *Perspectives on Marriage*, 3rd Ed., edited with Michael Warren (Oxford University Press, 2007); *Human Sexuality in the Catholic Tradition*, edited with Harold Daly Horell (Rowman and Littlefield, 2007); and "Illness and the Paradox of Power," in *Spiritual and Psychological Aspects of Illness*, edited by Beverly A. Musgrave and Neil J. McGettigan (Paulist Press, 2010).

Index